THE FIGURE OF ADAM IN ROMANS 5 AND 1 CORINTHIANS 15

THE FIGURE OF ADAM IN ROMANS 5 AND 1 CORINTHIANS 15

THE NEW CREATION AND ITS ETHICAL AND SOCIAL RECONFIGURATION

FELIPE DE JESÚS LEGARRETA-CASTILLO

Fortress Press
Minneapolis

THE FIGURE OF ADAM IN ROMANS 5 AND 1 CORINTHIANS 15

The New Creation and Its Ethical and Social Reconfiguration

Cover design: Alisha Lofgren

Library of Congress Cataloging-in-Publication Data is available

Print ISBN: 978-1-4514-7001-7

eBook ISBN: 978-1-4514-8024-5

The paper used in this publication meets the minimum requirements of American National Standard for Information Sciences — Permanence of Paper for Printed Library Materials, ANSI Z329.48-1984.

Manufactured in the U.S.A.

This book was produced using PressBooks.com, and PDF rendering was done by PrinceXML.

CONTENTS

Acknowledgements

I want to express my most sincere gratitude to Fortress Press. Neil Elliott encouraged me to submit my dissertation for publication and meticulously edited it. I thank the editorial staff of Fortress Press, Lisa Gruenisen, Marissa Wold, and Amy Sleper, for their insights and critical suggestions.

I also want to thank especially the faculty and administrative personal of the Department of Theology at Loyola University Chicago. First of all, the director of my dissertation, Professor Thomas Tobin, S.J., who patiently guided me with his biblical wisdom in every step of this dissertation and earlier in courses on Hellenistic Judaism and New Testament, in particular on the Letter to the Romans. I also earnestly thank the two readers of my dissertation: Professor Robert Di Vito and Professor Urban C. von Wahlde. Their critical analysis and encouragement guided me and supported me all the way on this journey. I want to extend my gratitude also to Professors Wendy Cotter, CSJ, and Pauline Viviano, who further enlightened me in the biblical sciences. Finally, I want to thank Catherine Wolf, Office Coordinator, and Marianne Wolfe, Administrative Assistant, at the Department of Theology at Loyola University Chicago for their friendship and most helpful assistance, and also to the staff at Cudahy Library.

Finalmente quiero agradecer de una manera muy especial a mi familia, mis padres Ignacio y María Inocencia, y a mis hermanos y hermanas José Ignacio, Ileana Patricia, Luis Noé, y Claudia, y demás familiares. Su fe en Dios y su amor al prójimo me han enseñado la esencia del mensaje de Jesucristo.

Abbreviations

AB Anchor Bible

ABRL Anchor Bible Reference Library

AGJU Arbeiten zur Geschichte des Spätjudentums und des Urchirstentums

AnBib Analecta Biblica

BAG W. Bauer, W. F. Arndt, and F. W. Gingrich, *Greek-English Lexicon of the New Testament and Other Early Christian Literature* (Chicago: University of Chicago Press, 1957)

BAGD W. Bauer, W. F. Arndt, F. W. Gingrich, and F. W. Danker, *Greek-English Lexicon of the New Testament and Other Early Christian Literature*, 2nd ed. (Chicago: University of Chicago Press, 1979)

BETL Bibliotheca ephemeridum theologicarum lovaniensium

BibOr Biblica et orientalia

BJS Brown Judaic Studies

CBQ *Catholic Biblical Quarterly*

CBQMS Catholic Biblical Quarterly Monograph Series Cicero

Nat. d. *De natura deorum*

CRINT Compendia rerum iudaicarum ad Novum Testamentum

HDR Harvard Dissertations in Religion

HSM Harvard Semitic Monographs

HSS Harvard Semitic Studies

HTR *Harvard Theological Review*

HTS Harvard Theological Studies

JBL *Journal of Biblical Literature* Josephus

Ant. *Antiquities*

JSHRZ *Jüdische Schriften aus hellenistisch-römischer Zeit*

JSJSup Supplements to the Journal for the Study of Judaism in the Persian, Hellenistic, and Roman Period

JSNT *Journal for the Study of the New Testament*

JSNTSup Journal for the Study of the New Testament: Supplement Series

JSPSup Journal for the Study of the Pseudepigrapha: Supplement Series

JSS *Journal of Semitic Studies*

L.A.E. *Life of Adam and Eve*

LCL Loeb Classical Library

LXX Septuagint

NICNT New International Commentary on the New Testament

NIGTC New International Greek Testament Commentary

NJBC *New Jerome Biblical Commentary,* ed. R. E. Brown, J. A. Fitzmyer, and R. E. Murphy (Englewood Cliffs, N.J.: Prentice-Hall, 1990)

NovT *Novum Testamentum*

NovTSup Supplements to Novum Testamentum

NTG New Testament Guides

NTS *New Testament Studies* Philo

Abr. *De Abrahamo*

Decal. *De decalogo*

Deus Imm. *Quot Deus sit immutabilis*

Leg. All. *Legum allegoriae*

Migr. *De migratione Abrahami*

Mos. *De vita Mosis*

Opif. *De opificio mundi*

Plant. *De plantatione*

Praem. *De praemiis et poenis*

Q.G. *Quaestiones et solutiones in Genesin*

Somn. *De somniis*

Spec. Leg. *De specialibus legibus*

L.A.B. *Liber Antiquitatum Biblicarum*

SBLDS Society of Biblical Literature Dissertation Series

SBLEJL Society of Biblical Literature Early Judaism and Its Literature

SBLSCS Society of Biblical Literature Septuagint and Cognate Studies

SBLSymS Society of Biblical Literature Symposium Series

SBT Studies in Biblical Theology

SNTSMS Society for New Testament Studies Monograph Series

StPB Studia Post-Biblica

ST *Studia theologica*

StudBib *Studia Biblica*

SVTP Studia in Veteris Testamenti pseudepigrapha

TDNT *Theological Dictionary of the New Testament,* edited by Gerhard Kittel and Gerhard Friedrich, translated by Geoffrey W. Bromiley (10 vols.; Grand Rapids: Eerdmans, 1964–76)

WMANT Wissenschaftliche Monographien zum Alten und Neuen Testament

WUNT Wissenschaftliche Untersuchungen zum Neuen Testament

Introduction

In Rom 5:12-21 and 1 Cor 15:21-22, 45-49, Adam represents an antithetical figure of the eschatological times inaugurated in Christ's resurrection. Historical-critical studies have looked into the background of the Pauline Adam motif and found that Paul and very likely the Christian communities in Rome and Corinth were acquainted with earlier traditions and interpretations of the story of the creation and fall of humanity (Genesis 3).[1] Thus, Joachim Jeremias suggested that behind the Adam motif in Paul was an Easter myth of the primordial man.[2] Others believed that Gnosticism influenced Paul's distinction between the heavenly and earthly man. Still others suggest that Philonic interpretations of the creation account reached the Christian community in Corinth via Apollos. Gregory E. Sterling compares the Corinthians' position on the resurrection of the body (1 Cor 15:44-49) with Philo's exegesis of the story of the creation in Gen 1:26-27 and 2:7 and concludes that "Philo's concept of the immortality of the soul and corresponding devaluation of the body makes the Corinthians' denial of a future

1. Peter C. Bouteneff (*Beginnings: Ancient Christian Readings of the Biblical Creation Narratives* [Grand Rapids: Baker Academic, 2008]) presents a summary on the figure of Adam from Genesis 1–3 to the Fathers of the Church. Other studies of the Adam motif in Paul include J. P. Versteeg, *Is Adam a "Teaching Model" in the New Testament? An Examination of One of the Central Points in the Views of H. M. Kuitert and Others,* trans. Richard B. Gaffin (Nutley, N.J.: Presbyterian and Reformed, 1977); A. J. M. Wedderburn, "Adam in Paul's Letters to the Romans," *StudBib* 3 (1978): 413–30, on Rom 1:18-23 and 7:7-12; Nicholas Thomas Wright, "Adam in Pauline Christology," in *SBL Seminar Papers,* vol. 22 (Chico, Calif.: Scholars Press, 1983), 359–89; C. Marvin Pate, *Adam Christology as Exegetical & Theological Substructure of 2 Corinthians 4:7—5:21* (Lanham, Md.: University Press of America, 1991); Seyoon Kim, *The Origin of Paul's Gospel* (WUNT 2/4; Tübingen: Mohr Siebeck, 1984), 162-92; James D. G. Dunn, *The Theology of Paul the Apostle* (Grand Rapids: Eerdmans, 1998), 281–92; idem, *Christology in the Making: A New Testament Inquiry into the Origins of the Doctrine of the Incarnation* (2nd ed.; Grand Rapids: Eerdmans, 1989); Sang-Won (Aaron) Son, *Corporate Elements in Pauline Anthropology: A Study of Selected Terms, Idioms and Concepts in the Light of Paul's Usage and Background* (AnBib 148; Rome: Pontificio Istituto Biblico, 2001), 55–59; and Aldo Martin, *La tipologia adamica nella lettera agli Efesini* (AnBib 159; Rome: Pontificio Istituto Biblico, 2005).

2. J. Jeremias argues that Paul was familiar with Jewish traditions that traced the Adam motif to an Easter redeemer myth that identified "the first man as an ideal man, together with the doctrine of the restitution by the Messiah of the glory which he lost at the fall"; and "by the doctrine of the pre-existent Messiah, בַּר נָשָׁא, which resulted from a fusion of Messianic expectation with the doctrine of the first man as redeemer," "Ἀδαμ, κτλ.," *TDNT* 1:141–43.

bodily resurrection fully explicable."[3] However, he explains that Philo was not the source of the Corinthians' position but simply "our major witness to them," and it may actually have been Apollos who brought these traditions to the synagogue in Corinth.[4]

These studies, however, have neglected the literary function of the figure of Adam, as well as the ethical implications Paul conveyed in 1 Cor 15:21-22, 45-49 and Rom 5:12-21. In order to grasp the meaning and function of Adam, it is necessary to pay attention to the literary context in which Paul introduces the contrast between Adam and Christ. This contrast is found within a broader comparison between the "old" and "new" creation,[5] and between "this age"

3. Gregory E. Sterling, "'Wisdom among the Perfect': Creation Traditions in Alexandrian Judaism and Corinthian Christianity," *NovT* 37 (1995): 366–67. See also Gregory E. Sterling, "The Place of Philo of Alexandria in the Study of Christian Origins," in *Philo und das Neue Testament: Wechselseitige Wahrnehmungen,* ed. Roland Deines and Karl-Wilhelm Niebuhr (WUNT 172; Tübingen: Mohr Siebeck, 2004), 21–52.

4. Sterling, "'Wisdom among the Perfect,'" 382. Citing Acts 18:24—19:1 he argues, "It is at least a distinct possibility that Apollo brought Greek-speaking Jewish sapiential traditions about the creation of humanity to Corinth which the Corinthians found appealing" (p. 383). See also W. D. Davies, *Paul and Rabbinic Judaism: Some Rabbinic Elements in Pauline Theology* (2nd ed.; New York and Evanston: Harper & Row, 1955), 51; Robin Scroggs, *The Last Adam: A Study in Pauline Anthropology* (Philadelphia: Fortress Press, 1966). Richard A. Horsley suggests that "the Hellenistic Jewish theology represented by Philo may be actually a source, mediated through the eloquent scriptural interpreter Apollos, who taught in the Corinthian community after Paul" ("'How Can Some of You Say That There Is No Resurrection of the Dead?' Spiritual Elitism in Corinth," *NovT* 20 [1978]: 203–31, here 207; cf. 229). See further John Gillman, "Transformation into the Future Life: A Study of 1 Cor 15:50-53, Its Context and Related Passages" (Ph.D. diss., Katholieke Universiteit Leuven, Belgium, 1980). Birger A. Pearson used the extrapolation of the second-century *Epistle of Barnabas* and the *Teachings of Silvanus* to point out the connections between these Alexandrian Christian traditions and 1 Corinthians 1–4 ("Cracking a Conundrum: Christian Origins in Egypt," *ST* 57 [2003]: 61–75). Specifically, "*Silvanus* retains . . . a good deal of the 'speculative wisdom' already encountered by Paul in first-century Corinth, presumably mediated by the Alexandrian Jewish teacher Apollos, [who] may very well have been a pupil of Philo" (p. 70). See also Birger A. Pearson, *The Pneumatikos-Psychikos Terminology in 1 Corinthians: A Study in the Theology of the Corinthian Opponents of Paul and Its relation to Gnosticism* (SBLDS 12; Missoula, Mont.: Society of Biblical Literature, 1973), 18. For the discussion of the use of Philo's works in the study of Paul, see Berndt Schaller, "Adam und Christus bei Paulus: Oder, Über Brauch und Fehlbrauch von Philo in der neutestamentlichen Forschung," in Deines and Niebuhr, *Philo und das Neue Testament,* 143–53.

5. See Davies, *Paul and Rabbinic Judaism,* 37–41. Robin Scroggs (*Last Adam,* 59–74) analyzes Paul's understanding of the last Adam within the schema of the new–old creation. See also Christina Hoegen-Rohls, "Κτίσις and καινὴ Κτίσις in Paul's Letters," in *Paul, Luke and the Graeco-Roman World: Essays in Honour of Alexander J. M. Wedderburn* ed. Alf Christophersen et al. (JSNTSup 217; Sheffield: Sheffield Academic Press, 2002), 102–22. In her analysis of "Creation" and "New Creation" in 2 Cor 5:17, Hoegen-Rohls identifies eschatological motifs in the description of the pangs of creation (p. 114). In the

(αἰῶνος τούτου) or "this world" (κόσμου τούτου) and "the age to come." This contrast usually had for Paul intrinsic ethical and social implications. Thus, the believer who belongs to the new aeon also is "in Christ," the heavenly man; the believer must be clothed with Christ and consequently is incorruptible. Therefore, those who belong to Christ must break with the old creation dominated by sin and represent in their lives the mystery of the new Adam if they want to participate in the age or world to come. Thus, being either in the old Adam or in the last Adam, Christ (ἐν Χριστῷ), or being either people of dust or people of heaven (cf. 1 Cor 15:48-50) implied a way of life according to the one they would follow and imitate.

Additionally, Paul sets the future resurrection of the believers in tension with their ethical commitment to the present. Thus, Paul emphatically argues, "If the dead are not raised, 'Let us drink and eat, for tomorrow we die.' Do not be deceived: 'Bad company ruins good morals.' Come to your right mind, and sin no more" (1 Cor 15:32-34). Paul concludes 1 Corinthians 15 with an exhortation, "Therefore, my beloved brethren, be steadfast, immovable, always abounding in the work of the Lord, knowing that in the Lord your labor is not in vain" (15:58). Although this element is less evident in Rom 5:12-21, its immediate context may reflect Paul's ethical concerns. The justification brought by Christ's expiatory death (5:1-11) requires believers to sin no more. Paul develops this implication through the explanation of baptism and its consequences in terms of dying, being buried with Christ, and walking in the newness of life (Rom 6:1-4). Paul also links Christ's death and resurrection to that of the believers as dying to sin and as living to God (6:10-11). In the subsequent verses, Paul exhorts, "let not sin reign in your mortal bodies" and asks, "What then? Are we to sin because we are not under law but under grace?

context of Rom 4:17, she also identifies the ethical consequences of the new creation; that is, Christians now recenter their lives from the once "self-centeredness toward an existence devoted to the Crucified and Risen One" (p. 118). In her analysis of the concepts "creation/new creation" in Paul, there is a correlation between the eschatological language and the ethical consequences of the new creation. See also Moyer V. Hubbard, *New Creation in Paul's Letters and Thought* (SNTSMS 119; Cambridge: Cambridge University Press, 2002). Hubbard analyzes the "new creation" motif in Paul, particularly in 2 Cor 5:12 and Gal 6:15 against the Jewish background, specifically of *Jubilees* and *Joseph and Aseneth*. He concludes that the "new creation" motif in Paul represents the newness of life of the individual brought by the Spirit, as well as the *demarcation* and *empowerment* of a new society (p. 233). Similarly, Bruce D. Chilton indicates that resurrection involves a new creative act by God that begins not simply at death. "Rather, a progressive transformation joins the realm of ethics together with the realm of metaphysics. Morally and existentially, the hope of the resurrection involves a fresh, fulfilled humanity" (Chilton and Jacob Neusner, *Classical Christianity and Rabbinic Judaism: Comparing Theologies* (Grand Rapids: Baker Academic, 2004), 231.

By no means!" (6:12–15). Then he concludes, "the wages of sin is death, but the free gift of God is eternal life in Christ Jesus our Lord" (6:23).

In sum, Paul uses the Adam Christology to explain the event of the resurrection as the new creation and the last aeon already inaugurated by Christ, which for the believer still lies in the future. With the Adam typology Paul challenges the believer to participate in the present in the resurrection of Christ through a new lifestyle, that of Christ. Although to rise with Christ is a future event, it can be anticipated in the present through ethical behavior.

In this dissertation, I analyze the Adamic traditions that may have come into contact with Paul or his communities in Corinth and Rome, as found in Rom 5:12-21 and 1 Cor 15:21-22, 45–49, and identify possible ethical and social implications that Paul may have applied to the Adam typology in these texts.

1

The *Status Questionis* of the Adam Typology in Paul

Modern scholars have sought to elucidate the Adam typology in Paul in light of his religious, cultural, and literary backgrounds. Among them, under the influence of the History-of-Religions School, there have been scholars who propose Gnosticism as the background to explain Paul's use of the Adam figure in 1 Corinthians 15 and in Romans 5. Another trend has been to look to early Judaism for the sources of Paul's understanding of the Adam typology. Nevertheless, in the end all agree that it is the stories of the creation and fall in Genesis 1–3 that influenced Paul's Adam typology most of all, as well as the later Hellenistic or Palestinian Jewish interpretations of the Genesis narratives. However, as we shall see, these studies have not identified two important aspects of the Adam typology in Paul. First, they have not explained adequately how the figure of Adam functions within the larger literary contexts of 1 Corinthians and Romans. Second, they have not noted the ethical and social implications that Paul may have drawn from the Adam motif.

Proponents of the Gnostic Hypothesis

Modern interpretations of the figure of Adam in Paul began with the theological debate between Rudolf Bultmann and Karl Barth.[1] Their exegetical and theological works reflect an anthropological concern. In his analysis of Romans 5, Barth states, "Man's essential and original nature is to be found,

1. David Paul Henry captures this debate between Barth and Bultmann. The dialogue begins as early as 1922, when the two authors agree that "the intent of biblical interpretation is to confront and involve the reader in the 'subject matter' of the text," which for Bultmann was "authentic human existence," whereas for Barth it was "the relationship between humanity and the transcendent God." See David Paul Henry, *The Early Development of the Hermeneutic of Karl Barth as Evidenced by his Appropriation of Romans 5:12-21* (NABPR Dissertation Series 5; Macon, Ga.: Mercer University Press, 1985), 203.

therefore, not in Adam but in Christ."[2] Bultmann replied that Paul "says nothing about the possibility of our recognizing in retrospect the ordering principle of the kingdom of Christ also in the world of Adam."[3] Although the former may emphasize the christological dimension and the latter the anthropological dimension of Paul's Adam typology, in the end both Barth and Bultmann agree that Paul's Adam typology is necessarily both christological and anthropological.

The more influential study for the Adam typology has been Bultmann's analysis of Rom 5:12–21 and 1 Cor 15:21 and 47–49. Bultmann argues that these texts reflect Gnostic influence: "The Adam Christ parallel, i.e. the thought of two mankinds (or two epochs of mankind) and their determination each by its originator, is a Gnostic idea which is conceived cosmologically and not in terms of salvation history."[4] In *The Old and the New Adam in the Letters of Paul,* Bultmann identifies "genuine analogies" between Paul and "the Hellenistic mystery religions and . . . Hellenistic mysticism."[5] Similarly, in his *Theology of the New Testament*, Bultmann finds what he calls "Gnostic mythology" speculation in Rom 5:12–21 and 1 Cor 15:21, 44–49: "The contrast 'psychic-pneumatic' ('man of soul'– 'man of Spirit') to designate two basically different classes of men . . . is an especially clear indication that Paul's anthropological concepts had already been formed under the influence of Gnosticism."[6] Indeed, taken together, the language, the myth of the fallen world, the descent of a redeemer into the material realm, and the dualistic view between the material and the spiritual world were particularly persuasive and led Bultmann to conclude that Paul and other texts of the NT were influenced by Gnostic material and mystery religions. As we shall see with other scholars who followed Bultmann's hypothesis, reliance on literary material that in fact

2. Karl Barth, *Christ and Adam: Man and Humanity in Romans 5* (New York: Collier Books, 1962), 39–40. He states, "*Jesus Christ is the secret truth about the essential nature of man, and even sinful man is still essentially related to Him. That is what we have learned from Rom. 5:12-21*" (pp. 107–8; emphasis in original translation)

3. Rudolf Bultmann, "Adam and Christ According to Romans 5," in *Current Issues in New Testament Interpretation: Essays in Honor of Otto A. Piper*, ed. William Klassen and Graydon F. Snyder (London: SCM, 1962), 163.

4. Bultmann, "Adam and Christ," 154; see also 160.

5. Rudolf Bultmann, *The Old and the New Adam in the Letters of Paul,* trans. Keith R. Crim (Richmond: John Knox, 1967), 18; see also 21.

6. Rudolf Bultmann, *Theology of the New Testament,* trans. Kendrick Grobel (2 vols. (New York: Scribner, 1951, 1955), 1:174.

postdated the New Testament documents makes this thesis methodologically untenable.

In a similar approach, Walter Schmithals argues that with the expression ἀνάθεμα Ἰησοῦς ("cursed be Jesus") found in 1 Cor 12:1-3 Paul is responding to some Christians in Corinth who, under the influence of Gnosticism, despised Jesus according to the flesh, but confessed the Christ according to the Spirit: "Thus the Christology of the Corinthian 'Christians' which is expressed in the ἀνάθεμα in 1 Cor 12.3 is the genuinely Gnostic Christology,"[7] Schmithals concludes. However, the distinction between "Jesus" and "Christ" in Paul seems rather artificial. Paul uses these terms interchangeably, and even preferably "Jesus Christ" together (Rom 8:34; 1 Cor 3:1; 8:6; 2 Cor 1:19; 13:5; Gal 3:1; Phil; 2:11). Furthermore, in his argument of 1 Corinthians 12 Paul is arguing about the spiritual gifts and not about spiritual people, spiritual gifts that each member should use to build up the unity of the community.

In her critique of Schmithals's thesis, Margaret M. Mitchell aptly summarizes the problems scholars found regarding the identity of Gnosticism or pre-Christian Gnosticism, as well as terminological inaccuracy and anachronistic "Christian heresiological designations of 'Gnostics' for a mid-first century Christian group."[8] Although the origins and nature of Gnosticism are still under debate,[9] we can conclude that the major difficulty is the reliance on documents that postdate the New Testament texts.

One of the most comprehensive modern works among the proponents of the "Gnostic hypothesis" for the Adam motif in Paul, particularly in Romans 5, is that of Egon Brandenburger.[10] In chapter 1 of *Adam und Christus,* he surveys the religious backgrounds of Rom 5:12-21. In chapter 2, he undertakes the exegetical analysis of Rom 5:12-21. Section A of chapter 1 is devoted to analyzing the Jewish understanding of sin and seath, and section B, to understanding the "two Adam-Anthropoi" in Palestinian and Hellenistic Judaism. Brandenburger claims that Paul's opponents in 1 Corinthians 15 are

7. See Walter Schmithals, "The Corinthian Christology," in *Christianity at Corinth: The Quest for the Pauline Church,* ed. Edward Adams and David G. Horrell (Louisville: Westminster John Knox, 2004), 77 (extracted from Walter Schmithals, *Gnosticism in Corinth: An Investigation of the Letters to the Corinthians,* trans. John E. Steely (Nashville, Abingdon, 1971], 124–30).

8. Margaret M. Mitchell, "Paul's Letters to Corinth: The Interpretive Intertwining of Literary and Historical Reconstruction," in *Urban Religion in Roman Corinth: Interdisciplinary Approaches,* ed. Daniel N. Schowalter and Steven J. Friesen (HTS 53; Cambridge, Mass.: Harvard University Press, 2003), 312–13.

9. See Pheme Perkins, *Gnosticism and the New Testament* (Minneapolis: Fortress Press, 1993); Birger A. Pearson, *Ancient Gnosticism: Traditions and Literature* (Minneapolis: Fortress Press, 2007).

10. Egon Brandenburger, *Adam und Christus: Exegetisch-religionsgeschichtliche Untersuchung zu Rom. 5, 12-21 (1 Kor 15)* (WMANT 7; Neukirchen: Kreis Moers, 1962).

identified with those represented in 2 Tim 2:18 who supposedly espoused a realized eschatology.[11] After his analysis of Jewish and Hellenistic Jewish literature,[12] including of Philo's interpretation of the creation of the human beings in Genesis 1–2,[13] Brandenburger concludes that "the scheme and basic underlying idea of the parallelism of Adam and Christ-Anthropos in 1 Cor 15:21f. 45ff and herewith also in Rom 5:12-21—alongside distinct motifs of the ancient Jewish tradition in Rom 5:12ff- becomes evident in the light of the Gnostic (*christlich*) Adam-Anthropos speculation background."[14] According to Brandenburger's hypothesis, the descent and ascension of the heavenly redeemer to save the physical man from his dreadful situation perfectly suited Paul's Christology and soteriology.[15]

Several scholars have extensively analyzed and criticized Brandenburger's thesis,[16] noting in particular three major difficulties. The first difficulty is the identification of Paul's opponents in Corinth as a Gnostic group. Apparently, in 1 Cor 15:12 Paul replied to some who denied the resurrection of the dead or questioned a bodily resurrection (15:35). However, the identity of Paul's opponents in Corinth is a matter of debate,[17] for Corinth's cultural and

11. Brandenburger, *Adam und Christus*, 69–77.

12. He surveyed the Adam motif in several Gnostic texts such as the Jewish-Gnostic prayers, the tradition of Zosimus, the Naassene reflections, the Apocryphon of John, *Poimandres* (*Corp Herm. 1*), and the Mandean texts, Adam, 77-109. Under the heading of " 'Pre, Early, and Late Jewish' texts," he analyzes 1QS 4.7-8, 23; 11.7-8; 1QH 17.15; CD 3.20. He also studies *Apoc. Mos.* and *Vit. Ad.*; *1–2 Enoch*; *4 Ezra* (syr.); Baruch; and rabbinic testimonies (*Adam und Christus*, 110–17).

13. Brandenburger, *Adam und Christus*, 117–31.

14. Brandenburger, *Adam und Christus*, 157 (my translation).

15. Brandenburger, *Adam und Christus*, 157: "In dem einen sarkisch-psychischen Anthropos ist die Menschheit insgesamt schicksalhaft dem verderblich-minderwertigen Seinsbereich, dem Herrschaftsbereich des Todes und versklavender Mächte verhaftet; aber durch Ab- und Aufstieg des himmlischen Erlöser-Anthropos ist ein Geschehen in Gang gekommen, durch das die Gesamtheit der nach Ursprung und Wesen pneumatsichen Menschen in den himmlisch-pneumatischen Anthropos hinein erlöst wird."

16. A. J. M. Wedderburn, "Adam and Christ: An Investigation into the Background of 1 Corinthians XV and Romans V. 12-21" (Ph.D. diss., Cambridge University, 1974), 22–34; Hans Conzelmann, *1 Corinthians: A Commentary on the First Epistle to the Corinthians*, trans. J. W. Leitch (Hermeneia, Philadelphia: Fortress Press, 1975), 284–86; Seyoon Kim, *The Origin of Paul's Gospel* (WUNT 2/4; Tübingen: Mohr Siebeck, 1984), 164–78; John R. Levison, *Portraits of Adam in Early Judaism: From Sirach to 2 Baruch* (JSPSup 1; Sheffield: JSOT Press, 1988), 17-18; Sang-Won (Aaron) Son, *Corporate Elements in Pauline Anthropology: A Study of Selected Terms, Idioms, and Concepts in the Light of Paul's Usage and Background* (AnBib 148; Rome: Pontificio Istituto Biblico, 2001), 66–70.

17. For instance, Robert Jewett (*Paul's Anthropological Terms: A Study of Their Use in Conflict Settings* [AGJU 10; Leiden: Brill, 1971]) argues that "the main opponents of Paul within the Corinthian

religious milieu was so heterogeneous that we cannot state with confidence that there was a single group or ideology that may have influenced the Christian community in this city.[18] Most important, the classification of Gnosticism and Gnostic groups is a rather conjectural construal of a phenomenon that appeared much later during the second century.

Related to the previous problem is Brandenburger's contention that Paul was using the language of his opponents. First, according to Brandenburger, the contrast between the heavenly and earthly man in 1 Cor 15:45-49 reflects the Gnostic myth of the "Primal man."[19] Yet in 1 Cor 15:21-22, 45-49 and Rom 5:12-21 Paul understands and interprets Adam and Christ as two antithetical historical figures and not as the abstract and ahistorical heavenly redeemer who evolves in two phases as proposed later in Gnosticism.[20] Furthermore, as Hans Conzelmann has concisely put it, "The figure in question belongs not so much to myth as to mythological speculation."[21] Instead, it is more likely that the contrast between the first and second Adam in Paul reflects earlier or contemporary Hellenistic Jewish traditions about the story of the creation of humanity in Gen 1:27 and 2:7, which some Corinthians may have known. A thesis that will be discussed in chapter 2 is that some in Corinth knew Philo's commentaries on the story of the creation.[22]

congregation itself were radical enthusiasts who can be termed Gnostics because of their belief in salvation through σοφία/γνώσις and because of their consistently dualistic world view" (p. 40; see also 28, 31, 34–40). On the other hand, Birger A. Pearson contends that Paul's adversaries were Hellenistic Jews in Corinth who, in interpreting Gen 2:7, "were espousing a doctrine of a-somatic immortality, and denying the bodily resurrection" (*The Pneumatikos-Psychikos Terminology in 1 Corinthians: A Study in the Theology of the Corinthian Opponents of Paul and Its Relation to Gnosticism* [SBLDS 12; Missoula, Mont.: Society of Biblical Literature, 1973], 24).

18. James D. G. Dunn aptly describes the Corinthian milieu as "a melting pot of religious ideas and philosophies, many of them Jewish in origin (the myth of Wisdom, as in Sir 24 and *1 En. I 42)*, others common in different religious systems" ("Reconstructions of Corinthian Christianity and the Interpretation of 1Corinthians," in Adams and Horrell, *Christianity at Corinth,* 300).

19. See Brandenburger, *Adam und Christus,* 77–131.

20. As noted by Son, *Corporate Elements*, 69.

21. Conzelmann, *1 Corinthians*, 285. In his excursus, he noted the complexity of the origins and meaning of this concept: "the *one* concept primal man is applied to heterogeneous things: the macrocosmos, the protoplast, the prototype, the redeemer ('redeemed redeemer'), to the God 'Man' in Gnosticism, where 'Man' mostly means the highest God, but then also the revealing power of the deity" (p. 284).

22. Gregory E. Sterling, "Wisdom among the Perfect: Creation Traditions in Alexandrian Judaism and Corinthian Christianity," *NovT* 37 (1995): 366–67; Wedderburn, "Adam and Christ," 120, 129. Furthermore, Wedderburn argues that Philo's interpretation of the man of Gen 1:26 "is described in the language of Plato's theory of forms," 157. "Philo is working here in a Hellenistic-Jewish tradition going

Second, Brandenburger also claims that the Corinthians borrowed the contrast between ψυχικόν and the πνευματικόν from a Gnostic group. Subsequent scholars have provided alternative solutions to this apparent dualism. Pearson argues that in 1 Cor 15:44–49 Paul was actually dealing not with Gnostic opponents but with competing Hellenistic-Jewish and rabbinic interpretations of Gen 2:7, to which Paul provided his own "eschatological 'targum.'"[23] He concludes that Paul introduced an eschatological dualism between the present age and the age to come as opposed to his adversaries in Corinth, who "were operating on a non-eschatological plane in dividing man's present existence into a duality of heavenly-earthly, spiritual-psychic, incorruptible-corruptible, immortal-mortal, level."[24] Although Pearson's critique of Brandenburger's thesis is right on target, his reliance on post–New Testament rabbinic literature may undermine his thesis. A similar solution is provided by Seyoon Kim, who argues that Paul himself introduced the distinction between the ψυχικόν and the πνευματικόν to the Corinthians and that "subsequently they abused it, rather than Paul borrowed it from them."[25] Whatever the case, what is at stake here is not really the identity of Paul's opponents so much as what Paul meant by using this contrast. Paul responds to those who rejected a bodily resurrection (1 Cor 15:35), using an analogy of the different bodies (15:40) to state that the body with which the believers will be raised is not physical, but spiritual (15:44). Then in v. 45 he supports his argument with his own interpretation of Gen 2:7. The contrast in v. 46 that the spiritual follows the physical (body) is then the logical outcome of his argument, and not necessarily Paul's reversal of his opponents' thesis.

Finally, Brandenburger argued that Paul counteracted his opponents' realized eschatology, as evidenced in 2 Tim 2:18.[26] However, 2 Timothy postdates both 1 Corinthians and Romans. Most important, the opponents of 2 Tim 2:18 claimed that the resurrection of the dead has already occurred, whereas in 1 Corinthians 15 Paul responds to those who claimed that "there

back to Plato's doctrine of ideas." See also Conzelmann, *1 Corinthians*, 286: Philo "distinguishes two types of man, the heavenly and the earthly, *Leg. all.*1:31f (on Gen 2:7) [Greek text and translation provided]. He distinguishes the idea[l] man from the historical man, *Op. mund.* 134 (likewise on Gen 2:7) [Greek text and translation provided]."

23. Pearson, *Pneumatikos-Psychikos Terminology*, 15–24.

24. Pearson, *Pneumatikos-Psychikos Terminology*, 26.

25. Kim, *Origin of Paul's Gospel*, 170–71, analyzing Gal 6:1 and 1 Cor 2:12-15. This is a verbatim expression from Wedderburn ("Adam and Christ," 187), who is cited in n. 3 but not quoted. Kim's contention (p. 266; cf. 267–68) that Paul himself derived the Adam Christology from the "Damascus Christophany," where Christ revealed to Paul "as the εἴκων τοῦ θεοῦ," is less convincing.

26. Brandenburger, *Adam und Christus*, 70–71.

is no resurrection of the dead" (vv. 12, 29) or who questioned the bodily resurrection (v. 35). Thus, in 1 Corinthians 15 Paul addresses the question of the future and of bodily, although as spiritual body, resurrection of the believers, and not a realized eschatology.

In his effort to elucidate the backgrounds of Rom 5:12-21 Brandenburger thus diverted his attention to what was initially intended as only a parenthetical analysis of 1 Corinthians 15 (as is shown in the title of his work). Indeed, this would be the logical process, since the earliest explicit comparison between Adam and Christ in Paul appears in 1 Corinthians 15. Brandenburger's contribution to the study of the Adam typology in Paul has illustrated the complexity of the Adam figure in Paul. His analysis of extensive Palestinian and Hellenistic Jewish interpretations of the story of the creation and fall of Adam in Genesis 1–3 led Brandenburger to postulate Gnosticism as the background for the contrast between Adam and Christ in Paul. On the contrary, further research has demonstrated that it is more plausible that the language found in 1 Corinthians has influenced later forms of Christian Gnosticism.[27] It is likely that Paul and his audience were familiar with a tradition about Adam's sin and death that was passed on to his descendants (1 Cor 15:21-22; Rom 5:12 and 18), and possibly also of the contrast between the "heavenly man" and the "earthly man" (1 Cor 15:42-49).[28] Furthermore, Jewish speculations about Adam and the effects of his disobedience often enough conveyed ethical implications. Some of these authors did not simply speculate about the origins of humankind or the ancestors of Israel, but they inferred ethical and social consequences for the communities they addressed. Eventually Paul inherited these traditions and creatively interpreted and adapted them into his argument in 1 Corinthians 15 and Rom 5:12-21. In other words, the story of Genesis 1–3 and its subsequent traditions intend to elicit an ethical and social reconfiguration in the audience. Thus, Paul creatively adapted these traditions in his letters to convey ethical and social implications. Our task in chapter 2 will be to identify these traditions among the Palestinian and Diaspora Jews who interpreted the Scriptures in

27. A. J. M. Wedderburn (*Baptism and Resurrection: Studies in Pauline Theology against Its Graeco-Roman Background* [WUNT 44; Tübingen: Mohr Siebeck, 1987], 21) argues that the conceptual similarities between 1 Corinthians and Gnosticism may possibly reflect "a type of Christianity *en route* to Gnosticism."

28. See Thomas H. Tobin, *Paul's Rhetoric in Its Contexts: The Arguments of Romans* (Peabody, Mass.: Hendrickson, 2004), 175–76. Tobin distinguishes two trends of traditions in 1 Corinthians 15, one that takes up Jewish traditions about Adam's sin and death (vv. 21-22) and the other (vv. 42-49) that reflects the Hellenistic Jewish speculations, as found in Philo, about the heavenly/earthly man of Gen 1:27 and 2:7, respectively.

a heterogeneous religious and cultural context like Paul's. Then, in chapter 3 we will analyze Paul's reworking of these traditions in his first letter to the Corinthians and that to the Romans.

Proponents of the Jewish Hypothesis

Since Gnosticism did not explain Paul's Adam motif in 1 Corinthians 15 and Romans 5, other scholars have investigated the possible background for Paul's use of the figure of Adam among Hellenistic and Palestinian Jewish interpretations of the story of the creation and fall of Genesis 1–3 of the turn of the first century.

In his influential investigation *Paul and Rabbinic Judaism*, W. D. Davies analyzes the antithesis between the old and the new creation, and thus between the old and the new humanity, the first and the second Adam.[29] Davies asserts that, "whereas the Christian Dispensation as a new creation was pre-Pauline, the conception of Christ as the Second Adam was probably introduced into the Church by Paul himself."[30] He claims that in 1 Corinthians 15, "Paul reverses the order found in Philo and identifies the Heavenly Man . . . with Jesus, the Son of David, who was later than the Adam of Genesis in time and therefore might be called the Second Adam."[31] In regard to Rom 5:12-21, Davies argues that, in addition to the "Rabbinic doctrine that through the Fall of the First Man, Adam, all men fell into sin," Paul incorporates and underscores the "Rabbinic speculation about the creation of the physical body of Adam" to demonstrate the unity of all humankind.[32] Then Paul applies this doctrine and explains that God now reconstitutes "the essential oneness of mankind in Christ as a spiritual community, as it was one in Adam in a physical sense."[33]

Davies's contribution has redirected Pauline studies to focus on Paul's Jewish identity. It is apparent that Paul and his audiences in Corinth and Rome

29. W. D. Davies, Paul and Rabbinic Judaism: Some Rabbinic Elements in Pauline Theology (2nd ed.; New York: Harper & Row, 1955), 36–57.

30. Davies, *Paul and Rabbinic Judaism*, 44. He argues that the story of the creation and fall in Genesis 1–3 is ultimately the background for the concept of Jesus the Messiah who restored the entire creation (pp. 37–41).

31. Davies, *Paul and Rabbinic Judaism*, 52. He suggests that Christians in Corinth were acquainted with "Philo's distinction between the Heavenly and the earthly man," via Apollos, but he also points out that "it is improbable, though not impossible, that Paul was directly acquainted with Philo's works."

32. Davies, *Paul and Rabbinic Judaism*, 53–55. In a later study, Davies confirms that Paul "draws upon well-defined elements from Judaism" (*Jewish and Pauline Studies* [Philadelphia: Fortress Press, 1984], 194–95).

33. Davies, *Paul and Rabbinic Judaism*, 57.

were familiar with some interpretations of the story of the creation and fall of Genesis 1–3. However, Davies's thesis faces two problems: first, his reliance on post–New Testament rabbinic literature makes his thesis methodologically untenable; and, second, his recourse to Jewish speculation about the creation of Adam's physical body to explain the solidarity of human race does not explain the polyvalent meaning in Paul.[34] To be sure, there is not a monolithic interpretation, but there are diverse Jewish understandings of the creation and fall of Adam, and not simply the creation of his body. This diversity could be identified even in the same document. For instance, *4 Ezra* interprets the creation of Adam both as the head of the human race and also as the ancestor of Israel called to rule over the whole creation and over the nations (*4 Ezra* 3:4–11). In *4 Ezra* 3:5, the body of Adam points to his creatureliness and weakness rather than to his solidarity with either Israel or the peoples. This solidarity is expressed by Adam's being the head of either Israel or the nations. *4 Ezra* 3:20 also uses the analogy of sowing, either of the evil heart or of the law, in order to explain the origins of evil in the world. Likewise, Paul used the story of the creation of Adam, including his body, diversely, even within the same context. He certainly assumed some kind of solidarity of humankind in 1 Corinthians 15 and Romans 5, but the noun σῶμα does not play any role in Rom 5:12-21 to make this point. Instead, Paul points to the contrast between Adam and Christ and the effects of their actions upon their descendants, without referring to their bodies. In 1 Cor 15:40-44, Paul uses the analogy of sowing different kinds of bodies to show the transformation from the physical and weak body into the spiritual and imperishable risen body, not to demonstrate the solidarity of humankind. Then Paul contrasts the first and the last Adam as heads of the physical and spiritual humankind, respectively (1 Cor 15:45-49). The solidarity is shown by their being the heads of two stages in humankind, and not simply by their respective physical and spiritual bodies. Davies also overlooks the different literary contexts of Rom 5:12-21 and 1 Cor 15:47 and therefore the different functions of the Adam motif in these texts due to the creativity of Paul, who addressed specific circumstances of two different communities. In 1 Corinthians 15, Paul addresses the question of the future and bodily resurrection of the believers who have died. In Rom 5:12-21 Paul emphasizes the greater effects of Christ's expiatory death. Davies also seems to have overlooked that by using the figure of Adam

34. E. Schweizer ("σῶμα, κτλ.," *TDNT* 7:1024–94) analyzes the history and polyvalence of this term, and demonstrates that Paul used it in more than one sense. See also Robert H. Gundry, *Sōma in Biblical Theology, with Emphasis on Pauline Anthropology* (SNTSMS 29; Cambridge: Cambridge University Press, 1976), 219–20. Jewett (*Paul's Anthropological Terms*, 240) also points out that the texts Davies cites "do not in themselves hint at such universalistic implications."

Paul instills an ethical dimension into the discussion that demands from the believers a change of life in order to participate in the future resurrection with Christ. The contrast between Adam and Christ is depicted as one of two very different lifestyles in Paul, the one leading to death, the other to resurrection.

Another approach that sought to interpret Paul against the background of Palestinian Judaism is found in E. P. Sanders.[35] He bases his analysis on his understanding of the "pattern of religion" and contends that "Paul presents an essentially different type of religiousness from any found in Palestinian Jewish literature."[36] Sanders argues that Paul's description of the human plight originates not in Judaism, Hellenism, or even Hellenistic Judaism, as represented by Philo, but from the solution he envisaged, that is, from the salvation that God brings to all who believe in Christ.[37] Seen in this way, Paul's contrast between Adam and Christ is concerned not with the status of humanity prior to the Christ-event, but with the significance and the consequences for the believer of Christ's death in the present, and the believer's future participation in Christ's resurrection. Thus, Sanders contends that Paul's main concern is not anthropological but soteriological and christological.[38] Furthermore, the Adam motif in Paul is set not within the Jewish "covenantal nomism," established already with Israel, but it derives from Paul's "participationist eschatology."[39] In other words, Sanders interprets the Adam motif in Paul under the light of the Christ-event and the effects that his death has brought to the believer in the present, but which are to be fulfilled in the future. Seen in this way, Sanders locates Paul closer to the apocalyptic trends of late Judaism. Paul interprets the Adam motif looking not to the origins of humankind in the old Adam but to the salvation that the death and resurrection of new Adam have brought to the believer, and to its fulfillment in the *eschaton*.

35. E. P. Sanders, *Paul and Palestinian Judaism: A Comparison of Patterns of Religion* (Philadelphia: Fortress Press, 1952).

36. Sanders, *Paul and Palestinian Judaism*, 543. For Sanders, the "pattern of religion" of Judaism is what he calls "covenantal nomism," that is, that God chose Israel and gave the Law, which should be kept in order for the Israelites to remain among the saved ones. On the other hand, Sanders calls Paul's pattern of religion "participationist eschatology" (see *Paul and Palestinian Judaism*, 552). "Thus, in all these essential points—the meaning of 'righteousness,' the role of repentance, the nature of sin, the nature of the saved 'group' and, most important, the necessity of transferring from the damned to the saved—Paul's thought can be sharply distinguished from anything to be found in Palestinian Judaism. . . . Further, the difference is not located in a supposed antithesis of grace and works . . . but in the total type of religion" (p. 548).

37. Sanders, *Paul and Palestinian Judaism*, 552–56.

38. Sanders, *Paul and Palestinian Judaism*, 446, *pace* Bultmann.

39. Sanders, *Paul and Palestinian Judaism*, 511–15, 549.

In addition to recognizing Paul's Jewish heritage, Sanders's most important contribution is in recognizing Paul's own creativity in highlighting the soteriological and eschatological significance of the contrast between Adam and Christ. The future tense used in Rom 5:17 and 1 Cor 15:22-23 shows that Paul considers the participation of the believer in Christ's resurrection to be a future event. Though Sanders admirably brings this to our attention, he overlooks Paul's ethical and social concerns for the believer in the present. For instance, in Romans Paul concludes his contrast between Adam and Christ with the contrast between sin and death, and grace and eternal life, "so that as sin reigned in death, grace also might reign (οὕτως καὶ ἡ χάρις βασιλεύσῃ) through righteousness to eternal life through Jesus Christ our Lord" (Rom 5:21). In the following chapter, Romans 6, Paul further develops the implications of the new status of those who are baptized into Christ, "so that as Christ was raised from the dead by the glory of the Father, we too might walk in newness of life" (οὕτως καὶ ἡμεῖς ἐν καινότητι ζωῆς περιπατήσωμεν) (Rom 6:4). Likewise, in 1 Corinthians 15 Paul concludes his discussion about the resurrection with the exhortation to "sin no more" (vv. 32b-34), and to "be steadfast, immovable, always abounding in the work of the Lord" (v. 58).

C. K. Barrett investigates the Adam typology in Paul within the Old Testament and early Judaism, underlining its corporate dimension.[40] He argues that "it is in the last resort in the event of Jesus Christ that the truth about man, and thus about the 'typical' men, Adam, Abraham, and Moses, is revealed."[41] Accordingly, Adam stands along with the figures of Abraham, Moses, and Christ as "representative figures" of every person.[42] Barrett claims, "What man needs is to return to the true Creator-creature relationship for which he was made."[43] Thus, according to Paul, Christ is the paradigm of God's original plan in creation. Finally, after a brief analysis of selected passages from Philo on the creation of man, Barrett excludes any possible influence of this author on Paul.[44] Barrett's thesis makes two important contributions: first, it explains Paul's Jewish notion of human solidarity, that is, that the actions and fate of one, Adam, and

40. C. K. Barrett, *From First Adam to Last: A Study in Pauline Theology* (New York: Scribner, 1962); see also his "The Significance of the Adam-Christ Typology for the Resurrection of the Dead: 1 Co 15, 20-22. 45-49," in *Résurrection du Christ et des Chrétiens*, ed. Lorenzo De Lorenzi (Série monographique de "Benedictina": Section biblico-oecuménique 8; Rome: Abbaye de S. Paul, 1985), 99–126. In this article he analyzes the relationship between 1 Cor 15:20-22 and vv. 45-49, and between Rom 5:12-21 and Romans 6.

41. Barrett, *From First Adam to Last*, 6.

42. Barrett, *From First Adam to Last*, 5. He states that "Paul believed that everything that could be said about Adam as a (supposed) historical figure could be said also about mankind as a whole" (p. 19).

43. Barrett, *From First Adam to Last*, 20.

then of Christ affect the rest of humanity. Second, although Barrett does not elaborate further, he identifies "the practical moral consequences of Christian belief . . . drawn in the middle of the chapter [1 Corinthians 15], with only a distant echo at the end in v. 58."[45]

Barrett's hypothesis presents some difficulties. First, although there is a corporate dimension in the figures of Adam and Christ, Paul clearly understands them primarily as individuals. Second, "the second man from heaven" (ὁ δεύτερος ἄνθρωπος ἐξ ουρανοῦ) (1 Cor 15:47b), understood as referring to the messianic and corporate figure coming from the clouds in Dan 7:13,[46] presents some textual difficulties.[47] Additionally, in 1 Cor 15:47b Paul refers to Christ as an individual, not as a collectivity, opposed to the individual Adam of Gen 2:7. Third, it is questionable that Paul identifies Christ's glory with the glory of the pre-fallen Adam. Instead, it is clear that Paul interprets the figure of Adam in a rather negative tone; that is, he sins and brings death to all. Furthermore, Paul emphasizes Christ's obedience and its salvific effects on all humanity in contrast to Adam's disobedience and its effects (πολλῷ μᾶλλον, Rom 5:9, 10, 15, 17; ὑπερεπερίσσευσεν, 5:20) and not simply a restoration of the order of creation established and originally intended by God. Fourth, Barrett's reliance on rabbinic literature that in fact postdated Paul also undermines his thesis. Even though these texts may point to later trends in the interpretation of the figure of Adam, they do not explain Paul's own interpretation, for he clearly did not have access to them.

In a similar approach, Robin Scroggs proposes that "Paul's Adamic Christology is based securely in Jewish theology about Adam and in Paul's own theological concerns."[48] From the "the general cultic and communal

44. See Barrett's appendix in *From First Adam to Last*. He makes the same point in his article "The Significance of the Adam-Christ Typology for the Resurrection of the Dead." There he discusses examples from Philo's exegesis of the double story of the creation of man in Genesis (pp. 103, 114–16).

45. Barrett, "Significance of the Adam-Christ Typology," 121.

46. See Barrett, "Significance of the Adam-Christ Typology," 116–20. He states, "Jesus like Adam was a representative person, for the Son of man in Dan 7 represents the people of the saints of the Most High" (p. 118; see also 120–21).

47. Other manuscripts render ο κυριος, 630; (McionA); ανθρωπος ο κυριος. **2א** A D1 K Λ Π Ψ 075. 81, 104, 365, 630, 1241, 1505, 1739mg. 1881. 2464 sy; ανθρωπος πνευματικος P46; *txt* **א*** B C D* F G 0243. 6. 33. 1175. 1739* latt bo; ο ουρανοις F G latt; Novum Testamentum Graece, Greek-English New Testament, Nestle Aland, 28th edition.

48. Robin Scroggs, *The Last Adam: A Study in Pauline Anthropology* (Philadelphia: Fortress Press), xxi–xxii. In a more recent contribution, Stephen Hultgren follows essentially the same argumentation ("The Origin of Paul's Doctrine of the Two Adams in 1 Corinthians 15.45-49," *JSNT* 25 [2003]: 343–70). He rules out Gnostic influences and Hellenistic Judaism such as Philo's interpretation of the

environment" of Jewish theology, Scroggs identifies three concepts that arguably Paul transforms from contemporary Jewish traditions. First, Paul interprets Christ as the last Adam, who is the model and mediator of what God intended for humanity.[49] Second, in his discussion of the resurrection in 1 Corinthians 15, Paul responds to "Jewish theologians" who altered the "original view" of a corporeal resurrection and held instead a "non-corporeal" resurrection.[50] Third, Paul introduced the concept of image, "Christ is the image of God. . . . The believer becomes God's image only through Christ."[51] Scroggs also identifies the apocalyptic context in which Paul correlates the original glory of Adam in the *Urzeit* and the glory that humanity, particularly Israel, will receive in the *Endzeit*.[52] Finally, Scroggs briefly discusses Philo's interpretation of Genesis 1–3 and his possible influence on Paul. He concludes that Philo used Jewish traditions and rabbinic concepts translated into Hellenistic concepts, but he states that "the ideas found in Philo cannot be said to be the background or foil for Paul's argument."[53] Scroggs advances the investigation of the Adam motif in Paul, noticing particularly Paul's originality within the Jewish context. Nevertheless, he also points out the methodological problem concerning the date of the literature of the Adam motif, since "much of the Apocrypha and Pseudepigrapha is . . . contemporary or later than Paul, and . . . no written rabbinic materials existed until probably at least a century after Paul's death."[54]

This literature suggests that there was a diverse array of Jewish traditions about Adam that underscored either his original glory or the sin and death that his transgression brought to humanity. Paul portrays Adam in a rather negative tone; that is, focusing on the sin and death he brought, in contrast to Christ's grace and life. Scroggs underestimates Paul's universalistic perspective on the

creation of man (see p. 355). Instead he claims that both rabbinic literature (pp. 360–63) and especially Paul's encounter with the risen Christ as the "image of God" (pp. 367–69) better explain Paul's background for the Adam motif. Nevertheless, Hultgren also acknowledges that the midrashim he explores (*Genesis Rabbah* 8.1; 14.2-5; and *Midrash Tehillim* on Ps 139:5) "are quite late" (p. 363). He concludes that "Christ was both the true representation of God in the likeness of human form and the true representation of humanity in the image of God" (p. 369).

49. Scroggs argues that Paul thinks of the new humanity as "no more no less than a restoration to that truly human reality God has always desired for man" (*Last Adam*, 64).

50. Scroggs, *Last Adam*, 65.

51. Scroggs, *Last Adam*, 69.

52. Scroggs, *Last Adam*, 21–31. Davies had already suggested this correlation (*Paul and Rabbinic Judaism*, 49).

53. Davies, *Paul and Rabbinic Judaism*, 49; Scroggs, *Last Adam*, 122.

54. Scroggs, *Last Adam*, 115; cf. 121–22.

Adam motif by which the effects of Christ, the last Adam, reach not only Israel but all peoples. Finally, Scroggs overlooks the literary context of the Jewish literature and Paul's letters to Romans and 1 Corinthians, thereby missing the ethical and social implications they inferred from the Adam figure. The literary context gives full meaning to the figure of Adam. Thus, Paul's comparison between Adam and Christ and the *Urzeit* and *Endzeit* they respectively inaugurated, is balanced by the demand of an ethical transformation of the believer in the present in order to participate in the resurrection with Christ in the future. On the one hand, Jesus' death and resurrection overcome Adam's past disobedience and its effects and inaugurate the eschatological times. On the other, Jesus' resurrection assures and enables the believer to share in the future resurrection. In the meantime, however, the believer is called to lead a life that accords with the new life in Christ.

A. J. M. Wedderburn's dissertation is perhaps the most comprehensive study that ruled out Gnosticism and turned to Paul's Jewish backgrounds, particularly Genesis 1–3 and subsequent Jewish interpretations of the story of the creation and fall of humankind, to explain the figure of Adam in 1 Corinthians 15 and Rom 5:12-21.[55]

In chapter 2 he systematically analyzes 1 Corinthians 15 against its Jewish backgrounds. He claims that "Paul's contrast of Adam and Christ is his own construction, using on the one hand Jewish ideas about the fallen Adam and on the other the early Christian tradition of Christ as God's appointed Man, or, as Jesus himself put it, 'the Son of Man.'"[56] Likewise, with regard to the contrast of being either "in Adam" or "in Christ" (1 Cor 15:22), Wedderburn contends that "Paul's ἐν Χριστῷ language is his own coinage or that of the early church."[57] Regarding 1 Cor 15:44-45 he claims that, drawing on Old Testament and Jewish traditions about the gift of the Spirit,[58] Paul introduced

55. A. J. M. Wedderburn, "Adam and Christ." In his "Adam in Paul's Letters to the Romans," *StudBib* 3 (1978): 413–30, Wedderburn focuses on other Adamic texts such as Rom 1:18-23 and 7:7-12. In a later work, Wedderburn rules out Gnosticism as the background for the denial of the resurrection in Corinth (*Baptism and Resurrection,* 12). He held a similar position in "The Theological Structure of Romans V.12" *NTS* 19 (1972–73): 339–54.

56. "Adam and Christ," 114. Therefore, he rules out both the "primal man" and the "Gnostic Man" to explain the contrast between Adam and Christ in 1 Corinthians 15. Regarding the latter he concludes that "there is no need to invoke a mythological Gnostic *Anthropos* to explain the traditions behind Philo's heavenly man; they are to be understood as Hellenistic interpretations of the legends surrounding the Biblical Adam in Jewish haggadah;" ibid., 162.

57. "Adam and Christ," 167, 171–75.

58. The Spirit as the gift of the end-time as an expression of a new creation; see Ezek 37:14 (Wedderburn, "Adam and Christ," 191–92).

the contrast between ψυχή and πνεῦμα, and between the heavenly man and the earthly man to correct the negative esteem the Corinthians had of ψυχή.[59] Similarly, regarding the order of the spiritual and the physical (1 Cor 15:46), Wedderburn contends that Paul reminds the Corinthians that "there is a present existence on the natural level to be lived out before the new creation could be ushered in."[60] Finally, after skipping 1 Cor 15:47-48, he claims that Paul reinterpreted the Jewish concept "image" as the garment of glory that human beings are to wear in the future, to introduce the contrast between "bearing the image" of the man of dust, or "bearing the image" of the man of heaven (15:49).[61]

In a comparatively briefer chapter 3, Wedderburn analyzes Rom 5:12-21. In regard to Rom 5:12, he claims that Paul drew on Jewish texts that point to the origin of sin in Adam and/or Eve,[62] and texts that describe sin as a power.[63] However, Wedderburn rightly claims that Paul did not imply that Adam was responsible for other human sins.[64] Likewise, he contends that Paul relied on Old Testament and Jewish ideas that spoke of death as "as a personified power which reigns over men," and as "the judgment of God" against humankind.[65] Yet Paul develops this thought to introduce the paradox that Christ's death brought life into the world and that "we must only be conformed to that death that we may enjoy his life."[66] Thus, despite the oppressive power of sin and death over all humanity, Paul claimed that the power of grace and righteousness has abounded even more for all humanity. Wedderburn also analyzes Rom 5:13-14a within the previous context where Paul discussed the relationship between sin and the law (Rom 2:12-16) and claims that here Paul "must say how all could sin regardless of whether the law was there or not."[67] Finally, regarding

59. Wedderburn argues that the expression πνεῦμα/πνευματικοί may have been introduced by Paul himself "to the Corinthians and that they then abused it rather than invented it or borrowed it from elsewhere," as evidenced earlier in Galatians 6 ("Adam and Christ," 187. Likewise, the term ψυχή "was introduced, perhaps by Paul himself, to the Corinthians" (p. 196).

60. "Adam and Christ," 204. Although he acknowledges Philo's distinction between the heavenly and earthly men, this might be no more than "an indirect witness" in 1 Cor 15:46 ("Adam and Christ," 199–200.

61. "Adam and Christ," 206–9, an idea also used in the early Christian symbolism of baptism.

62. In addition to Genesis 3, see Wis 2:24; Sir 25:24; *Apoc. Mos.* 32:2; *2 En.* 41:1; *2. Bar.* 43:42-43; *T. Adam* 3:16; "Adam and Christ," 213-5.

63. "Adam and Christ," 216.

64. "Adam and Christ," 221; see also 215, 219, 233–35.

65. He cites among other texts Exod 12:23; 1 Chr 21:12, 15; Job 15:21 (see "Adam and Christ," 222–23.

66. "Adam and Christ," 223.

the contrast between the one and the many/all in Rom 5:18-19, Wedderburn argues that Paul is indebted to Old Testament traditions that explained the solidarity of all humankind with Adam (although not in his act of sin) and also the responsibility of God's people for keeping the covenant.[68] Thus, the new covenant that God made through Christ's death for the salvation of all sinful mankind is "the foundation of Paul's schema of the 'one' and the 'many.'"[69]

Wedderburn's study represents an important turning point toward Paul's Jewish background to understand the Adam motif in 1 Corinthians 15 and Rom 5:12-21.[70] He correctly interprets Paul's Adam motif against the story of the creation as found in Genesis 1–3 along with Jewish and Hellenistic Jewish traditions about the story of Adam and Eve and the effects of their actions on their descendants. Nevertheless, his thesis presents several difficulties. First, he overlooks the diversity of Jewish interpretations of the creation and fall of Adam, and even the tensions within some documents, as the background for Paul's interpretation of the figure of Adam in both 1 Corinthians 15 and Rom 5:12-21[71] Second, he also neglects the overall structure of each document and the way each author put the figure of Adam into the service of their message. In other words, he decontextualized the figure of Adam from the intended message of each author. Third, he also overlooks the eschatological dimension of most of these Jewish interpretations. They interpret the dreadful present situation of humankind as a consequence of their disobedience, as was the case with Adam, but they envision a recreation in the near future that would abolish sin and death. Finally and most importantly, although Wedderburn parenthetically identifies the ethical overtones that Philo inferred from his exegesis of the story of the creation of humans,[72] he overlooks the ethical implications that most Jewish interpreters found in the story of the creation and fall of Adam. Quite often, as we will see in chapter 2, these authors addressed a current situation using the story of Genesis 1–3 as an example of the consequences of the disobedience to God's commandments and to exhort their audiences to abide

67. "Adam and Christ," 236; see also 237. This in accordance with the wider context of Romans (2:14-16).

68. "Adam and Christ," 244.

69. "Adam and Christ," 245.

70. Wedderburn concludes his work with a challenge: "In a sense all that we have done in the preceding pages is to clear away misunderstandings that have accumulated around Paul's view as the new Man; certainly there remains a great deal of interpretative work that needs to be built upon this cleared site" ("Adam and Christ," 248).

71. A point already noted by Levison, *Portraits*, 23.

72. In *Leg. All.* 1.31-39, "Philo is quite deliberately combining the ethical and the physical" ("Adam and Christ," 152 n. 3.

by God's statutes. This insight may support the thesis that the traditions about the story of the creation and fall were not merely anthropological speculations about the origin of humanity or the dire situation of humans in the present, but that these traditions also elicited a transformation in the present regarding hope for a better situation in the future. This is the case of Paul who, in Rom 5:12-21 and 1 Corinthians 15, may have used different interpretations of the creation and fall of Adam that he put into the service of the respective arguments of 1 Corinthians and Romans. The novelty he introduced in both cases is that he contrasted Adam to Christ, who brought the last aeon with his death and resurrection. As for the believer, Paul placed his participation in Christ's resurrection in the future on the condition that the believer may participate in Christ's death in terms of an ethical transformation in the present.

There have been other contributions to the Adam motif in Paul that we will analyze in the following section. James D. G. Dunn represents a transition between proponents of the Gnostic hypothesis and proponents of the Jewish hypothesis in regard to the Adam motif in Paul. In what appears to be his first contribution,[73] he contends that, in 1 Cor 15:45, Paul responds to some Gnostics who claimed that through the experience of the Spirit they were already participating in a spiritual unbodily resurrection. Dunn suggests that Paul identifies "the last Adam" with the "risen Lord" who became πνεῦμα ζῳοποιοῦν ("life-giving Spirit"). Furthermore, he claims that "*the believer's experience of the life giving Spirit is for Paul proof that the risen Jesus is* σῶμα πνευματικόν" ("spiritual body"; 15:44).[74] Although at the end of his article Dunn makes a distinction between Christ and the Spirit,[75] throughout his argument he identifies the experience of the risen Lord with the experience of the Spirit,[76] reducing the πνεῦμα ζῳοποιοῦν to the subjective spiritual experience of the believers.

73. James D. G. Dunn, "1 Corinthians 15.45—Last Adam, Life-Giving Spirit," in *Christ and Spirit in the New Testament,* ed. Barnabas Lindars and Stephen S. Smalley (Cambridge: Cambridge University Press, 1973), 127–41.

74. Dunn, "1 Corinthians 15.45," 131 (emphasis original). According to Dunn, Paul based his argument on two assumptions. First, Christians in Corinth experienced the exalted Jesus as a πνεῦμα ζῳοποιοῦν. This is exemplified when they confess Jesus as Lord (1 Cor 12:3) and also in their experience as sons of God (Rom 8:15-16; Gal 4:6) (p. 133). Second, "Jesus has a representative capacity in his existence as πνεῦμα ζῳοποιοῦν" (p. 135).

75. Dunn, "1 Corinthians 15.45," 139.

76. Dunn, "1 Corinthians, 15.45," 127, 132, 137, 138, 139, 140. More clearly, in his closing statement he says that "Christ has become Spirit, *Christ is now experienced as Spirit*—that is true. But it is only because *the Spirit is now experienced as Christ* that the experience of the Spirit is valid and essential for Paul" (p. 141, emphasis on the original).

Later, Dunn rules out the "Gnostic redeemer myth" as the background for Paul or his readers.[77] Instead, he acknowledges that Paul was reacting against the heavenly/earthly man antithesis, as attested in Philo's exegesis of Genesis 1–2,[78] but he claims that ultimately "Paul derived his exegesis *from the resurrection of Christ*."[79] Dunn argues that Jewish interpretations of the story of the creation and fall of humans in Genesis 1–3 as well as earlier Christian interpretations of the story of the creation along with Ps 8:4-6 (and Ps 110:1) provided "an Adam christology which embraced both the earthly as well as the exalted Jesus,"[80] as reflected in 2 Cor 8:9; Phil 2:6-11; and 1 Cor 15:45-47. He surmises that Phil 2:6-11 is an expression of traditional Adam Christology that presents two stages of Christ, first the earthly Jesus who shares humans' lot, including death, and, second, Christ's exaltation.[81] Dunn concludes that 2 Cor 8:9; Phil 2:6-11; and 1 Cor 15:45-47 do not represent a typology of a preexistent Adam,[82] but rather that Paul emphasizes the eschatological dimension of Christ as the Last Adam

77. "On the contrary all indications are that it was a *post*-Christian (second-century) development using Christian beliefs about Jesus as one of its building blocks" (James D. G. Dunn, *Christology in the Making: A New Testament Inquiry into the Origins of the Doctrine of the Incarnation* (2nd ed.; Grand Rapids: Eerdmans, 1989), 99; cf. also 124–25. In his *1 Corinthians* (NTG; Sheffield: Sheffield Academic Press, 1995), Dunn again rules out the Gnostic hypothesis (p. 84).

78. "Paul himself seems to be aware of some such distinction . . . his *denial* that the spiritual (= heavenly) man *precedes* the earthly in his own interpretation of Gen 2.7 being possibly directed against something like Philo's heavenly man/earthly man interpretation of Gen 1.26f and 2.7" (Dunn, *Christology in the Making*, 100).[

79. Dunn states that Paul's "Adam christology focused not on some original man who had descended from heaven but on the second man whom he expected to return from heaven shortly, whose image as the resurrected one Christians would share" (*Christology in the Making*, 124).

80. He claims, "This development . . . probably predates Paul's letters too, since it seems to be reflected in 1 Cor 15 and to provide the backcloth for Rom 5.12-19" (*Christology in the Making*, 111). He previously argued that Ps 8:6 "was drawn in to supplement the latter half of Ps 110:1," "again and again in earliest Christian apologetic and in proclamation of the resurrection of Jesus (Mark 12.36 pars.; 14.62 pars.; Acts 2.3f; Rom 8.34; 1 Cor 15.25; Eph 1.20; Col 3.1; Heb 1.3, 13; 8.1; 10.12f; 12.2; I Peter 3.22)" (p. 108).

81. "*The Christ of Phil. 2.6-11 therefore is the man who undid Adam's wrong*: confronted with the same choice, he rejected Adam's sin, but nevertheless freely followed Adam's course as fallen man to the bitter end of death; wherefore God bestowed on him the status not simply that Adam lost, but the status which Adam was intended to come to, God's final prototype, the last Adam" (Dunn, *Christology in the Making*, 119).

82. "It would seem therefore that the point of the parallel between Adam and Christ is not dependent on any particular time scale—pre-existence, prehistory or whatever" (Dunn, *Christology in the Making*, 119; cf. also 126 and 128).

(cf. 1 Cor 15:45), whose role "begins and stems from his resurrection, not from pre-existence, or even from his earthly ministry."[83]

Finally, in *The Theology of Paul the Apostle,* Dunn surveys seven Jewish interpretations of the story of the creation and fall in Genesis 1–3 that prepare for Paul's understanding of sin and death.[84] For instance, Ben Sira contends that hardships and death were the natural lot of humankind.[85] More significant are the similarities between Wis 2:23-24 and Rom 1:19—2:6, where the language ("incorruption," "image," "eternity," and the entrance of death into the world) shows literary contact between these documents. Likewise the interpretation of the story of Adam's disobedience and sentence of death found in *Jub.* 3:17-31 is similar to the way Paul associates Adam's sin and death in Rom 5:12. A different trend of interpretation of the creation of humans is that of Philo, who points to two kinds of humans, one living according to reason, the other according to the flesh. According to Philo, death does not seem to be the result of human sin. The *Life of Adam and Eve* also has striking similarities to Paul; for instance "the identification of *epithymia* . . . as the root of all sin; and the theme of 'death gaining rule over all our race' as a result of Adam and Eve's transgression," as well as the promise of resurrection to a faithful Adam.[86] Dunn also identifies several similarities between Rom 5:12-14 and *4 Ezra* 3:7-10 and 3:21-26, which attribute to Adam's transgression the entrance of sin and death into the world.[87] Finally, 2 *Baruch* tries to balance Adam's sin and death as something transmitted to his descendants with personal responsibility. Dunn argues that these Jewish interpretations of the story of the creation and fall of Adam in Genesis 1–3 identify a play between Adam as individual and *'ādām* as a representative of all humankind in an effort to deal with the dire human experience of sin and death, and he concludes that "Paul was entering into an already well-developed debate and that his own views were not uninfluenced by its earlier participants."[88]

83. Dunn, *Christology in the Making,* 126. Indeed, in his later work on 1 Corinthians, Dunn underscores the eschatological and apocalyptic dimension of the gospel for Paul and states that "the fundamental structure of his thought [particularly in 1 Corinthians 15] is drawn primarily from Jewish apocalypticism" (*1 Corinthians*, 87).

84. Dunn discusses the figure of Adam, under the heading "Humankind under Indictment," in chapter 3; see *The Theology of Paul the Apostle* (Grand Rapids: Eerdmans, 1998), 83–90.

85. With the exception of Sir 25:24, which blames woman's sin for humankind's death.

86. Although the Latin and the Greek version of (*Apocalypse of Moses*) might be dated later than Paul's letters, Dunn claims that it may reflect an earlier original Hebrew text (*Theology of Paul,* 88).

87. Dunn, *Theology of Paul,* 88–89.

88. Dunn, *Theology of Paul,* 90.

Although earlier Dunn claimed that Phil 2:6-11 does not represent a typology of a preexistent Adam, in *The Theology of Paul,* he analyzes this text under the heading of the preexistent one and claims that "the Philippians hymn is, after Heb 2.5-6, the fullest expression of Adam Christology in the NT."[89] Now Dunn argues that Phil 2:6-11 is "an extended metaphor" that speaks of a preexistent stage of Christ as the ideal "Adam that God intended."[90]

This series of studies shows that Dunn developed his thought about Paul's Adamic typology only to arrive at the same conclusion, that is, that the hymn found in Phil 2:6-11 represents an Adam Christology that speaks of Jesus as the Last Adam. He initially proposed that in 1 Corinthians 15 Paul reacted against Gnostic proponents of an unbodily resurrection. Then he rejected the Gnostic hypothesis and focused on Paul's Jewish heritage. Thus, he rightly identified the story of the creation and fall of humanity in Genesis 1–3 and subsequent Jewish interpretations as the general background of the Adam typology in Paul. Nevertheless, Dunn's interpretation of Adam's typology is not without problems.[91] First, he does not account for the diversity of these Jewish interpretations of the story of creation and fall of Adam (and Eve), even in the same texts, as we will see in the next chapter. Second, he does not take into consideration the historical and literary contexts of these interpretations, and he overlooks the literary function of the figure of Adam, which in some cases may convey implicit ethical or social ideas such as an exhortation to obey God's commands. Third, he likewise overlooks the different literary contexts where Paul evokes the figure of Adam and the ethical connotations he elicits from them. The most notorious difficulty is his interpretation of Phil 2:6-11 in *The Theology of Paul.* It is fair to acknowledge that there is an implicit contrast between Adam's disobedience and Christ's obedience, but to identify other details of the story of the creation account(s) from Genesis 1–3 in Phil 2:6-11 is beyond what the text simply says. First of all, it seems that Paul understood Adam not as humankind but as an individual, as attested earlier in the Greek translation of both accounts of the creation, Gen 1:26-27 and 2:7, which translate אָדָם as ἄνθρωπος, not as the proper name "Adam," whereas Gen 3:9-24 אָדָם is retained in the Greek as Αδαμ. Second, although ἐν μορφῇ and κατ' εἰκόνα may be translated as synonyms, Phil 2:6c says that Christ "did not count equality with God (ἴσα θεῷ)" whereas Gen 1:26b states that God created man according to his "likeness," καθ' ὁμοίωσιν. It seems that

89. Dunn, *Theology of Paul,* 286.

90. Dunn, *Theology of Paul,* 288.

91. For a critique of Dunn's thesis of the Adam typology in Phil 2:6-11, see also L. D. Hurst, "Re-enter the Existent Christ in Philippians 2.5-11?" *NTS* 32 (1986): 449–57.

ἴσα in Phil 2:6c may evoke ἰσάγγελοι, as in παρ' ἀγγέλους (LXX Ps 8:6).[92] Thus, Phil 2:6-11 may refer to the human condition and dignity of Jesus Christ, a "little less than an angel, crowned with glory and honor" (cf. Ps 8:6), who, despite his dignity, "emptied himself" (Phil 2:7). Although Phil 2:6-11 may allude obliquely to the theme of Adam's disobedience, the focus of this passage is Jesus, who, despite his dignity and honor, became obedient to death. This interpretation better responds to the literary context, which shows that some Philippians, perhaps thinking too highly of themselves, quarreled among themselves and disobeyed the apostle. Thus, Paul exhorts his readers to "do nothing from selfishness or conceit, but in humility" (Phil 2:3) and to obey (2:12). Even in the event that Paul has in mind the story of Adam's disobedience in Phil 2:6-11, it shows that Paul used the Adam motif differently than in 1 Corinthians 15 and Rom 5:12-21. It seems that Paul knew a wide range of Jewish interpretations of the creation and fall of Adam and interpreted them diversely accordingly to different contexts. Thus, Phil 2:6-11 may reflect an early Christian interpretation of the story of Adam's disobedience, but other texts such as 1 Cor 15:21 and Rom 5:12-21, speak also of Adam's sin and death, whereas 1 Cor 15:45-47 refers to his earthly and mortal nature. In sum, Dunn advanced in the right direction the investigation of the Adam motif in Paul from its Gnostic background to its Jewish milieu, but he failed to note the literary context and function of the figure of Adam in Paul and his Jewish antecedents or contemporaries, as well as the social and ethical implications they elicited from the Adam motif.

N. T. Wright also interprets Paul's Adam typology in the context of the Old Testament and Jewish traditions.[93] His thesis is that the Adam typology in intertestamental and rabbinic literature "is not about 'man in general.' It is about Israel, the people of God."[94] Wright argues that Paul's Adam Christology is a

92. The focus of the discussions has been on whether εἰκόνα and μορφῇ are synonyms or not, but the discussion should also include ὁμοίωσιν and ἴσα. This could be supported if ἴσα can be linked to ἰσάγγελοι, since "This rare word corresponds to such analogous constructions as ἰσόθεος and ἰσοβασιλεύς." It is especially likely when Luke 20:36 "tells us that the resurrected will know neither mortality nor sexual intercourse, since they are like angels," as G. Kittel argues ("ἄγγελος, κτλ," *TDNT* 1:87).

93. N. T. Wright, "Adam in Pauline Christology," in *SBL Seminar Papers,* vol. 22 (Chico, Calif.: Scholars Press, 1983), 359–89.

94. Wright, "Adam," 360. He continues, "God's purposes for the human race in general have developed on to, and will be fulfilled in, Israel in particular. Israel is, or will become God's true humanity. What God intended for Adam will be given to the seed of Abraham. . . . If there is a 'last Adam' in the relevant Jewish literature, he is not an individual . . . he is the whole eschatological people of God" (p. 361). Wright reviews the motif of blessings and "God's purposes for Israel" in the Old Testament,

revision of these traditional Jewish understandings of God's purposes for Israel applied now to Jesus Christ.[95] Wright selects "relevant passages" to prove this: 1 Cor 15:20–57; Rom 5:12–21; Phil 2:5–11; and Col 1:15. In the analysis of 1 Cor 15:20–57, Wright argues first that in 15:20–28 Paul explains the resurrection as "a two stage process" within a modified "Jewish apocalyptic scheme," which considers Jesus as "the one upon whom has now developed the vocation of Israel."[96] Then, leaving out the analysis of 15:29-34, which he considers to be "a more personal appeal,"[97] Wright focuses on the question of the future bodily resurrection in 15:35–57, particularly 15:42–49. Wright concludes, "The Last Adam is the eschatological Israel. . . . Paul's claim is that Jesus, as Messiah, is the realization of Israel's hope."[98]

Wright's creative interpretation of 1 Cor 15:20–57 is questionable for several reasons. First, there is no evidence that Paul's Adam Christology is "an Israel-Christology." On the contrary, Paul explicitly explains that "in Adam *all* die" and that "in Christ shall *all* be alive" (1 Cor 15:22). Second, Wright's appraisal of v. 45 "as an aside" contradicts Paul's explicit reference to the Scripture, οὕτως καὶ γέγραπται (very likely a reference to Gen 2:7, καὶ ἐγένετο ὁ ἄνθρωπος εἰς ψυχὴν ζῶσαν), which supports his argument. Third, Wright translates ἄνθρωπος in v. 47 as "humanity."[99] It is evident, however, that Paul understands ἄνθρωπος here as individuals, as is suggested by the explicit contrast between ὁ πρῶτος ἄνθρωπος Ἀδάμ ("the first man Adam") and ὁ ἔσχατος Ἀδάμ ("the last Adam"), and between one "from the earth" and the other "from heaven," respectively. Finally, Wright's reductionist claim that Christ stands as the representative of Israel contradicts 1 Cor 15:22, where Paul clearly states that the consequences of Adam and Christ affect "all."

In the analysis of Rom 5:12–21, Wright contends that "Christ, and his people, form the true humanity which Israel was called to be but, by the law alone, could not be."[100] He interprets this passage within the larger context

intertestamental Judaism, and "post-biblical Jewish theology," so that the Messiah would embody the blessings of the whole nation of Israel (pp. 361–65). After the crisis of the exile, he argues, the messianic expectations grew. "Thus a Messiah, if one is envisaged, draws on to himself the hope and destiny of the people itself. He, like the nation, is called the son of God" (p. 365).

95. "Paul now regarded him, not Israel, as God's true humanity" (Wright, "Adam," 365).

96. Wright, "Adam," 366. "Paul's Adam-Christology is basically an Israel-Christology: Jesus, as the Messiah, is the true Man, through whom God is now ruling the world as he always intended (vv. 25-28)" (p. 366–67).

97. That is to say, the question of the baptism "on behalf of the dead" (Wright, "Adam," 368).

98. Wright, "Adam," 370.

99. Wright, "Adam," 367–68. Then he continues, "Adam and Christ as individuals are not the main subject of discussion, but a buttress to the anthropological assertions of vv. 42-44, 46-47" (p. 368).

of Rom 1:18—5:11 and chapters 6–8, and he brings in Phil 2:5-11 to point out Christ's obedience in contrast to Adam's disobedience. Although Paul might have in mind the traditional hymn of Phil 2:6-11, especially Christ's obedience vis-à-vis Adam's disobedience, each text plays a different role in each letter. Thus, the hymn in Phil 2:6-11 supports Paul's appeals to the Philippians to endure in their sufferings (1:29) and to be humble (2:3), imitating Christ's humility and obedience; whereas the emphasis of Rom 5:12-21 is on the incommensurable contrasts between Christ and Adam and the grace and death they respectively brought to all humanity. There is, in short, nothing in Rom 5:12-21 or in Phil 2:6-11 to suggest Paul had envisioned Christ as the embodiment of the true Israel.

Yet in his analysis of Phil 2:5-11 and Col 1:15, Wright claims that Paul integrated the Adam Christology with the Servant Christology and Wisdom Christology respectively. He claims that both cases are "*Israel*-Christologies."[101] In Phil 2:5-11, Paul argues that Israel, in the figure of Adam, failed to obey God, but then the obedience of the Servant in Isaiah 40–55 has been fulfilled in Christ (Phil 2:7).[102] On the other hand, according to Wright, in Col 1:15, Christ as the εἰκὼν τοῦ θεοῦ ("image of God") echoes the story of creation in Genesis, and therefore the Adam motif. Then Wright associates this image with wisdom; "Wisdom, like Adam, is God's vice-gerent, his obedient servant, who is set in authority over the world."[103]

Wright's analysis of Phil 2:6-11 and Col 1:15 presents several problems. First, the Adam motif is not explicit in these passages. The possible allusion to Adam in Phil 2:6-11 is not to Adam as God's image but to Adam's disobedience. Second, although it seems that Paul is reinterpreting Jewish traditions, and possibly an Adam Christology, there is no evidence of so-called Israel Christologies. Wright presumes that there was a unified tradition about Adam. However, as we will see in the next chapter, the various Jewish traditions about Adam regarded him both positively and negatively. Sometimes Adam was viewed as an individual and other times as a representative for all humankind. Paul also uses the figure of Adam in different ways, according to the flow of his argument. We cannot say that the figure of Adam is presented the same way in all the texts. For example, the way in which Paul uses the figure of

100. Wright, "Adam," 371.

101. Wright, "Adam," 382, 385.

102. Wright claims that in Phil 2:10-11 "Paul credits Jesus with a rank and honor which is not only in one sense appropriate for the true Man, the Lord of the world, but is also the rank and honor explicitly reserved, according to the scriptures, for Israel's God and him alone" ("Adam," 377).

103. Wright, "Adam," 385.

Adam in 1 Cor 15:21-22, 45-49 and Rom 5:12-21 is quite different from the way he uses it in Phil 2:6-11 and Col 1:15— if indeed he uses it at all there. Third, Paul envisioned Adam as an individual and contrasted him negatively to Christ the individual. Both individuals and their actions had an impact on their descendants. Paul's interpretation also looked to the future resurrection, something that none of the Jewish interpretations envisioned for Adam.

Summary

In this chapter I have reviewed previous investigations into the Adam typology in 1 Cor 15:21-22, 45-49 and Rom 5:12-21 that concentrated on the analysis of Paul's literary and cultural backgrounds for the Adam motif.[104] One trend of investigations sought to interpret Paul's Adam motif against Gnosticism, represented by Rudolf Bultmann, Walter Schmithals, and more extensively by Egon Brandenburger. Another line of investigation has looked instead into Paul's Jewish backgrounds, represented by W. D. Davies and E. P. Sanders, who sought to interpret Paul against the background of Palestinian Judaism. Supporters of this position are Robin Scroggs, C. K. Barrett, and, more prominently A. J. M. Wedderburn. They are right on target in identifying Paul's Jewish inheritance regarding the Adam motif, in addition to Paul's own interpretation.

104. To be sure, there have been other studies on the Adam typology in Paul, but those surveyed in this chapter are the most representative studies on the Adam motif in Paul. Among other studies are those by Quek Swee-Hwa, "Adam and Christ according to Paul," in *Pauline Studies: Essays Presented to Professor F. F. Bruce on His 70th Birthday*, ed. Donald A. Hagner and Murray J. Harris (Grand Rapids: Eerdmans, 1980), 67–79. Quek builds on the studies of Paul's backgrounds developed by the *religionsgeschichtliche Schule* and concentrates on the rhetorical structure of 1 Cor 15:21, 45-49 and Rom 5:12-21. He points to the different functions of the Adam analogy in these passages: "In 1 Corinthians 15 all the formulations concern the nature of each Adam whereas in Romans 5 it is rather the respective act of each Adam and its impact" (p. 69). Although he notes the eschatological dimension in these passages, he does not identify the changes in the present for the believers. *See* also Richard H. Bell, "The Myth of Adam and the Myth of Christ in Romans 5.12-21," in *Paul, Luke and the Graeco-Roman World: Essays in Honour of Alexander J. M. Wedderburn*, ed. Alf Christophersen, Carsten Claussen, Jörg Frey, and Bruce Longenecker (JSNTSup 217; London: Sheffield Academic Press, 2002), 21–36. Bell approaches the analysis of Rom 5:12-21 as a "myth." His analysis renews the anthropological and existential debate, as exemplified by Augustine and Luther, about the meaning of sin and responsibility. "From the theoretical perspective Adam's sin is manifest in our sinning (stressing our personal responsibility). But from a practical perspective we sin in Adam (stressing rather predestination)" (p. 29). Although he distinguishes between the Adam myth and the Christ myth and the inadequacy of the latter, Bell introduces the question of predestination and responsibility with a language (myth) alien to Paul's theology. Nevertheless, as we have noted before, Paul's emphasis is on the asymmetric contrast between Adam and Christ, and the greater and better effect of the latter on the believers.

James D. G. Dunn initially suggested the Gnostic background for the Adam motif in Paul; then he sought Paul's Adam motif against his Jewish background. He also claimed that Paul actually received an earlier Christian interpretation of the Adam motif, derived from Psalm 8 and Psalm 110 to describe Christ's resurrection. However, it is a question to be explored whether Paul received an earlier Christian interpretation of the Adam motif, or if he is actually the precursor of this Christian Adam tradition. More problematic was N. T. Wright's thesis that Paul's Adam Christology is "an Israel-Christology." Although indeed Paul assumed that the deeds of Adam and Christ had effects upon their descendants, he understood them primarily as individuals, and the effects of their actions were felt not only by Israel but by all humanity.

The analysis of these contributions correctly points to early Jewish interpretations of the story of the creation and fall of humanity from Genesis 1–3 as the most likely milieu to understand Paul's Adam typology. Nevertheless, these studies have overlooked essential elements in the process of interpreting the Adam motif in both early Judaism and Paul. First, previous interpretations of the Adam motif in Paul have underestimated the diversity of Jewish interpretations and have selected instances where the figure of Adam is mentioned without paying attention to the historical and literal context of each document. In some instances, the figure of Adam is cast in a negative fashion in order to warn the audience about the consequences for those who disobey God. In other cases, Adam is presented in a positive way as the ancestor of Israel endowed with power to rule over the world. In the case of Paul, I will demonstrate that Adam is presented in a rather negative fashion to contrast him to Christ. Second, these studies have failed to note the function of the figure of Adam in each document. It is my contention that Jewish authors used the figure of Adam to explain the dire situation of the sufferings and death of humankind, sometimes putting the blame on Adam (and/or on Eve). More importantly, they used the figure of Adam in order to convey ethical and social implications to the audience, warning them of the consequences of disobeying God's commandments. Thus, inasmuch as the historical backgrounds are important to understand the figure of Adam, it is still more important to identify the way each author interpreted the narrative and the function each one gave to the story of the creation and fall of Adam.

In the same vein, quite often these studies have also neglected the larger literary context of 1 Corinthians 15 and Rom 5:12-21 and the rhetorical function the figure of Adam plays in Paul's argumentation. Although some scholars have recognized Paul's creativity in interpreting the stories of Genesis 1–3, they have not noted the unique literary context and concerns of each letter, 1 Corinthians and Romans, where Paul introduces the Adam motif. Furthermore, more attention should be paid both to the different traditions Paul may have received and to the different ways he applied the Adam figure in each of these letters.

Additionally for Paul, Adam and Christ as representative figures stand as two types of humans, the former as the representative of the old order dominated by sin and destined to die like Adam; the latter as the representative of the new creation dominated by grace and destined to share in Christ's resurrection. Thus, being in Christ gives the believer a new identity from which Paul infers ethical and social implications for the believer and the community. Being in Christ both demands that believers walk according to the Spirit, according to Christ, and enables them to do so.

Finally, more attention should be paid to the eschatological dimension of the figure of Adam in 1 Corinthians 15 and Rom 5:12–21. Indeed, the emphasis in Paul is not much on the first Adam but on Christ the last or second Adam who inaugurated the eschaton. Thus, the figure of Adam is not much explicative of the current situation of humankind; rather it contrasts to the eschatological dimension of Christ as the last Adam. In other words, Paul's perspective is not etiological but eschatological. Paul created a tension between the past and the future, emphasizing the present implications of being in Christ or in Adam. Adam's past action explains the dire present situation of humanity, particularly of sin and death. Christ's resurrection gives to the believer hope of a future resurrection. However, in order to participate in the future resurrection, the Christian is required to replicate Christ's life in the present. Thus, in 1 Corinthians 15 Paul exhorted the Corinthians, "come to your right mind, and sin no more" (v. 34); be "steadfast, immovable, always abounding in the work of the Lord" (v. 58). Although the ethical implications are less evident in Rom 5:12–21, Romans 6 points to them. The reiterated question in Rom 6:1 and 6:15 makes quite clear that Paul wants to convey to the audience that the consequences of being reconciled through Christ is "to walk in newness of life" (v. 4). In baptism "our old self" (ὁ παλαιὸς ἡμῶν ἄνθρωπος) was crucified with Christ (Rom 6:6). Thus, the literary context illuminates the function of the figure of Adam in Paul. Adam represents the old order and the old creation, but now being in Christ believers must reflect in their lives this newness in the present so as to participate also in the future in Christ's resurrection. In sum, on the one hand, the resurrection of Christ enables believers to lead a new life in Christ; on the other, in order to participate in the future resurrection with Christ, they need to be modeled after the example of Christ, as the new and last Adam.

In the next chapter, I will analyze Jewish interpretations of the story of the creation and fall in order to identify the literary function and the ethical inferences the authors may have conveyed in the Adam motif.

2

The Figure of Adam in Ancient Jewish Sources

Introduction

In this chapter, I explore ten Jewish interpretations of the story of the creation and fall of Adam as the context and background for Paul's interpretation of the figure of Adam in 1 Cor 15:21-22, 45-49, and Rom 5:12-21.[1] These interpretations see in the story of the creation and fall of Adam the drama of their own time. They cope with the dilemma of human freedom and responsibility and divine justice. Therefore, often enough they also draw ethical implications that exhort the keeping of God's commandments in order to restore the design of the creation as it was in the beginning. Nevertheless, each interpretation is marked by its specific historical and cultural context, and consequently they portray Adam in different ways.[2] In a few instances, Adam represents the ideal of the paradisiacal state before the fall and therefore is an example of a virtuous and blissful life. In most cases, however, Adam is an example of disobedience and its consequences to illustrate every person's actions and consequences, whether confined to this life or open to some sort of retribution in an afterlife. In any case, the emphasis of these interpretations is not primarily on the past but on the present, and in some cases on a future retribution. Although in most cases Paul or his audiences were probably not directly influenced by these Jewish interpreters, the analysis of other interpretations of the figure of Adam exemplifies ways of appropriating the story of the creation of humankind and the fall during this period in order

1. John R. Levison (*Portraits of Adam in Early Judaism: From Sirach to 2 Baruch* [JSPSup 1; Sheffield: JSOT Press, 1988]) concludes his thesis encouraging his readers to interpret Paul's interpretation of Adam "*alongside* the writing of other authors of Early Judaism" (p. 161; emphasis original).

2. Levison claims that "early Jewish interpretations of Adam are remarkably diversified because each author employs and adapts Adam according to his *Tendenz* (*Portraits of Adam*, 14).

to convey ethical implications in the present that may have an effect in the future. In other words, Adam is an etiological figure that evokes eschatological implications.

This chapter focuses on two aspects: first, the literary function of the Adam figure within the larger context of each passage, and, second, the ethical and social implications the authors may convey with the figure of Adam. Following a brief analysis of story of the creation and fall of Adam in Genesis 1–3, we divide this chapter into three sections that contain Jewish interpretations according to their dominant historical and cultural influence.[3] These interpretations usually incorporate more than one *Tendenz*; however, for methodological purposes we venture a threefold classification. The first group typically integrates Hellenistic concepts into their interpretations of the Scripture, to respond to their Hellenistic context: Sirach, Wisdom, and Philo's *De Opificio Mundi*. The second group, classified as "Rewritten Bible," interprets the story of the creation and the fall to explain the place of Israel among the nations: *Jubilees*, Josephus's *Antiquities*, Pseudo-Philo's *Liber Antiquitatum Biblicarum*, *Sibylline Oracles*, and *Life of Adam and Eve* (*L.A.E.*). The third group represents apocalyptic interpretations of the story of the creation and the fall as the background of a new and eschatological creation: *4 Ezra* and *2 Baruch*. It must be kept in mind that all of them are concerned with the present human situation and attempt to infer ethical implications from the story of Adam.[4]

Contemporary Exegesis of Genesis 1–3

When Paul introduced the figure of Adam in 1 Corinthians 15 and Romans 5:12-21, he certainly did not tackle the narrative of Genesis 1–3 with the critical eyes of contemporary interpreters. He simply presumed that his audiences were familiar with the drama of the creation and fall of the protoplasts. Yet he and

3. Levison classifies in three groups the books in which the figure of Adam appears according to their own *Tendenzen*: wisdom, apocalyptic, and Greco-Roman categories. He determines four criteria to select the texts: (1) "they must be Jewish"; (2) they need to be dated between 200 b.c.e. and 135 c.e.; (3) they "must have an adequate number of allusions and references to *adam*"; and (4) they "must have a discernible *Tendenz* to establish the contexts in which interpretations of Adam occur" (*Portraits of Adam*, 29). On the other hand, Thomas H. Tobin classifies these texts according to the function of Adam: (1) "to explain the general human condition, especially its mortality (Sirach and Wisdom); (2) "as exemplary of the human condition" (Josephus and Philo); and (3) as "explanatory . . . of the present condition of human beings" (*Sibylline Oracles*, *Jubilees*, *Apocalypse of Moses*, 4 Ezra, *2 Baruch*, and Pseudo Philo's *Liber antiquitatum biblicarum*) (Thomas H. Tobin, *Paul's Rhetoric in its* Contexts, 167–75).

4. See Benjamin G. Wright III and Lawrence M. Wills, eds., *Conflicted Boundaries in Wisdom and Apocalypticism* (SBLSymS 35; Atlanta: Society of Biblical Literature, 2005).

some of his contemporaries were also aware of some of the difficulties of the narrative of Genesis 1–3. Before we explore interpretations of the story of the fall of Adam (and Eve) during the turn of the first century, it is worthwhile to start with an overview of some conclusions of contemporary interpretations of Genesis 1–3 that eventually may elucidate some of the intricacies of the biblical text and of its Jewish interpreters.

First of all, the interpretation of the story of the creation and fall of Adam is best explained within the larger narrative of the Primeval History (Genesis 1–11), as a preface to the history of the patriarchs and Israel (Genesis 12–50).[5] The story of Genesis 1–3 epitomizes the larger introduction of Genesis 1–11 that describes "the problematic nature of human existence, the reality of sin and judgment, and the character of a God who does not give up on his creation."[6] Second, the etiologies of Genesis 1–11 drew elements from the Sumerian cosmogonies, namely, Atrahasis and Enuma Elish,[7] which were interpreted and transformed according to the Jewish faith.[8] They were concerned not so much with the past as with the present.[9] Third, according to most scholars, there

5. See Joseph Blenkinsopp, *The Pentateuch: An Introduction to the First Books of the Bible* (ABRL; New York: Doubleday, 1992), 93. Richard J. Clifford points out that the "prefatory function of Genesis 1 extends even beyond chapters 1–11 to chapters 12–50 . . . and indeed to the Pentateuch itself" (*Creation Accounts in the Ancient Near East and the Bible* [CBQMS 26; Washington, D.C.: Catholic Biblical Association of America, 1994], 139). Clifford further explains that the emphasis on Genesis 1–3 attained special attention in Christian circles with "Paul's New Adam Christology" (pp. 144–45 n. 19). Most scholars recognize a fivefold structure in Genesis 1–11, identified by the *tôlĕdôt* formula that describes the "origins," or still better the "begetting" of "heavens and earth" and humankind (Gen 2:4a; cf. 5:1; 6:9; 10:1; 11:10, 27; 25:19), attributed to a Priestly (P) editor. See Jean Louis Ska, *Introduzione alla lettura del Pentateuco: Chiavi per l'interpretazione dei primi cinque libri della Bibbia* (Collana Biblica; Rome: Dehoniane, 1998), 30; Blenkinsopp, *Pentateuch*, 59.

6. Blenkinsopp, *Pentateuch*, 94.

7. Although other ancient Eastern traditions also played a role in Genesis 1–11, Atrahasis and Enuma Elish are the most influential on the story of the creation and fall. See Clifford, *Creation Accounts;* Richard J. Clifford and John J. Collins, "Introduction: The Theology of Creation Traditions," in *Creation in Biblical Traditions*, ed. Richard J. Clifford and John J. Collins (CBQMS 24; Washington, D.C.: Catholic Biblical Association of America, 1992), 1–7; and, in the same volume, Bernard F. Batto, "Creation Theology in Genesis,"; and Robert A. Di Vito, "The Demarcation of Divine and Human Realms in Genesis 2–11," 39–56. See also Ed Noort, "The Creation of Man and Woman in Biblical and Ancient Near Easter Traditions," in *The Creation of Man and Woman: Interpretations of the Biblical Narratives in Jewish and Christian Traditions*, ed. Gerard P. Luttikhuizen (Themes in Biblical Narrative 3; Leiden: Brill, 2000), 1–18.

8. According to Clifford and Collins, "Yahweh, the God of Israel, is the sole deity; the focus of interest is earth and the doings of the human race, not heaven and the doings of the gods. Yahewh's holiness makes an ethical claim on Israel" ("Introduction," 11).

were two redactors of the Primeval History, the Priestly (P) and the Yahwist (J). According to P, humankind is made according to God's image and likeness (בְּצַלְמֵנוּ כִּדְמוּתֵנוּ וְיִרְדּוּ / κατ' εἰκόνα . . . καὶ καθ' ὁμοίωσιν), male and female (1:26-27).[10] According to J, God "formed man (אָדָם/ ἄνθρωπον) out of the clay of the ground (הָאֲדָמָה/ χοῦν ἀπὸ τῆς γῆς) and blew into his nostrils the breath of life (נִשְׁמַת חַיִּים / πνοὴν ζωῆς), and so man became a living being (לְנֶפֶשׁ חַיָּה / ψυχὴν ζῶσαν)" (Gen 2:7).[11] The second account forms a literary unit with the story of the fall that describes the placing and expulsion of the molded man from the garden.[12] Ultimately, the story of the creation and fall in J explains the dire existence of human beings as a consequence of the disruption of the original order in creation caused by their disobedience to God's command not to eat from the tree of knowledge of good and evil.[13]

The story of the creation and fall of Adam has been continuously revisited throughout the history of Israel and Christianity.[14] In its final form, it exemplifies the dynamics of the creation of Israel and the world and their

9. See Clifford and Collins, "Introduction," 7. Likewise Robert A. Di Vito argues that the authors' concern of the stories of the creation in the Bible was "the present, if not immediate, moment and its context" ("Demarcation of Divine and Human Realms," 56).

10. P, Gen 1:1—2:3 (sixth century BCE), addressing the needs and concerns of the exilic community, served as a preface to the earlier redactor J, 2:4-11. See Clifford, *Creation Accounts*, 137–50; Batto, "Creation Theology in Genesis," 26–38; E. A. Speiser, *Genesis: Introduction, Translation, and Notes* (AB 1; Garden City, N.Y.: Doubleday, 1964), 3–28. P "depicts the first man [and woman] in royal terms, using the nouns 'image' and 'likeness' . . . and the verbs 'rule' and 'subdue'" (Clifford, *Creation Accounts,* 143, citing Phyllis Bird, "'Male and Female He Created Them': Gen 1:27b in the Context of the Priestly Account of Creation," *HTR* 74 [1981]: 140–44). Scholars still debate, however, the exact extent of P and J, and the date of J, possibly ninth century b.c.e. See Claus Westermann, *Genesis 1–11. A Continental Commentary,* trans. John J. Scullion (Minneapolis: Fortress Press, 1994), 147–58 ("The History of the Exegesis of Gen 1:26-27").

11. The *tôlĕdôt* formula in 2:4a links the first to the second account of the creation, J, 2:4b-25. Blenkinsopp argues that 2:4a has been placed here "to make way for the solemn exordium of Gen 1:1 and to effect the transition between the origin of heaven and earth and what happened subsequently on earth" (*Pentateuch, 6*0). The second account of the creation of humanity is part of the narrative of the garden and the fall (Gen 3:1-24) and of the larger narrative of decay that ends with the flood. Clifford argues that the plot of Genesis 2–11 "is the typical plot of the creation-flood genre," as attested in Mesopotamian literature, but promptly transformed by J (*Creation Accounts* 145).

12. Claus Westermann calls the paradise story "a primeval narrative of crime and punishment," as part of the larger narrative of Genesis 1–11 (*Genesis 1–11,* 193). Some scholars consider the trees of life, and of the knowledge of good and evil (Gen 2:8-9) to be later additions; see Blenkinsopp, *Pentateuch,* 63.

13. According to Di Vito, eating from the tree of the knowledge of good and evil allowed "Adam and Eve simply choose to have the knowledge that is proper to humankind, that knowledge which likens them to the gods and sets them apart from all else on earth. Their aspiration is not for a change of ontological status" ("Demarcation of Divine and Humans Realms," 47).

destruction because of human wickedness. Yet, because Israel and humankind are God's creation, annihilation is not the last word; after the fall and the flood there is hope of restoration. Nevertheless, later interpreters, mindful of the tensions in the narrative, emphasized certain aspects of the narrative. On the one hand, being created in God's image and likeness, humankind is close to God and stands at the summit of the creation and has dominion over it as God's administrator. Humankind's likeness to God also conveyed the implicit command to respect the human dignity of each person. Thus, any transgression against a kinsman would be a transgression against God.[15] On the other hand, that humans were molded out of clay makes humankind another living being, close to the earth and bound to return to it. As the first human being, Adam stands as the father and representative of Israel and of all peoples.[16] More importantly, the creation of the earthly man is typically interpreted along with the story of Adam's fall and the punishments and the expulsion from the garden. Thus, it explains the dire situation of Israel throughout its history—and to a certain extent of all humankind—as the consequence of their disobedience and infidelity.

14. Speiser suggests that both accounts, J and P, "were concerned with the story of a society and more particularly, a society as the embodiment of an ideal, that is, a way of life" (*Genesis*, LVII). Jacob Neusner comments that later rabbinic Judaism found in the Scripture a pattern that allowed the rabbinic sages to "compare the story of Israel's possession and loss of the Land with the story of Creation and Adam's and Eve's possession and loss of Eden . . . but it is a pattern with a difference: Adam and Eve lost paradise, never to return, but Israel after its exile returned to the Land and, with the Torah for guidance, would endure there" (Bruce D. Chilton and Jacob Neusner, *Classical Christianity and Rabbinic Judaism: Comparing Theologies* [Grand Rapids: Baker Academic, 2004], 43). Neusner later explains that "Israel above all embodies God's abode in humanity, his resting place on earth" (p. 46). It should be noted that the Priestly redactor addressed specifically the community of exiles, who understood their restoration in cosmic dimensions.

15. See Katell Berthelot (*L' "humanité de l'autre homme" dans la pensée juive ancienne* [JSJSup 87; Leiden: Brill, 2004], 166–68) argues that ancient Jewish interpreters combined Gen 1:26-27 with Gen 9:6 to infer ethical implications from the story of the creation of humanity in God's image. He concludes that the human being as God's image had to imitate a benevolent God, "Les textes étudiés ci-dessus insistent surtout sur l'obligation d'imiter la bienfaisance et la miséricorde divines (dont la portée est *a priori* universelle), mais logiquement l'*imitatio Dei* conduit aussi a la condamnation des personnes qui remplissent pas leurs devoirs de créatures, et en premier lieu de celles qui refusent de reconnaître le Dieu Un" (p. 238).

16. The Greek translator understood the creation of the earthly man as an individual, that is, אָדָם as Ἀδάμ instead of ἄνθρωπος. The LXX renders Ἀδάμ as a proper name in Gen 2:16, 19-23, 25; 3:8-9, 12, 17, 20-22, 24; 4:1, 25; 5:1-5; Deut 32:8; and 1 Chr 1:1. In other instances, it translates אָדָם as ἄνθρωπος. See Peter C. Bouteneff, *Beginnings: Ancient Christian Readings of the Biblical Creation Narratives* (Grand Rapids: Baker Academic, 2008), 9–12, and the appendix, 185.

Although Jewish authors and eventually Paul were mindful of the tensions of the text, it was the final literary product that they read and interpreted. However, each author emphasized one aspect over the other in the narrative to respond to the specific circumstances and needs of their audiences. As part of the larger biblical narrative, the story of the creation and fall of Adam underwent a long history of interpretation that stemmed from the biblical text itself.[17] The following classification is simply methodological.

Hellenistic Interpretations of the Figure of Adam

The authors discussed here interpret the story of the creation of Adam and the fall incorporating Hellenistic traditions and thoughts to preserve Judaism or accommodate it to their larger historical and cultural milieu. They portray Adam as paradigm of humankind and the ancestor of Israel who faces the dilemma of freedom and its implications. On the one hand, Hellenistic Jewish authors relate God's image (Gen 1:26-27) to "the breath of life" of the earthly man (Gen 2:7). These features represent the intellectual attributes of the human soul and psyche as the locus of human freedom and responsibility. On the other hand, the creation of the earthly man is interpreted in conjunction with the story of the fall. Thus, Adam and his descendants are earthbound and mortal. Adam's disobedience to God's command "not to eat from the tree of knowledge of good and evil" (Gen 2:16-17) exemplifies Israel's disobedience to God's commandments and the passions and vices of all humankind that bring distress to the wicked. Conversely, a virtuous life would bring happiness and bliss to the righteous. Ultimately, their actions and retribution are confined essentially to this life.

Sirach

The prologue of Sirach provides important information regarding the location and composition of the book.[18] The author belonged to priestly and scribal

17. See Michael Fishbane, "Inner-Biblical Exegesis, in *Hebrew Bible/Old Testament: The History of Its Interpretation*, vol. 1, *From the Beginnings to the Middle Ages*, part 1, *Antiquity*, ed. Magne Saebø (Göttingen: Vandenhoeck & Ruprecht, 1996), 33–48: "The Hebrew Bible (HB) is thus a thick texture of traditions received and produced over many generations. In the process, a complex dynamic between tradition (*traditum*) and transmission (*traditio*) developed—since every act of *traditio* selected, revised, and reconstituted the overall *traditum*" (p. 34).

18. The author of the prologue explains that his grandfather "Jesus, son of Eleazar, son of Sirach" (Sir 50:27), originally wrote this book, apparently in Hebrew, and that he translated it "into another language," presumably Greek, when he arrived in Egypt "in the thirty-eighth year of the reign of King Euregetes" (Ptolemy VIII Physcon [170–164, 146–117). For the dating of Sirach, see Alexander A. Di

circles in Jerusalem.[19] He addressed young men, usually called "my son" in a sort of school (οἴκῳ παιδείας; see 51:23) in order to preserve them from Hellenistic influences. The central motif in Sirach is the Law, which is identified with wisdom, created by God (1:1; 24:3), and with the fear of the Lord (1:25-27; 24:23).[20]

Sirach belongs to the genre of wisdom literature.[21] Apart from two major sections, 1:1—23:27 and 24:1—50:24,[22] the book is woven by means of catchwords and recurrent topics. Adam appears explicitly three times in Ben Sira, 33:10; 40:1; 49:16, and implicitly four times, 15:14; 17:1-7, 32; 24:28, and possibly 25:24.[23] The figure of Adam is located within the larger context of the

Lella, O.F.M., "Sirach," *NJBC,* 496–97; Patrick W. Skehan and Alexander A. Di Lella, *The Wisdom of Ben Sira: A New Translation with Notes* (AB 39; Garden City, N.Y.: Doubleday, 1987), 8–16; Craig A. Evans, *Ancient Texts for New Testament Studies: A Guide to the Background Literature* (Peabody, Mass.: Hendrickson, 2005), 15. The author of the prologue also says that his grandfather wrote "in the nature of instruction and wisdom, in order that those who love wisdom might . . . make even greater progress in living in conformity within divine Law."

19. See Benjamin G. Wright III, "Putting the Puzzle Together: Some Suggestions Concerning the Social Location of the Wisdom of Ben Sira," in Wright and Wills, *Conflicted Boundaries,* 106–7; and, in the same volume, Richard A. Horsley, "The Politics of Cultural Production in Second Temple Judea: Historical Context and Political-Religious Relations of the Scribes Who Produced 1 Enoch, Sirach, and Daniel," 123–45, esp. 133–37. He argues that the author of Sirach was a sage-scribe at the service of the priestly aristocracy: "Ben Sira represents a nonpriestly scribal faction that supported the Oniad incumbents and propagandized for the authority of the Aaronids. He and his circle of scribes had adjusted to imperial rule and found an honorable life in service of the high priesthood sponsored by the imperial regime" (p. 144).

20. B. G. Wright claims that Sirach responds also to "inner Jewish concerns" regarding the cult in Jerusalem and the proper interpretation of the Law, particularly regarding the calendar for the Jewish festivities ("Putting the Puzzle Together," 97, 106, 109, 111).

21. It contains different literary form such as the proverb "*mashal* . . . , hymn of praise, prayer of petition, autobiographical narrative, lists or onomastica, and didactic narrative" (Di Lella, "Sirach," *NJBC,* 497; see also Skehan and Di Lella, *Wisdom of Ben Sira,* 21–30).

22. Each section starts with a poem that introduces the creation motif, where Wisdom is both God's creation and his agent in the creation of the world. In each poem, Wisdom is identified with the Torah (1:25-27; 24:23) and has a special place in the creation of the world. In the first poem (1:1-10), Wisdom is presented in the third person as being created before all things and poured out upon all God's works (1:4, 9). In the second poem (24:1-33), Wisdom speaks in the first person as coming out of the mouth of the Most High, being created from before the beginning of the world, and being eternal (24:3, 9, 18). Craig A. Evans suggests that "Sirach is probably intended to be two volumes, consisting of chapters 1-23 and 24-51" (*Ancient Texts,* 15). Only chapters 44:1—50:24, "Praise of the Ancestors of Old," whose title is extant only in the Cairo ms. B, follow a distinct structure; see Di Lella, "Sirach," *NJBC,* 507.

23. *Pace* John R. Levison, "Is Eve to Blame? A Contextual Analysis of Sir 25:24," *CBQ* 47 (1985): 617–23.

story of the creation and fall, and its immediate literary contexts provide further specific connotations.[24]

The first Adamic passage, Sir 33:10 (cf. Gen 2:7; *Jub.* 2:19), occurs in the "poem on the polarities in creation" (33:7–15).[25] This poem presents a parallelism between the division of the days and the division of humankind.

The Division of the Days and of Humankind[26]

Why is one day more important than another, since the light of every day of the year comes from the sun? (33:7).	So too all people come from clay (ἀπὸ ἐδάφους), and Adam too was created for from earth (ἐκ γῆς) (33:10).
It is by the knowledge of the Lord that they were *separated* (διεχωρίσθησαν) (33:8a), and He made the seasons and feasts different (ἠλλοίωσεν) (33:8).	With abundant knowledge the Lord has *separated* (διεχώρισεν) them, and He made their ways different (ἠλλοίωσεν) (33:11).
Some He exalted (ἀνύψωσεν) and sanctified (ἡγίασεν) (33:9a);	Some of them He has blessed (εὐλόγησεν) and exalted (ἀνύψωσεν), and some of them he sanctified (ἡγίασεν), and set near himself (33:12a);

24. Levison argues that Sirach "ignores the original context [of Genesis 1–3], extracting elements and assimilating their meaning to the contexts of which they are part in his own composition" (*Portraits of Adam*, 48). He claims that this would allow Sirach to offer three different interpretations of the story of Adam, that is, as "a glorious ancestor of Israel" (49:16), as "the first man" who lacked wisdom (24:28), and as an earthly and mortal being (chapters 17; 33; and 40) (p. 47).

25. Di Lella argues that "Ben Sirach attributes the differences between the opposites in creation and between the pious/wise and the impious/foolish to God's ordering of the universe in general and of humans in particular" ("Sirach," *NJBC*, 506). Clifford and Collins note a similar contrast between opposites made by the Stoics Chrysippus and Cleanthes ("Introduction," 12). Indeed, Chrysippus also tried to solve the problem of the existence of evil in the world, "The evil . . . is not without usefulness in relation to the whole. For without it there could be no good (Plut. quoting Chrysippus, *Comm. not.* 1065b)," in A. A. Long, *Hellenistic Philosophy. Stoics, Epicureans, Sceptics* (2nd ed.; Berkeley: University of California Press, 1986), 169.

26. My translation.

while others He established as ordinary days (33:9b).	while some of them He has cursed, humiliated, and expelled them from their places (33:12b).

Although all days receive the light of the sun, and all men are made from the ground, the Lord separated them, days and men, by his knowledge. This act of "separating" evokes the first account of creation (Gen 1:4, 6-7, 14, 18). The separating between peoples comes at God's will (Sir 33:13). The author explains that this division ultimately follows the larger schema of the cosmos established by "the Most High" (33:14-15). The blessing of the days and people evokes the blessing of the seventh day (Gen 2:3; cf. Sir 44:22-23; Gen 2:28; 12:2-3). This passage points to the earthly condition of Adam and all humankind, that is, their mortal nature, but also to the division between humans and their ways established by God (33:11).[27] Although the division is primarily between Israel and the nations and the blessings the former receives, the previous context points to the division between the wise who fear the Lord and keep his Law, and the lawless who are without wisdom (Sir 33:1-4). Therefore, the identity of Israel is defined primarily by the observance of the Law.

The second passage is found in Sir 40:1: "Great anxiety is created for every human being, and a heavy yoke is upon the sons of Adam (υἱοὺς Ἀδάμ), from the day that they go out of their mother's womb, till the day that they return to the mother of all things." This passage belongs to the first (40:1-11) of five poems about the "miseries and joys of life" (40:1-41:13),[28] located after the author praises God for the goodness of creation (39:12-35). In this passage the author first points to the toil every human being has to endure to survive (cf. Gen 3:17-19a), and then to the earthly and mortal human condition (cf. Gen 3:19b; Sir 33:10; 40:11). Although the author evidently evokes the punishments God allotted to Adam because of his disobedience, for Sirach the toils and death are not the consequence of humanity's disobedience but part of God's design: death is inherent in human life (17:30; 18:9; 37:25; 40:1-11; 41:3-4), regardless of a person's social status (40:3-4). Furthermore, death even releases humankind from the sufferings of this life (cf. 41:2). For Sirach, retribution occurs in this life and has an effect on people's descendants (cf. 40:12-15). Thus, in this passage Adam simply represents the human condition; humans are bound to return to the earth from which they came—that is, they are mortal by nature. Yet, for

27. Although human freedom and responsibility are upheld in 15:11-20.

28. Thus, God is not to blame for human hardships; see Skehan and Di Lella, *Wisdom of Ben Sira*, 469; see also Di Lella, "Sirach," *NJBC*, 507.

Sirach, the death that sinners experience is harsher, "seven times more" (40:8), and it is expressed in terms of "plague and bloodshed, wrath and the sword, plunder and ruin, famine and death. For the wicked, these were created evil, and it is they who bring on destruction" (40:9–10).

The third passage is Sir 49:16: "Shem and Seth were glorified (ἐδοξάσθησαν) among men, and likewise Adam above every living thing in creation (ὑπὲρ πᾶν ζῷον ἐν τῇ κτίσει)." It belongs to the larger section of the exaltation of Israel's ancestors (44:1—50:24).[29] This is the only case in Sirach where Adam is presented explicitly as an individual in the list of Israel's ancestors.[30] There is no indication in Genesis that Adam was "glorified," but the author conflates the command that humankind received to rule over all the living things (Gen 1:26, 28) with "the glory and honor" (δόξῃ καὶ τιμῇ) that God gave humankind to "rule over the works of your hands" (Ps 8:6-7). However, in these cases the glory and power are bestowed on both male and female and not on Adam as an individual. Thus, it seems that the author adapts the reference to Gen 1:26 and 28 and possibly to Psalm 8 to mention Adam first in the list of Israel's ancestors whose glory the author praises (see Sir 44:1-2). Adam is included primarily to place Israel within the wider schema of creation, which is predominant in the rest of Sirach.

More numerous are the oblique allusions to Adam in Sirach. The author substitutes the name "Adam" for "man" in order to contemporize the story of Genesis 1–3 and infer ethical implications for a wider audience, perhaps unfamiliar with Adamic traditions. The first allusion, "He himself made man from the beginning (ἐξ ἀρχῆς) and left him in the hand of his deliberation (διαβουλίου)" (15:14), belongs to the first of four stanzas of an exhortation not to blame God for humanity's sins and to be responsible for one's actions (15:11-20).[31] The author contemporizes the creation of humankind (Gen 1:27) changing and introducing several elements into the story. First, he changes the

29. This reference is an awkward interruption of the semihistorical sequence after the praise of Nehemiah (Sir 49:13), as an effort to enclose the succession that began with Enoch, who was taken up from the earth (Sir 44:16 [μετετέθη]; 49:14 [ἀνελήμφθη ἀπὸ τῆς γῆς]). Likewise Joseph, Shem, and Seth (49:15-16a) are mentioned out of order, only to mention Adam last (v. 16b) and then return again to the semihistorical sequence with the long praise of the priest Simon in 50:1-24. The inclusion of Adam here may be an extrapolation that forms an awkward inclusion with Enoch (44:16; 49:14).

30. Levison notes the textual difficulties of this verse, "In the light of these uncertainties, any definitive statement of the passage's meaning is unfeasible" (*Portraits of Adam,* 44) and concludes that "the attribution of glory to Adam should be regarded as an expression of the contextual interest of Ben Sirach" to exalt Israel's past in Sir 44–50, "claiming the first human for Israel, attributing the glory which characterizes Israel to him" (p. 45).

31. See Skehan and Di Lella, *Wisdom of Ben Sira*, 271.

preposition ἐν (Gen 1:1) to ἐξ to express that God has made all humankind, from the beginning until the present time. Second, he interprets the creation of humankind after the image of God (Gen 1:27) as endowed with διαβούλιον ("counsel, deliberation"), that is, the human ability of self-determination (cf. Sir 17:6) to underline that each person is responsible for his/her actions.[32] Third, he explains διαβούλιον in the context of the Deuteronomistic axiom of freedom and responsibility (Sir 17: 15-20).[33] Thus, the author contemporizes the story of the creation of humankind to infer ethical implications applicable to people of all time; that is, people of each generation are free and responsible for their actions.

In the second passage, Sir 17:1-7, the author conflates the two creation accounts of humankind (Gen 1:26-27 and 2:7) and the charge to return to the earth (Gen 3:19). He also relates the creation to the Sinaitic theophany as the manifestation of God's glory (Exod 19:2—20:17; 24:15-17).[34] First, as part of the earthly beings described at the end of the previous poem, the Lord created humankind (ἄνθρωπον) from the earth, to which they will return as the other earthly beings do (Sir 17:1; cf. Sir 16:30b; 41:10; Gen 2:7; 3:19), and consequently the Lord assigned *them* a short time (17:2a)—that is, made them mortal.[35] Although Sirach omits the duality "male" and "female" (cf. Gen 1:27), he changes here and in the following verses to the plural to show that he is referring to humankind in general, and not to Adam the individual.[36] Second, God gave *them* power over the earthly things (Sir 17:2b) and clothed *them* with strength, and made *them* according to his image (καθ' εἰκόνα αὐτοῦ) (Sir 17:3; cf. 49:16). Here the author conflates Gen 1:26-27, humankind as God's image,

32. Levison argues that Sirach "removes the reference to the יצר from the flood narrative [as an evil inclination] and places it into the context of creation," with a neutral meaning (*Portraits of Adam,* 35). However, there is no need to remove יצר from its original context to render its neutral meaning. As a matter of fact, the LXX renders יצר (*yetzer*) as διανοεῖται in Gen 6:5, and as ἡ διάνοια in Gen 8:21. In these cases it has a neutral meaning, "counsel." It is possible that the negative connotation of יצר is due to later Jewish interpretations.

33. "I set before you today life and prosperity, death and destruction," and "I have set before you life and death, blessings and curses. Now choose life, so that you and your children may live" (Deut 30:15, 19; cf. 11:26-28).

34. This passage belongs to the second (17:1-24) of four poems that praise God's wisdom manifested in the creation of the world and humankind (16:24—18:14); see Di Lella, "Sirach," *NJBC*, 501.

35. As opposed to the heavenly bodies, which do not change or cease in their work (16:27). That humankind is mortal is evident in Sirach (17:30; 18:9; 37:25; 40:1-11; 41:3-4). However, human perpetuity somehow could be achieved in progeny (39:11; 44:11-14) and wisdom (37:26; 44:15).

36. Verse 4b returns to the singular. Although the author turns his attention momentarily to Israel, in 17:11-14, he addresses humankind in general, Israel being God's portion among the nations (17:17).

and Ps 8:3-8, where the author praises God for the power that humankind received to rule over beasts and birds (17:4). God gave *them* also counsel (διαβούλιον; cf. Sir 15:14), the senses of perception to ponder (διανοέομαι), and filled them with understanding (ἐπιστήμην συνέσεως) to show them good and evil (17:6-7; cf. Gen 2:9).[37] Sirach transforms the negative tale of the tree of good and evil (Gen 2:16-17) into a positive faculty that God bestowed on humankind. Thus, this knowledge is the wisdom required to praise the Lord for his marvelous works (Sir 17:8-9). Third, the author introduces the Sinaitic motif to associate the creation with the giving of the Law and the covenant, so that both the creation of the world and the theophany at Sinai reveal God's glory and his Law and judgments (17:9-14). Finally, Sirach returns to the fools' presumption that he and his deeds are hidden to God (see 16:17-23) and concludes that all the ways and sins of humankind are before God and therefore human beings are accountable for their actions (17:19-24).[38] Therefore, this allusion to the creation of humankind underscores human mortality set in its immediate context, which points to the accountability of every human being because their actions are always known to God.

The third passage, "all people are dust and ashes" (ἄνθρωποι πάντες γῆ καὶ σποδός, 17:32b; cf. Gen 2:7), comes at the end of the third poem (17:25-32), which makes an exhortation to return to the Lord.[39] Human beings are to return to the Lord because of their mortal condition (17:27-28, 30, 32) and because of God's generosity and compassion (ἡ ἐλεημοσύνη, ἐξιλασμός, 17:29). In the following poem, 18:1-14, the author contrasts human mortality

37. Cf. Philo, *De Opificio Mundi*, 153-54.

38. Levison reaches a similar conclusion, but he divides this section differently (15:9—18:14; 16:17—17:24; 17:25—18:14), perhaps driven by his assumption that the author is rebutting some opponents who thought they and their actions were hidden to God (*Portraits of Adam*, 34–38). I regard this section, instead, as a series of instructions that Ben Sira gives to his students on how both the works of creation and the Torah reveal God's mercy for humankind. *Pace* Levison, who claims that Ben Sira "argues from the universal to the specific" (p. 38), the author draws a parallel between the understanding bestowed by God on humankind on their creation and the knowledge and wisdom that God gave Israel at Mount Sinai. Thus, the story of the creation helps Sirach to expand the perspective to make of the event of the creation of the world and humankind an inclusive event that embraced all humankind; Ben Sira makes of wisdom for all what the Torah was for Israel. For a similar perspective, see Luis Alonso Shökel, "The Vision of Man in Sirach 16:24—17:14," in *Israelite Wisdom: Theological and Literary Essays in Honor of Samuel Terrien*, ed. John G. Gammie, Walter A. Brueggemann, W. L. Humphreys, and J. M. Ward (Homage Series 3; Missoula, Mont.: Scholars Press, 1978), 235-45. He concludes that "Ben Sira is talking from the beginning to the end about *man in general*" 243 (emphasis original). Overall Sirach tries to convince his audience that the Law is appealing and addressed ultimately to all.

39. It also forms an *inclusio* with the opening of the second poem, 17:1.

to God's eternity and righteousness. Ultimately, the realm of human beings is consigned to this age because they are mortal. Thus, Sirach exhorts his audience to return to God while they are alive so they may praise the Lord.

The fourth allusion, "The first man (ὁ πρῶτος) knew her [Wisdom] not perfectly; no more shall the last (ὁ ἔσχατος) find her out" (24:28), is an evident reference to Adam's transgression (Genesis 3).[40] Sirach interprets the story of the fall as the innate limitation humans have to acquire Wisdom by themselves. The juxtaposition, "the first/the last man," means that no one can grasp Wisdom; instead, it comes as a gift, primarily to Israel (24:8–12, 18, 23) but also to all who seek wisdom (24:33–34).[41] Although there are no explicit ethical inferences in this passage, the identification of Wisdom and Torah (24:23) may point to the ethical and social demands of the Torah given primarily to Israel and secondarily to all humankind.

The last allusion is a reference not to Adam but to his wife, "from a woman (γυνή) [came] the beginning of sin, and through her we all die (ἀποθνῄσκομεν πάντες)" (Sir 25:24; cf. Gen 2:17; 3:3–6).[42] This passage is part of a contrast between the wicked (25:13–26) and virtuous wife (26:1–18). Although this passage does not explicitly refer to Eve, the context suggests that Sirach has in mind the story of the fall.[43] In 25:24 Sirach evokes the story of the fall to explain that, as sin began with a woman, it also happens today. That is, she may lead her husband to sin, although this does not make him innocent.[44] Although for

40. This passage is part of a poem, 24:1–33, that introduces the second part of the book, where Wisdom speaks of herself, her role in creation, and her identification with Torah (24:23).

41. ὁ πρῶτος in 24:28 may also be identified with the πρωτογόνῳ in 36:11, which refers to Israel. This passage is part of a lament (36:1–17) where the author invokes God's intervention in favor of his people, so that they also may know him. Thus, Israel is the "firstborn" and becomes the people through whom God manifests his Law to all the nations.

42. Cf. *L.A.E.* 7.1; 9.2; 10.1–2; 14.1; Josephus, *Ant.* 1.47–51; Philo, *Opif.* 151.

43. As a matter of fact, Eve's name appears only in Gen 3:20 (the Greek renders it as Ζωή). In Gen 4:1, the Hebrew חַוָּה is translated into Greek as 'Ευαν (cf. also 4:25). Previously, she is simply called "woman" (אִשָּׁה/γυνή). Levison ("Is Eve to Blame?" 617–23) argues that this passage does not refer to Eve. He rightly mentions that Sirach describes death as an intrinsic aspect of human life and that the context of Sir 25:24 refers to the wicked wife, not to Eve. However, the context suggests that Sirach has in mind Gen 2:17 (which is probably what Levison meant, and not 2:7 [p. 618]) and the story of the fall, 3:19. Indeed, in the previous allusions to Adam, his name is not mentioned either, yet the context clearly evokes the creation of the first human. For a critique of Levison's argument, see Skehan and Di Lella, Wisdom of Ben Sira, 349.

44. In his advice regarding the wicked and virtuous wife, he includes also advice in regard to daughters (26:10–12). In further recommendations regarding daughters, Ben Sira also attributes to woman the beginning of misfortunes, "For just as moth comes out from garments, so too the wickedness of a woman comes from a woman" (42:13). My translation.

Sirach mortality is connatural to human beings (17:30; 18:9; 37:25; 40:1–11; 41:3–4), he asserts that sin may hasten and worsen death. Conversely, a virtuous wife would help her husband to double the number of his days (26:1). For Sirach, God is not ultimately to blame for sinful humankind, but each person is responsible for his or her own actions, and death constitutes part of the human fabric. The negative description of woman in Sir 25:24 reflects the overall negative portrayal of women in Sirach.

In sum, the references to the creation of humankind in Sirach are part of the larger context of the creation motif. As God revealed himself on Mount Sinai to Israel and gave them his Law, so he does to all humankind in creation. With the exception of Sir 49:16, where Adam stands as an individual, gifted with glory along with the other ancestors of Israel, the figure of Adam in Sirach represents all humankind. The most salient feature of Adam in Sirach is that all human beings are mortal by nature (17:1, 30–32; 33:10; 40:1, 11), not as a consequence of their disobedience; it is part of God's ultimate plan for humankind and the whole creation. Furthermore, death can release humankind from the burdens of life. The immortality of humankind could be achieved through their progeny or by means of their wisdom. The knowledge of good and evil becomes for Sirach a positive quality required to praise God in his creation and to discover his Law. Yet no one, "the first" or "the last man," could attain wisdom; it is a gift that comes from God. However, when humans disobey God's commands, they are responsible for their own actions (Sir 15:14; 17:6–7). Sirach also incorporates into the context of the story of the creation of humankind exhortations to repent and to follow God's commands (see 17:32b). However, human retribution or reward remains a matter for this age; there are no repercussions after death. Humankind is mortal by nature.

Wisdom of Solomon

Wisdom of Solomon was written in Greek during the Hellenistic period, sometime between 100 BCE and 30 CE, possibly in Alexandria. Although the style varies in different sections, most scholars defend the unity of the book.[45] The book is structured in three sections: (1) reward of the righteous with immortality through Wisdom (1:1—6:21); (2) Solomon as the paradigm in the quest for Wisdom (6:22—11:1); (3) the exodus as the paradigm of God's

45. See Addison G. Wright, "Wisdom," *NJBC*, 510; John M. G. Barclay, *Jews in the Mediterranean Diaspora: From Alexander to Trajan (323 BCE–117 CE)* (Berkeley: University of California Press, 1996), 181; David Winston, *The Wisdom of Solomon: A New Translation with Introduction and Commentary* (AB 43; Garden City, N.Y.: Doubleday, 1979). The dissenting voice is Dieter Georgi, *Weisheit Salomos* (JSHRZ 3.4; Gütersloh: Gerd Mohn, 1980), 392–94.

salvation through Wisdom (11:2—19:22).[46] The book of Wisdom is a "protreptic discourse or didactic exhortation."[47] The author interprets the Jewish Scriptures in Hellenistic terms to address his fellow Diaspora Jews, who either deserted or were in danger of deserting because of the cultural and religious challenges they faced. Σοφία becomes a personified agent or consort in God's creation (chs. 6–10), and during the events of the exodus.[48] Thus, the author interprets the creation of humanity under the wider concept of creation.

Although the author deliberately avoids proper names, the context provides enough information to identify them. He portrays characters simply as the "righteous" or the "wicked" and identifies Israel primarily, though not exclusively, with the former (cf. 11:2-19:22; 10:17, 20; 12:6, 21; 18:1, 6, 9).[49] Thus, the righteous Israelites are examples for the Diaspora Jews to remain faithful to God and his Law in the midst of their sufferings and to assure them

46. Most scholars agree with this division. A. G. Wright identifies section two (6:22—11:1) as the second part of 1:1—11:1; however, it is evident that 6:1-21 is an exhortation to the kings, clearly defined by the *inclusio* in 6:1 and 6:21, which prepares for the section 6:22—11:1, which implicitly presents the figure of King Solomon as the paradigm in the quest for Wisdom.

47. According to A. G. Wright, it is "a blend of philosophy and rhetoric, it is not an abstract treatise but a practical appeal that one's learning should have an impact on one's moral life." It incorporates other genres such as diatribe (1:1—6:9, 13-15), the philosophical inquiry (6:10—9:18), the proof from example (10), and the *synkrisis* (11–19) ("Wisdom," 511). George W. E. Nickelsburg also identifies apocalyptic and prophetic (Isaiah 52–53) traits in Wisdom of Solomon ("Wisdom and Apocalypticism in Early Judaism: Some Points for Discussion," in *Conflicted Boundaries in Wisdom and Apocalypticism*, ed. Benjamin G. Wright III and Lawrence M. Wills [SBLSymS 35; Atlanta: Society of Biblical Literature, 2005], 28-29).

48. John S. Kloppenborg makes a case for the similarities between Wisdom and Isis: "the peculiar configuration of Sophia's characteristics is a result of and a response to the immediate and powerful challenge to Judaism presented by another feminine figure, savior and revealer, a goddess linked to the pursuit of wisdom and one associated with the throne: Isis" ("Isis and Sophia in the Book of Wisdom," *HTR* 75 [1982]: 67). Nevertheless, he clarifies that the author did not borrow "Egyptian legends" but relied on biblical traditions, which he translated into a new cultural context (p. 72). Michael Kolarcik ("Creation and Salvation in the Book of Wisdom," in Clifford and Collins, *Creation*, 97-107) convincingly argues that the author interprets "the exodus events through the lens of creation theology [and] finally unites creation, the exodus, and salvation into a continuous spectrum" (p. 105). He notices the apocalyptic feature of Wisdom 5, the "ultimate judgment" against the wicked, as an act of justice and destruction of evil (cf. p. 107).

49. The author avoided proper names either to elude open confrontation with the surrounding audience or to make his message more appealing to them. The universalistic perspective (1:13; 6:7; 9:1; 11:23) was intended to attract sympathizers of Judaism and to address his fellow Diaspora Jews who were familiar with the biblical stories so they may identify themselves with each "righteous" character presented in the book.

that at the end they will be vindicated in the afterlife, whereas the wicked will be punished with death.

There are five references to the story of the creation and fall from Genesis. The first allusion appears in Wis 2:23–24, "For God created man to be immortal (ἐπ' ἀφθαρσίᾳ), and made him an image of his own eternity (ἀϊδιότητος). However, through the devil's envy, death came into the world; and those who put to test him (the devil), they experience it (death) (πειράζουσιν δὲ αὐτὸν οἱ τῆς ἐκείνου μερίδος ὄντες)."[50] In the context of this passage the author replies to the wicked who do not believe in life after death and consequently lead a dissolute lifestyle (2:1–20). The author introduces the concept of ἀφθαρσία (2:23b), which means both some sort of immortality and moral incorruption.[51] Thus, only the righteous who keep the commandments may share in God's ἀφθαρσία and ἀθανασία (see 1:15; 3:4; 6:18–19). Conversely, the lot of the wicked is death. This is what the Sage underlines in v. 24 with the reference to the story of the fall to explain that the devil, not God, is the cause of death.[52] The context suggests that θάνατος is a hypostatized power that exercises its dominion over those who belong to it (1:16; 2:24b). Thus, death transcends physical death and implies a sort of spiritual death as being separated from God even after physical death.[53] On the other hand, ἀφθαρσία is a spiritual existence with God that continues even after death (3:1–9; 5:15; 6:19). Whereas the righteous ones hope to share immortality with God in the future (2:23); the hope of the impious is in vain (3:11), for they belong to death and death's kingdom (1:16; 2:24b). Therefore, obedience to the Law and a blameless life give the righteous a share in God's immortality. Conversely, the wicked who disobey the Law belong to death and death's kingdom. Whereas hope in their immortality leads the pious to a virtuous life, hopelessness leads the wicked to a dissolute lifestyle.

50. My translation. Some manuscripts read ἰδιότητετος, "nature" or "identity."

51. The Sage relates ἀφθαρσία and ἀθανασία (cf. Wis 1:15; 3:4; 6:18–19; 12:1; 18:4; cf. also 4 Macc 9:22; 17:12); "To keep her [Wisdom] commandments is the basis of ἀφθαρσίας" (Wis 6:18–19); cf. G. Harder, φθείρω, κτλ, *TDNT* 9:100–102. The root of ἀφθαρσία was frequently used in the LXX (Hos 9:9; Gen 6:11; Deut 9:12), and Hellenistic Judaism (Philo, *Spec. Leg.* 3.167; *Leg. All.* 3.220; *Deus Imm.* 142) with moral nuances; see Winston, *Wisdom of Solomon*, 121.

52. *Pace* Levison, who claims that the Sage refers to Cain (Genesis 4) (*Portraits of Adam*, 51–52). However, the first allusion to Cain does not appear until the implicit comparison between Adam and Cain in 10:1-4. For the view that the Sage refers to Genesis 3 and not to Genesis 4, see Winston, *Wisdom of Solomon*, 121; and A. G. Wright, "Wisdom," 514.

53. Winston (*Wisdom of Solomon*, 122) and A. G. Wright ("Wisdom," 514) interpret death as "spiritual" death. Levison (*Portraits of Adam*, 52) interprets death with Brandenburger (*Adam und Christus*, 51–52) as "an independent power which brings people to eternal destruction."

The second reference, Wis 7:1-6, is found in the context of Solomon as the paradigm in the quest for Wisdom (6:22—11:1). The Sage portrays Solomon as mortal, earthborn (γηγενούς), and a descendant of the "first man made of the earth" (πρωτοπλάστου). The emphasis on the mortal condition that King Solomon shares with all people is indicated by the *inclusio* ἴσος ἅπασιν (v. 1), and πάντων ἴση (v. 6).[54] The Sage also substituted πρωτόπλαστος for πρωτότοκος ("firstborn") to refer to Adam, made out of the clay of the ground (see Wis 10:1; Gen 2:7).[55] Thus Solomon, as a descendant from the first man made out of clay, ultimately shares with Adam and all his descendants their mortal condition (see Sir 40:1). Because of Adam's mortal condition (διὰ τοῦτο) he prays for wisdom (7:7-12; 9:1-18).

The third reference, Wis 9:1-3, belongs to the first strophe of Solomon's prayer asking God for wisdom to rule his people (9:1-18).[56] As God made all things by his word (ὁ ποιήσας τὰ πάντα ἐν λόγῳ σου, vv. 1-3) so his Wisdom made humankind in order that they may rule and manage (ἵνα δεσπόζῃ . . . καὶ διέπῃ) over the other creatures and the cosmos (cf. Gen 1:26-28). God's mercy is related to the moral qualities required to rule the cosmos in holiness and justice (ἐν ὁσιότητι καὶ δικαιοσύνῃ) and to judge in integrity of heart (ἐν εὐθύτητι ψυχῆς). As humankind required wisdom to rule over creation, now Solomon requests it to rule God's people (9:4). Therefore, given human constraints and their mortal condition, the author emphasizes the need for wisdom in order to rule the cosmos and God's people and to share in God's immortality and incorruptibility (9:5-6, 14-15; cf. 7:1-6).

In the two previous passages (7:1-6 and 9:1-5), the Sage invokes the story of the creation of humankind in Genesis to underline the mortal condition of Solomon and of all humankind, and their need of divine Wisdom in order to partake in God's immortality and incorruption, and to rule and administer the cosmos and society properly. Divine wisdom and mercy are to be reflected in the human moral qualities required to live incorruptibly, to share in God's immortality and to rule the cosmos and God's people. Therefore, only the wise and the righteous would participate somehow in some sort of immortality with God.

54. See A. G. Wright, "Wisdom," 515. Winston provides examples of the motif of the mortal condition that kings share with the rest of humankind (*Wisdom of Solomon,* 162–63).

55. πρωτότοκος and πρωτόγονος are found in Greek literature, in the LXX, and in Philo; see Levison, *Portraits of Adam,* 55; W. Michaelis, "πρωτότοκος, κτλ," *TDNT* 6:871–76; see also the Latin rendition in *L.A.B.* 13:8.

56. For parallels and inclusions in 9:1-18, see Winston, *Wisdom of Solomon,* 200; A. G. Wright, "Wisdom," 517.

The fourth passage (10:1-2) represents a transition between the previous section, Solomon as paradigm in the quest of wisdom (6:22—11:1) and the following section, the exodus as the paradigm of God's salvation through wisdom (11:2—19:22). The Sage picks up the previous verse (9:18), "For so the ways of them which lived on the earth were reformed (διωρθώθησαν), and men were taught the things that are pleasing unto thee, and were saved (ἐσώθησαν) through wisdom." Then he develops this theme in the list of righteous saved by Wisdom,[57] vis-à-vis the impious punished by her (10:1—11:1). Thus, the πρωτόπλαστον πατέρα κόσμου (cf. Wis 7:1) stands at the head of the list of seven unnamed righteous men whom Wisdom protected and rescued (διεφύλαξεν καὶ ἐξείλατο) from his sin (ἐκ παραπτώματος ἰδίου),[58] and "gave him power to rule all things (ἰσχὺν κρατῆσαι ἁπάντων)." Although Adam is not named nor is he called righteous, the πρωτόπλαστον in 10:1 clearly alludes to Gen 2:7. With this term the author underlines the earthly and mortal condition of Adam and of all humankind. Then he evokes with different wording the power bestowed on humankind (10:2; cf. Gen 1:26-28). Therefore, the Sage attributes to Wisdom the function that Genesis 1 ascribed to God's word in the creation of the world; now, by saving the pious, Wisdom restores the dominion that humans lost after their transgression. In this way, the unnamed Adam represents the first virtuous Israelite saved by Wisdom, who was called to rule over creation. This text may indicate the author's agenda of instilling a virtuous life among the Israelites in order to play an active role in the leadership of their community. In this way the righteous Israelites function not only as paradigms who give hope to the Diaspora Jews in the midst of challenges, but they also represent the wise called to rule them by means of their virtuous life.

Finally, Wis 15:7-13 is part of a satiric digression (13:1—15:17) that scorns the potter because he knows that he makes fragile idols out of clay (15:13).[59]

57. In this section the author uses several verbs interchangeably such as σῴζω (9:18), διεφυλάσσειν (10:1),ʹ ῥύομαι (10:6, 9, 13, 15), which belong to the semantic group "to save," "to rescue," and the like; *pace* Levison, who translates διεφυλάσσειν distinctively as "to preserve" (*Portraits of Adam*, 60).

58. For other lists of righteous Israelites, see Winston, *Wisdom of Solomon*, 212. These lists may have been a common topos to encourage distressed communities to stand firm in their faith and identity (see Hebrews 11; Philo, *De virtutibus* 198-210). For catalogues in ancient Greek literature, see John T. Fitzgerald, "The Catalogues in Ancient Greek Literature," in *The Rhetorical Analysis of Scripture: Essays from the 1995 London Conference*, ed. Stanley E. Porter and Thomas H. Olbricht (JSNTSup 146; Sheffield: Sheffield Academic Press, 1997), 274–93.

59. Wisdom 15:7-13 also belongs to the section of the exodus as the paradigm of God's salvation through Wisdom (11:2—19:22). After a short introduction (11:2-5), the author organizes this section in "five antithetical diptychs" that contrast God's salvation in favor of the Israelites as opposed to his

In 15:8b, the Sage conflates Gen 2:7 and 3:19b to point out that the potter himself was made out of the ground (ἐκ γῆς γενηθείς), to which he is to return. The Sage charges that the potter's life "is more ignoble than clay because he did not know the one who fashioned him and breathed into him a working soul, and infused a vital spirit (τὸν ἐμπνεύσαντα αὐτῷ ψυχὴν ἐνεργοῦσαν καὶ ἐμφυσήσαντα πνεῦμα ζωτικόν)" (Wis 15:10b–11; cf. Gen 2:7). Evidently the synonymous parallelism, ψυχὴν ἐνεργοῦσαν and πνεῦμα ζωτικόν, betrays the Sage's Hellenistic influence, which views the spirit as capable of subsisting after death, independent of the body.[60] Consequently, because the potter ignores his maker who gave him a πνεῦμα ζωτικόν, he viewed this life as "a plaything" (παίγνιον) and "a holyday for gain" (πανηγυρισμὸν ἐπικερδῆ) (v.12). This leads him to make the best of this life without regard to righteousness and virtue, to "profit every way, be it even out of evil" (v. 12).[61] In this passage, the author insists on the earthly condition of the idol maker but already introduces his spiritual dimension to convey that despite his mortal nature, he is better than the idol he made, "a dead thing," for "he lived once, but they never" (v. 17). Therefore, ignoring his Maker leads the potter to ignore his earthly and spiritual nature and any sort of spiritual existence after death. This leads the potter, and ultimately anyone, to live a futile and dissolute life. In the view of the Sage, hopelessness leads one to wickedness. It is evident that the understanding of the nature of humankind and the expectations after death would affect the decisions in the present life.

In sum, the Sage integrates implicit references to the story of the creation of humankind and the exodus imbued with Hellenistic concepts. For the Sage "Sophia" is God's agent in the process of creation and salvation. According to the Sage, "God created humankind to be immortal (ἐπ' ἀφθαρσίᾳ), and made him an image of his own eternity (ἀϊδιότητος). However, through envy of the devil, death came into the world; and those who put to test him (the devil), they experience it (death)" (Wis 2:23–24). Thus, only the righteous may participate in God's ἀφθαρσίᾳ.

Philo's De Opificio Mundi

Philo is one of the most prolific and sophisticated Hellenistic Jews living in Alexandria in the turn of the Common Era (20 b.c.e.–50 c.e.).[62] Philo's most

punishing of the Egyptians. See A. G. Wright, "Wisdom," 518. This comparison or *synkrisis,* found in the previous section between the Israelite heroes and the wicked ones (10:1-21), is applied now to the Israelites and the Egyptians.

60. See Levison, *Portraits of Adam,* 53; Winston, *Wisdom of Solomon,* 287.

61. These are common Greek topoi; see Winston, *Wisdom of Solomon,* 288; cf. 1 Cor 15:32.

important legacy, preserved only by Christian authors, is his interpretations of the Jewish Scriptures in Greek, which are part of a richer stream of interpretations of both Greek and Jewish traditions.[63]

Philo's interpretations of the Scriptures are built on two hermeneutical principles. First, for Philo the whole cosmos somehow is interconnected.[64] Thus, the Law revealed by God to Moses ordains the prescriptions for living according to this cosmic order (see *Opif.* 1-3).[65] Second, he believes that every detail of the biblical text is inspired by God and conveys an important meaning. However, he is also a critical reader and is aware of the inconsistencies of the biblical text. Consequently, he resorts to a methodology that integrates the whole and full meaning of the biblical text. Thus, he upholds its literal interpretation (cf. *Migr.* 89-93) but finds in the allegorical method the hermeneutical key to interpret its inner and full meaning.[66]

62. For Philo's historical and cultural context, see Barclay, *Jews in the Mediterranean Diaspora*, 158–63; David T. Runia, *Philo of Alexandria, On the Creation of the Cosmos according to Moses* (Philo of Alexandria Commentary Series 1; Leiden: Brill, 2001), 19–36; F. H. Colson and G. H. Whitaker, "General Introduction," in *Philo* (11 vols.; LCL; London: Heinemann, 1929–62), 1:ix–xxii. Thomas H. Tobin (*The Creation of Man: Philo and the History of Interpretation* [CBQMS 14; Washington, D.C.: Catholic Biblical Association of America, 1983], 9–19) points more specifically to the Middle Platonism of Alexandria of the turn of the first century as the milieu that influenced Philo's works.

63. See Gregory E. Sterling, "The Place of Philo of Alexandria in the Study of Christian Origins," in Philo und das Neue Testament: Wechselseitige Wahrnehmungen. 1. Internationales Symposium zum Corpus Judaeo-Hellenisticum, 1.–4. Mai 2003, Eisenach, Jena, ed. Roland Deines and Karl Wilhelm Niebuhr (WUNT 172; Tübingen: Mohr Siebeck, 2004), 21–52; and, in the same volume, George W. E. Nickelsburg, "Philo among Greeks, Jews and Christians," 69; and Larry W. Hurtado, "Does Philo Help Explain Christianity?" 73–92. See also David T. Runia, Philo in Early Christian Literature: A Survey (CRINT, Section 3, Jewish Traditions in Early Christian Literature 3; Assen: Van Gorcum; Minneapolis: Fortress Press, 1993), 66–74; and Peder C. Borgen, "Philo of Alexandria: Reviewing and Rewriting Biblical Material," Studia Philonica Annual 9 (1997): 37–53.

64. See Folker Siegert, "Philo of Alexandria," in Saebø, *Hebrew Bible/Old Testament*, vol. 1, part 1, 187.

65. Philo's interpretations of the Scriptures are concentrated on the Pentateuch. According to H. A. Wolfson, Philo revises "the ethical theories of Greek philosophy [Socrates, Plato, Aristotle, and the Stoics], and modifies them in conformity with certain presuppositions derived from Scripture" (*Philo: Foundations of Religious Philosophy in Judaism, Christianity, and Islam* [2 vols.; Structure and Growth of Philosophic Systems from Plato to Spinoza 2; Cambridge, Mass.: Harvard University Press, 1948], 2:165). He claims, "Men are therefore urged by Philo, in the language of philosophy, to follow reason and virtue and, in the language of Scripture, to obey the commandments of the Lord their God, and as a reward for such a life of reason and virtue and obedience of the commandments he promises, in the language of philosophy, happiness and, in the language of Scripture, blessings" (2:290). This is more evident when Philo interprets the lives of Abraham, Joseph, and Moses as historical figures and as examples that "have a lesson for edification apart from allegory" (Colson and Whitaker, "General Introduction," xiii–xiv).

The interpretation of the creation and fall of humankind occurs in Philo's three exegetical works (*Questions and Answers on Genesis* and on *Exodus* and the *Allegorical Commentary* on Genesis [Gen 2:1—37:41]) and in the *Exposition of the Law*[67] and *De Opificio Mundi.*

De Opificio Mundi is the most complete systematic treatise (σύνταξις) of the story of the creation and fall of humankind, which functions as an exordium to the entire *Exposition of the Law* (see *Opif.* 1-3).[68] In this treatise, Philo draws most of the ethical implications from the narrative of Genesis 1–3 in order to live "in harmony with the Law, and the Law with the world, and that the man who observes the Law is constituted thereby a loyal citizen of the world"

66. Although "Philo considers both of these levels of interpretation legitimate," the allegorical method "dominates *Legum Allegoriae* and the latter part of *De Opificio Mundi*" (Tobin, *Creation of Man*, 34–35). Tobin explains that "Philo's notion of an 'allegorical' interpretation involves 1) the internalization of the interpretation and 2) the recognition of multiple levels of interpretations" (pp. 34–35 n. 23). Additionally, Philo resorts to a third kind of interpretation called "mystical," which "consists of a series of efforts to obtain a true and even intimate knowledge of God" (Siegert, "Philo of Alexandria," 185). For further discussions of Philo's method of interpretation, see A. A. Long, "Allegory in Philo and Etymology in Stoicism: A Plea for Drawing Distinctions," *Studia Philonica Annual* 9 (1997): 198-210; Wolfson, *Philo: Foundations*, 1:115–37.

67. For a systematic classification of Philo's works, see Runia, *Philo in Early Christian Literature*, 37. For the chronological order of Philo's exegetical works, see Ralph Marcus, *Philo, Questions on Genesis* (LCL: Cambridge, Mass.: Harvard University Press, 1953), x; Abraham Terian, "The Priority of the *Questiones* among Philo's Exegetical Commentaries," in *Both Literal and Allegorical: Studies in Philo of Alexandria's* Questions and Answers on Genesis and Exodus, ed. David M. Hay (BJS 232; Atlanta: Scholars Press, 1991), 29-–46; and, in the same volume, Gregory E. Sterling, "Philo's *Questiones*: Prolegomena or Afterthought?" 99-123. For the place of *De Opificio* in the Philonic corpus, see Abraham Terian, "Back to Creation: The Beginning of Philo's Third Grand Commentary," *Studia Philonica Annual* 9 (1997): 19-36. On the grounds of external (he contests Eusebius's catalogue) and internal evidence (*Opif.* 1-3; *Abr.* 2; *Mos.* 2.46-47; *Praem.* 1-3), Terian concludes that "*De opificio* was written after *Legum allegoriae* and in anticipation of the rest of the *Exposition*, which by virtue of its literary progression (whether exegetical, allegorical or apologetic) could not have preceded the *Allegorical Commentary*" (p. 36). On the other hand, Runia argues that *Opificio* is the opening of the *Exposition of the Law*, the *Allegorical Commentary*, and *Question and Answers on Genesis and Exodus* (*Philo of Alexandria, On the Creation of the Cosmos*, 2).

68. Apparently *Legum Allegoriae* and *Questiones et Solutiones in Genesim* also originally contained an interpretation of Genesis 1, but it is no longer extant. See Thomas H. Tobin, "The Beginning of Philo's *Legum Allegoriae*," *Studia Philonica Annual* 12 (2000): 27-43. For charts on Philo's interpretation of the creation and fall of humankind, see David M. Hay, "Philo's Anthropology, the Spiritual Regimen of the Therapeutae, and a Possible Connection with Corinth," in Deines and Niebuhr, *Philo und das Neue Testament*, 132–33; Anita Méasson and Jacques Cazeaux, "From Grammar to Discourse: A Study of the *Questiones in Genesim* in Relation to the Treatises," in Hay, *Both Literal and Allegorical*, 132–34; and Tobin, *Creation of Man*, 162–64.

(*Opif.* 2-3).[69] He sums up his objective in the conclusion (170-72): the one who understands these things, "will lead a happy and blessed life, moulded by the doctrines of piety and holiness" (172). Between the prologue and the conclusion of *De Opificio* Philo develops sophisticated interpretations of the stories of the creation and the fall of humankind.[70]

In *De Opificio Mundi,* Philo incorporates earlier traditions of the creation and fall.[71] He resorts to both the literal and allegorical methods, although the latter is more prevalent in his interpretations of the fall, where he conveys most of his ethical lessons.

According to Philo, God created the intelligible world on day one (*Opif.* 15-35; cf. Gen 1:1-5), including the intelligible humankind created after the Divine *image,* which is "the very Logos of God" (*Opif.* 25).[72] Then, from the second through the sixth day God made the sense-perceptible world (*Opif.* 36-88; cf. Gen 1:6—2:1). On the fifth-sixth day,[73] God created the animated beings; and last of all, as the crown of all creation, he made the man "and bestowed on him mind (νοῦς) *par excellence*, life-principle of the life principle itself," "great Ruler" (μέγας ἡγεμών) (*Opif.* 66).[74] Philo explains that the creation

69. See also *Opif.* 143. Translations are from Colson and Whitaker in the Loeb Classical Library, and Runia, *Philo of Alexandria, On the Creation of the Cosmos*, 5-8. I have made slight modifications to highlight some nuances in the translation. . For Philo's ethical theory, see Wolfson, *Philo: Foundations,* 2:165, 290; Levison, *Portraits of Adam*, 64; Runia, *Philo of Alexandria, On the Creation of the Cosmos*, 25. Hay also identifies ethical tones in *De Vita Contemplativa* ("Philo's Anthropology, 137).

70. For the structure of *De Opificio,* see Runia, *Philo of Alexandria, On the Creation of the Cosmos,* 8-10.

71. Tobin argues that Philo drew on and interpreted traditional material, especially interpretations of the *Timaeus* in Middle Platonism (*Creation of Man*, 11-13, 18). Tobin states, "Interpretations, then, of the creation of man as a double creation take over prior interpretations of Gen 1:27 and Gen 2:7 as complementary accounts of the creation of a single man and re-interpret them to refer to the creation of two different men, one heavenly and the other earthly" (pp. 26–27). Furthermore, "The interpretations of Gen 1:26-27 [in which man in created in the image of God, i.e. God's *Logos*] are Platonic in their thought structure […] On the other hand, the interpretation of Gen 2:7 in which man has a divine spirit, a fragment of the divinity, is Stoic in outlook," (p. 28). He concludes, "The Stoic interpretation of Gen 2:7 was not rejected but integrated into and finally reinterpreted in the light of Platonic interpretation of Gen 1:26-27" (p. 101). These were traditional "anti-anthropological" interpretations meant to counter interpretations, mostly literal, that portrayed God in human terms. See also Tobin, "Interpretations of the Creation of the World in Philo of Alexandria," in Clifford and Collins, *Creation,* 109–12.

72. "The *Logos* stands between God and man and is the representation (ἀπεικόνισμα) of God and the paradigm (παράδειγμα) of the human mind," (*Opif.* 25; see also *Leg. All.* 3.95-96; *Spec. Leg.* 1.80-81; 3.83, 207; and *Q.G.* 2.62. Tobin argues that these interpretations are modeled after the interpretations found in Plato's *Timaeus* (*The Creation of Man,* 58–59).

73. Philo's distinction between the fifth and the sixth day is "blurry"; see Runia, *Philo of Alexandria, On the Creation of Cosmos,* 211–13.

of humankind after the image of God and after his likeness (Gen 1:26) refers not to the body but to "the Mind, the director of the soul (κατὰ τὸν τῆς ψυχῆς ἡγεμόνα νοῦν) . . . for after the pattern of the single Mind, even the Mind of the universe as an archetype, the mind in each of those who successively came into being was moulded" (*Opif.* 69).[75] Philo compares the function of the human mind as the ruler of soul (ψυχή)[76] to the function of the Mind of the "great Ruler" (μέγας ἡγεμὼὼν) as the ruler of the cosmos.[77] Thus, as the great Ruler governs the universe under his laws, so people ought to order their lives under the guidance of the mind, a principle that humankind eventually fails to accomplish, as the story of the fall describes.

Philo explains that the plural "*Let us* make man after *our* image and likeness" (*Opif.* 72-75; cf. Gen 1:26) indicates that other coworkers took part in the fashioning of the "mixed nature" of a "creature so puny and perishable as man" (*Opif.* 72).[78] This explains that the "mixed nature" of human beings is "liable to *contraries*, wisdom and folly, self-mastery and licentiousness, courage and cowardice, justice and injustice, and (in a word) to things good and evil, fair and foul, to virtue and vice" (*Opif.* 73). When one's "thoughts and deeds are blameless, God the universal Ruler may be owed as their source; while others from the number of His subordinates are held responsible for thoughts and deeds of a contrary sort" (*Opif.* 75). In this way Philo exonerates God of any wrongdoing in the creation of humanity and introduces a list of opposite virtues and vices to explain the ethical predicament and ambivalence of humankind. At this point this is explained by intermediate agents that participated in the creation.[79] It is not until his allegorical interpretation of the fall that Philo will

74. Philo explains why man was created "last," so that the "Ruler of all things" (ὅλων ἡγεμών) may prepare the banquet beforehand for man (*Opif.* 77-78).

75. Philo explains this to counter anthropomorphic representations of God; see Tobin, *Creation of Man*, 36-55.

76. In *Opif.* 81, Philo uses the metaphor of the war in the soul that struggles against passions and vices and to pursuit virtue; see also *Leg. All.* 3.115-17.

77. However, Philo preserves the distinction between the human and the divine mind; cf. the "flight of the soul" (*Opif.* 70-71); see Runia, *Philo of Alexandria, On the Creation of the Cosmos*, 224-33.

78. Here Philo refers to the man of mixed nature (Gen 2:7), but the emphasis is now on the function of "reason" to distinguish the three orders in the cosmos: (a) the plants and animals, "devoid of reason" (ἄλογα) "partake neither of virtue nor of vice . . . for mind and reason (νοῦν καὶ λόγον) are as it were the dwelling place of vice and virtue"; (b) the heavenly bodies, "endowed with mind, or rather each of them a mind in itself, excellent through and through and unsusceptible of any evil" participate in virtue only; and (c) those "of mixed nature (τῆς μικτῆς ἐστι φύσεως), as humankind."

79. In his interpretation of the meaning of the "tree that discerns between good and evil things" Philo will explain that humankind can "distinguish things by nature contrary the one to the other," that is,

interpret the external world—the man, the woman, and the serpent—as the internal dynamics of the human soul. Thus, Philo builds his ethical theory on cosmological and ontological grounds.

Then Philo gives four reasons why man was created last (*Opif.* 65-66; 77-88). First, he refers to the explanation given by others (77-78).[80] The second explanation is his, that is, "for the instruction of future generations," so that "like the first father of the race (τὸν ἀρχηγέτην τοῦ γένους) they were to spend their days without turmoil or trouble. . . . And this will be if (ἐάν) irrational pleasures (ἄλογοι ἡδοναί) do not get control of the soul (ψυχῆς)" (79). "But now that (νυνὶ μὲν γάρ) all these evils" have overcome humankind,[81] "a fitting penalty is incurred, due punishment of impious courses. That penalty is difficulty to obtain the necessaries of life" (80).[82] He concludes that *if* self-control (εἰ δὲ σωφροσύνη μὲν . . .) were to alleviate the immoderate impulses of the passions . . . God will provide for our race good things all coming spontaneously ready for consumption" (81). Thus, Philo infers an ethical lesson not from the main point he is addressing, that is, why humankind was created last, but from the story of the fall (Genesis 3), where he resorts mainly to allegorical interpretation. He also relates the original bliss before the fall to the abundance of good things that humankind would enjoy in the eschaton, provided that they subdue their passions and lead a virtuous life. In the third explanation, Philo also relates the creation of heaven in the beginning to the creation of man "last," so that the latter, as "a miniature heaven has capacities . . . for science and art, for knowledge, and for the noble lore of the several virtues" (82).[83] In the last

good and evil, by means of the virtue of "intermediate practical insight/prudence" (φρόνησιν τὴν μένσην, *Opif.* 154). For the philosophical background of φρόνησις and parallel passages in Philo, see Runia, *Philo of Alexandria, On the Creation of the Cosmos*, 367–68. However, the relevance of this passage is not the intermediate character of this virtue, as Runia suggests, but the ability of this virtue to distinguish and choose between "things by nature contrary," that is, good and evil. Thus, this virtue is not of mixed nature, but its middle position (φρόνησιν τὴν μένσην) enables one to choose between two external and opposite things, good and evil, virtue and vice. In other words, the relationship between the two passages is the "contraries" between which one can choose by means of φρόνησις.

80. They "maintain (λέγουσιν) that God . . . made ready for him beforehand all things in the world" for humankind's "living and living well" (77). Philo illustrates this answer with the images of the banquet and contest that "the Ruler of all things" (ὅλων ἡγεμών) prepares for his guests (78). For Philo's philosophical background in this section, see Runia, who notes the similarities with Plato's *Timaeus* and *Phaedrus*, and Stoic influence (Cicero's *Nat. d.* 2.131-67) (*Philo of Alexandria, On the Creation of the Cosmos*, 248–51).

81. Philo provides a list of vices: greediness and lust, desires (ἐπιθυμίαι) for fame, money, and power; grief, folly, cowardice, and injustice (79).

82. Philo provides examples of natural disasters that tamper with human labor for their sustenance.

explanation, *Opif.* 83–88, Philo returns to the interpretations provided earlier by others that emphasize the place of human beings over the created earthly beings "like a governor subordinate (ὕπαρχος) to the chief and great King" (88), but here ethical implications are not drawn either.[84] This analysis shows that in the sections where Philo refers to earlier interpretations, ethical inferences are not drawn, whereas in his own interpretation he draws ethical implications from the biblical text, as found later in his allegorical interpretation of the fall. Nevertheless, unlike his interpretation of the fall, the explanations still refer to the external world; that is, God will provide good things for human sustenance if humans overcome vices and lead a virtuous life. This interpretation is in accordance with Philo's plan stated in the prologue and in the conclusion, that is, that humankind may live according to the Law in order to "lead a life of bliss and blessedness" (173).[85]

Subsequently, Philo moves on to the creation of the earthly man (*Opif.* 134–47; Gen 2:7).[86] First, he distinguishes between the man "formed after the image of God and this man: for the man so formed is an object of sense-perception . . . consisting of body and soul (ἐκ σώματος καὶ ψυχῆς), man or woman, by nature mortal (φύσει θνητός); while he that was after the image (κατὰ τὴν εἰκόνα) was an idea (ἰδέα) or type (γένος) or seal (σφραγίς), intelligible (νοητός), incorporeal (ἀσώματος), neither male or female, by nature incorruptible (ἄφθαρτος φύσει)" (134). However, Philo's distinction between the two men is not without difficulties. Indeed, earlier he had described the first man as being mortal (θνητὸς) (77) and earthborn and perishable (γηγενῶν καὶ φθαρτῶν) (82). Furthermore, in the interpretation of the first creation account,

83. Once again, Philo resorts to interpretations of the *Timaeus;* see Runia, *Philo of Alexandria, On the Creation of the Cosmos,* 253–54. Philo contrasts the "imperishable" heaven to man, who belongs to the things "earthborn and perishable" (82).

84. The verb λέγεται in *Opif.* 83, which introduces this part may indicate the interpretations given by others; cf. also *Opif* 156, where Philo explicitly alludes to what has been said in ancient times. In *Opif.* 87–88 Philo concludes with the metaphors of the drivers and pilots.

85. Philo concludes the section on the first creation account with a long commentary on the significance of the seventh day, Gen 2:2-3 (*Opif.* 89–128).

86. Philo introduces this section by interpreting Gen 2:4-5 as a "summary" (ἐπιλογιζόμενος) of the previous creation account and as a transition to what follows, *Opif.* 129-30. He interprets "in the day (ᾗ ἡμέρᾳ) in which God created heaven and the earth and every herb of the field *before* (πρὸ) it appeared upon the earth, and all the grass of the field *before* it sprang up," as referring to "the incorporeal and intelligible ideas" (ἀσωμάτους καὶ νοητὰς ἰδέας) (129). This interpretation is reinforced by the verb "preexist" (προϋπῆρκε). Thus, it seems that "in the day" refers to "day one" on which God created the intelligible world (*Opif.* 15-35, esp. 16; Gen 1:1-5). Afterwards, Philo comments on the separation of the fresh water from the salt water (131-33).

Philo seems to distinguish between the intelligible man created on "day one," and the man of the sense-perception world created on the fifth–sixth day. However, after his interpretation of Gen 2:5, "the creation of the heavenly man (Gen 1:27) falls within the creation of the intelligible world, and the creation of the earthly man (Gen 2:7) falls within the creation of the sensible world."[87] Philo attempts to solve the problem by asserting that "the formation of the individual man (ἐπὶ μέρους ἀνθρωπου) is the object of sense (αἰσθητοῦ), a composite one made up of earthly substance (γεώδους οὐσίας) and of Divine breath (πνεύματος θείου)" (135), as opposed to the generic humankind (γένος) made after the divine image of Gen 1:27. Their composite nature is what places humans in the borderline in creation and makes them partakers of both mortality due to their earthly nature, and immortality due to the soul inbreathed by God. In this interpretation, Philo links God's image (Gen 1:27) with the divine breath (Gen 2:7), described as the human soul (ψυχή) or mind (διάνοια). Later on, Philo states that the Creator employed his own word (ἑαυτοῦ λόγῳ) as the pattern for the soul of the first man and breathed it into his face (*Opif.* 139). Rather than a direct identification between the Logos and *nous* (Gen 1:27) and the divine breath (Gen 2:7), Philo moves from the generic human being of Gen 1:27 to the individual and composite man created of Gen 2:7.[88]

Then Philo compares the superior qualities of "the first man, earth born, ancestor of our whole race" (*Opif.* 136–39), with his descendants, who are formed as "inferior copies" of the original first molded man (140–41).[89] Thus, the first man excels in moral qualities (142–44), whereas the moral qualities of his descendants dim compared to their ancestor (145).[90] Up to this point

87. Tobin, *Creation of Man,* 134. Contra Tobin, Runia interprets "the human being after the image" as the "ideal" person, that is, an idealization of human nature in terms of intellect," but he ultimately leaves the question open and blames Philo "for this lack of clarity" (*Philo of Alexandria, On the Creation of the Cosmos,* 323).

88. So Runia, *Philo of Alexandria, On the Creation of the Cosmos,* 323–24. In *Opif.* 66-71, Philo had interpreted the creation of man after the image of God as the mind (νοῦς), "the life-principle of the life principle itself" and "the faculty of reasoning," and related the order ruled by the divine Mind in the cosmos with the moral order the human mind was supposed to rule in man. In *Opif.* 135, Philo is concerned with the composite nature of humans, being mortal because of their earthly origins and immortal because of the divine inbreathing; however, no ethical implications are raised here.

89. "As generation follows generation the powers and qualities of body and soul which men receive are feebler" (*Opif.* 141).

90. Thus, the original forefather is also called "the only citizen of the world" (*Opif.* 142), for he abides by the "divine law" (νόμος θεῖος) (143). He does so because "the divine spirit (θείου πνεύματος) had flowed into him in full current . . . and so all his words and actions were undertaken to please the Father and King, following Him step by step in the highways cut out by virtues (ἀρεταί)" (144). Philo also

Philo has interpreted the two creation accounts of humankind *before the fall* and has described the forefather of the human race as an ideal and example of virtue, wisdom, and happiness. He integrated earlier traditions of the creation of humankind and provided his own interpretations, in which he introduced ethical implications that describe the forefather before the fall as the virtuous ideal for his descendants. His righteousness proceeds from his closer likeness to his maker, whereas his descendants have a lesser share in the original bliss.

Finally, Philo interprets the story of the fall, *Opif.* 151–170a. It is in his interpretation of the fall that he draws most of the ethical implications from the biblical text. In his interpretations of the creation of humankind in Gen 1:26-27 and 2:7, the characters represented the external world; however, in his interpretation of the fall, while preserving to a certain extent the literal meaning of the text, he turns mostly to allegorical interpretation: "This description is, I think, intended symbolically (συμβολικῶς) rather than literally (κυρίως)" (*Opif.* 154a)."[91] Thus, in the story of the fall the characters represent the internal phenomena of the human soul; thus, "the man created in Gen 2:7 becomes a symbol of 'mind' (νοῦς), the woman of 'sense perception' (ἄσθησις), and the serpent of 'pleasure' (ἡδονή)."[92] The structure of this section is complex, for Philo departs from the biblical text (Gen 2:8—3:24) and occasionally digresses to expand on particular details of the account: (a) the formation of woman (*Opif.* 151–52); (b) the interpretation of paradise and its trees (153-55); (c) the allegorical interpretation of the snake, the woman, and the man (156-66); and (d) the punishments that follow the fall (167-70a).

Philo states that the first man, inasmuch as he was created mortal and liable to changes, "should experience ill fortune (κακοπραγίας)" (*Opif.* 151a). He explains abruptly that "woman became for him the beginning of blameworthy life (ἀρχὴ ὑπαιτίου ζωῆς) for man" (151b).[93] He states that before the woman was created, the first man enjoyed a life of solitude (μόνωσις), growing in similitude (ὡμοιοῦτο) to God and to the world (151c).[94] Then the woman was

explains that the first man gives the names [to the animals, Gen 2:19-20], because it is a task of royalty and because he "was taught by Wisdom's own lips" (148-50). On the other hand, the first man's descendants participate in a limited way, "in the original form in which [their forefather] was formed" (145). This kinship makes every person a participant in the divine Reason by means of one's mind, and of the four elements of the cosmos by means of one's body (146-47).

91. He criticizes others' interpretations: "Now these are not mythical fictions, such as poets and sophists delight in, but modes of making ideas visible, bidding us resort to allegorical interpretations (ἀλληγορίαν παρακαλοῦντα) guided in our rendering by what lies beneath the surface" (*Opif.* 157; see also 164).

92. Tobin, *Creation of Man,* 34. Tobin extensively develops this question in chapter 6.

93. See similar attitudes regarding woman in Sir 25:24.

"molded" (ἐπλάσθη), "a figure like his own and a kindred form (εἶδος καὶ συγγενῆ)" (151d), but Philo omits the detail about the rib (Gen 2:21-22).[95] Their encounter initially aroused "in each of them a desire (πόθος) for fellowship with the other with a view to the production of their like," but then this desire "begat bodily pleasure (σωμάτικων ἡδονήν), which is the beginning of wrongs and violation of law," a pleasure "by which men bring on themselves the life of mortality and wretchedness (κακοδαίμονα) in lieu of that of immortality and bliss (εὐδαίμονος)" (152). Thus, what actually leads humankind to mortality is not sexuality as such, but bodily desire.[96] However, mortality represents the troublesome existence of the wicked,[97] whereas immortality represents the bliss of the righteous. What Philo does in this section is to introduce the basis for his allegorical interpretation of the fall, where the external reality becomes the inner experience of the human soul.

Philo briefly reintroduces the status of solitude of the man (τοῦ ἀνδρός) before woman was formed and then interprets the significance of paradise (παράδεισον) and its trees (*Opif.* 153-55). Philo first alludes to the literal interpretations by others (λόγος ἔχει),[98] which describe the excelling physical qualities of paradise, where the wood is "soulless" (ἄψυχος) and provides abundance for humankind and even for wild beasts (153a). Then he introduces an allegorical interpretation:

94. Runia argues that Philo draws on Plato's *Timaeus* 30-31 for the "unicity" between the divinity, the cosmos, and the first human being, but he educes also an ethical or even a mystical resemblance between the divinity and the human being. This is not evident in the text, but may reflect the cosmological foundation Philo envisioned for his ethical theory.

95. While for Philo the first man was made after the image of God and received the divine breathing, the woman instead was molded after the first man. In this way, Philo lays down the foundation for his allegorical interpretation where, while man represents the "mind" (νοῦς), the woman will symbolize "sense perception" (ἄσθησις).

96. Philo's opinion about sexuality overall is positive, for implicitly it responds to God's command to be fertile and multiply. Likewise Philo's attitude regarding women should be interpreted within the larger context of his interpretation of the fall, which he claims is not meant literally but "symbolically" (see *Opif.* 154, 157, 163); see Runia, *Philo of Alexandria, On the Creation of the Cosmos,* 359–61.

97. A "troublesome" life is said to be worse than death (see *Opif.* 164).

98. *Pace* Runia (*Philo of Alexandria, On the Creation of the Cosmos*, 364), who claims that this phrase refers to the biblical account. Cf. *Opif.* 100, where Philo refers to earlier exegetes whose interpretations he initially accepts but that he then takes to a deeper—that is, allegorical—meaning; see also 77 and 83. Runia notes, "The differences in interpretation of the garden and its trees reflects a diversity of Alexandrian exegetical traditions anterior to Philo" (*Philo of Alexandria, On the Creation of the Cosmos,* 366). To illustrate this diversity, Runia (p. 371) includes other Philonic interpretations of this passage: *Leg. All.* 1.43-108; 2.71-108; 3.52, 107 *Q.G.* 1.6-16, 32-40; 2.12; *Plant.* 32-45; *Migr.* 37; *Somn.* 2.70.

> But in the divine park (τὸν θεῖον παράδεισον) all plants (φυθά) are endowed with soul (ἔμψυχα) and reason (λογικά), bearing the virtues (τὰς ἀρετάς) for fruit, and beside these insight (σύνεσιν) and discernment (ἀγχίνοιαν) that never fail, by which are recognized things that are good (καλά) and evil (αίσχαρά), and life free from disease, and incorruption (ἀφθαρσίαν), and all that is of a like nature (*Opif.* 153b).

Although paradise and the trees symbolize incorporeal qualities, they still refer to external realities and not to the psychological dynamics of the human soul. In the following interpretation, which Philo attributes to Moses, paradise and its trees represent virtues and the internal phenomena of the human soul,

> By the paradise he signifies the ruling power of the soul (τὸ τῆς ψυχῆς ἡγεμονικόν) . . . and by the tree of life (δένδρου τῆς ζωῆς) he signifies reverence toward God (θεοσέβειαν), the greatest of all the virtues, by means of which the soul attains to immortality (ἀθανατίζεται); while by [the tree] that discerns (γνωριστικοῦ) between good (καλῶν) and evil things (πονηρῶν) he signifies intermediate practical insight/prudence (φρόνεσιν τὴν μέσην), which enables us to distinguish things by nature contrary the one to the other (*Opif.* 154b).

Earlier, Philo explained that by "image" Moses meant the "*Mind*, the director of the soul (τῆς ψυχῆς ἡγεμόνα νοῦν) (*Opif.* 69).[99] Likewise, he interpreted the "mind and reason" (νοῦς καὶ λόγος) as "the dwelling-place of vice and virtue" (κακίας καὶ ἀρετῆς) (73).[100] Now, "paradise" represents the "ruling power" of the soul, that is, the *nous* responsible for one's moral choices. Correspondingly, the soul would attain immortality by means of the tree of life.[101] Then, although he does not mention that it was *in the middle* of the garden, he interprets the tree that discerns good and evil things as the "intermediate practical insight."

99. In both passages, 69 and 154, Philo explicitly states that these are Moses' interpretations. In the first instance, Philo was referring to the creation of the first man, the generic human being; in the second case, the interpretation of paradise comes after his discussion of the creation of the second man, the molded individual, male and female. That is why Philo refers here to the status of man *before* the formation of woman.

100. Philo explains that in the creation of "the mixed nature of man" other agents are responsible for the vices that exist in man, whereas God is the sole cause for the virtues in man.

101. By immortality he means "an existence long and happy" (μακραίωνα καὶ εὐδαίμονα βίον) (156; cf. 172).

Philo explains that after the boundaries in the soul (ἐν ψυχῇ) were established, God waited to see to which tree it would incline; but seeing that it inclined toward wickedness (πανουργίαν), "and disregarded reverence of God (εὐσεβείας) and holiness, out of which comes immortal life, he expelled it from paradise, giving the soul . . . no hope of a subsequent return" (*Opif.* 155).[102] Philo makes a quick and awkward move here, for before he interpreted "paradise" as the ruling power of the soul, but now he says that the soul is expelled from paradise. Without solving this contradiction, Philo moves on to the next question.[103]

In *Opif.* 156–66 Philo integrates literal and allegorical interpretations of the story of the fall. He first mentions earlier interpretations (λέγεται τὸ παλαιόν) that believed that the snake approached and spoke to "the wife of the first man,"[104] who took of the fruit and gave some of it to her husband (156a).[105] He explains that this action "transformed (μετέβαλεν) them both from a state of simplicity (ἀκακίας) and innocence (ἁπλότητος) into one of wickedness (πανουργίαν) (156b).[106] Thus, they took from the tree that discerns what is good and evil; that is, they chose "ephemeral and mortal existence, which is not an existence but a life full of misery" (156; cf. 165). They forfeited the tree of life, skipping complete virtue (ἀρετῆς παντέλειαν) and missed its fruit of a "happy and long life" (156c). It is likely but not definitive that Philo introduced here this allegorical and ethical turn into the story.

Then Philo claims that these stories are not "mythical fictions (μύθου πλάσματα) . . . but indications of types (τύπων), which invite to allegorical interpretation (ἀλληγορίαν) through the explanation of hidden underlying meaning (ὑπονοιῶν)" (*Opif.* 157a).[107] Thus, he interprets the snake as "a symbol

102. Cf. the analogy of "the warfare of the soul," where Philo suggests that there is place for hope "that God . . . would provide for our race good things" (*Opif.* 81).

103. Runia points out that ἦν οὐκ ἄξιον παρασιωπῆσαι, as in *Opif.* 6, "introduces the next stage of the exegesis" (*Philo of Alexandria, On the Creation of the Cosmos*, 369).

104. It was believed that before the fall all the animals in paradise were able to speak; cf. *Jub.* 3:28; Josephus, *Ant.* 1.41.

105. However, Philo qualifies the fruit, not the tree (cf. Gen 3:6), as having "power to recognize things good and evil" (γνωρίζειν ἀγαθά τε καὶ κακά). He anticipates his allegorical interpretation by describing the woman as lacking in "further reflection" (ἀνεξετάστως), of "an unreliable conviction (γνώμης ἀνβεβαίου) and devoid of steadfastness and firm resolution" (156).

106. Runia persuasively suggests that this transformation is an "ethical" change that brought them out of a state of "genuine virtue and goodness" (cf. *Opif.* 170) into that of wickedness (*Philo of Alexandria, On the Creation of the Cosmos*, 370). Philo withholds his interpretation of the punishments until 167–70a.

107. Philo preserves the literal meaning of the biblical text but also incorporates his allegorical interpretation; see Runia, *Philo of Alexandria, On the Creation of the Cosmos*, 374–75.

of pleasure" (ἡδονῆς σύμβολον) (157-64; cf. *Q.G.* 1.31-33). First, he provides three reasons why the snake represents pleasure (157b).[108] Second, he identifies the snake with "the lover of pleasure" (φιλήδονος), who resembles similarly the three features of the snake.[109] Third, Philo interprets the human voice of the snake as the "doctrine" of many who advocate the sovereignty of pleasure (160).[110] Finally, Philo contrasts the serpent as a symbol of pleasure to "the snake-fighter" (ὀφιομάκης) (163b), representing "self-control" (ἐγκράτεια), which fights "intemperance (ἀκρασίαν) and pleasure" (ἡδονήν).[111] This contrast is applied to the opposite lifestyles, "austere (φιλαθστήρω) and honorable (σεμνῷ) life," on the one hand, and "troublesome life" (χαλεπτωτέραν),[112] which is "worse than death," on the other. This contrast anticipates the punishments that Philo will interpret in the next section, 167-70a.

Philo continues with his allegorical interpretation, where "the man" (ἀνδρί) represents the mind (νοῦς),[113] and "the woman" (γυναικί) stands for "sense-perception" (αἴσθησις) (*Opif.* 165-66).[114] Thus, "Pleasure" comes first to the "senses" and through them "she" also ensnares "the sovereign mind" (ἡγεμόνα νοῦν). Then Philo compares the actions of four of the senses to "handmaids" who offer "to the Reason (λογισμῷ) as to a master (δεσπότῃ)" the result of their perceptions. Ultimately, Reason is ensnared and "becomes

108. (1) Because without feet he is prone upon his belly (γαστέρα); (2) because he eats earth; and (3) because with his poison he destroys those he bites (*Opif.* 157c).

109. (1) He is bent downward because of his lack of self-control (ἀκρασίας; cf. 164). (2) "He feeds not on heavenly food, which wisdom provides to lovers of contemplation by means of words and doctrines, but on what is provided from the earth . . . and which produces drunkenness, and delicacies [οψοπαγιαι, "delicacies" indeed], and greediness" (158). (3) The resemblance of the teeth carries on the idea of gluttony and not of poison. Philo profusely describes the gastric pleasures of the lover of pleasure, which reflect the banquets of which Philo was certainly aware. For the philosophical background, see Runia, *Philo of Alexandria, On the Creation of the Cosmos,* 377-78.

110. Philo describes the doctrine of these advocates, who explain the function of "pleasure" in the attraction between male and female at birth, and the infant's displeasure when s/he experience any suffering, to the extent that "every living creature hastens after pleasure as its most necessary and essential end, and man above all," whose pleasures include not only "the taste and the organs of reproduction" but "the other senses as well," (161-63a).

111. Philo aptly interprets this insect (ὀφιομάκης) which Moses allows to eat (cf. Lev 11:22), as a symbol of "simplicity" (εὐτέλειαν) and "abstemiousness" (ὀλιγοδεῖαν) in the context of the over-indulgences some have with food.

112. On this term, in the sense of "suffering," see 4 Macc 8:1; 9:4; 16:8; as "troublesome life," Sir 3:21; as "violence," Wis 19:13; cf. also *Opif.* 156c, though using a different term, κακοδαιμονίας.

113. ἐν ἡμῖν γὰρ ἀνδρὸς μὲν ἔχει λόγον ὁ νοῦς.

114. Philo does not use the term "snake" anymore, but "pleasure."

subject instead of a ruler (ἡγεμόνος) . . . and a mortal instead of immortal" (165). Finally, to highlight the negative effects of "Pleasure" Philo compares her to a prostitute who entices and "brings the mind (νοῦν) under her control" (166a).[115]

In the last section, Philo explains the punishments that follow the fall (*Opif.* 167-70a; cf. Gen 3:16-19).[116] Philo paraphrases the punishments against the woman and man, but he omits those against the snake now called "Pleasure" (167; cf. Genesis 3). Then Philo draws out two moral lessons from man's need to till the ground for his sustenance. First, from the earth's failure to produce abundantly without cultivation,[117] he infers that "now that wickedness (κακία) has begun to abound at the expense of the virtues, the ever-flowing fountains of God's grace have been blocked, *that they might not* bring supplies to the unworthy (ἀναξίοις)" (168).[118] Second, he explains that God did not "provide food ready to hand in the same way as before, *that they might not,* by indulging the twin evils of laziness (ἀργία) and overindulgence (κόρῳ), go astray and become insolent in their behavior" (169).[119]

The conclusion summarizes the interpretation of the story of the fall (*Opif.* 151-70a),[120] but most importantly it provides the hermeneutical key for its interpretation, "Such was the life of those who in the beginning acted with innocence (ἀκακίᾳ) and simplicity (ἁπλότητι), but then preferred (προτιμώντων) wickedness (κακίᾳ) instead of virtue (ἀρετῆς)" (170a). Therefore, the interpretation of the story of the fall—and to a certain extent of the entire treatise—illustrates the consequences of turning away from virtue and choosing wickedness. It teaches a moral lesson, so that one "will lead a happy (μακαρίαν) and blessed (εὐδαίμονα) life, molded by the doctrines of piety (εὐσεβείας) and holiness (ὁσιότητος)" (172).

In sum, previous studies of *De Opificio Mundi* have demonstrated that Philo drew on earlier interpretations and traditions of the creation of the world, particularly interpretations of Plato's *Timaeus.* He integrated the literal meaning into allegorical interpretations of the biblical text. In those sections where

115. Philo concludes with an explanation of the function and need of the senses in the process of knowledge that is borrowed from Stoic epistemology; see Runia, *Philo of Alexandria, On the Creation of the Cosmos,* 382.

116. Cf. *Opif.* 79-81; *Leg. All.* 3; and *Q.G.* 1.49-51.

117. He compares this to the light that the sun and the moon continue to provide.

118. Besides the examples Runia (*Philo of Alexandria, On the Creation of the Cosmos,* 388) mentions from Cicero *Nat. d.* 2.79; *Sib. Or.* 4:15, it may well be the case that Philo also has in mind the streams that watered the earth (Gen 2:6).

119. Philo explains that this was a moderated punishment on account of God's nature and compassion.

120. So Runia, *Philo of Alexandria, On the Creation of the Cosmos,* 389.

Philo incorporates earlier interpretations, there is hardly any ethical inference. Conversely, in his allegorical interpretation, he draws ethical implications. This is most evident in his interpretation of the story of the fall, where, while preserving the literal and the allegorical meanings, he transfers their significance from the external world to the internal phenomena of the human soul. Thus, paradise represents the ruling power of the soul; the tree of life signifies reverence toward God; and the tree of the middle of the garden that discerns between good and evil stands for the intermediate practical insight. Similarly, the three characters of the fall represent human faculties, the man represents the mind, and the woman stands for sense perception, whereas the serpent signifies "pleasure." It is from his overly allegorical interpretation that he draws most of the ethical implications from the text. This explanation of the creation of humankind and particularly the story of the fall responds to Philo's objective in *De Opificio,* which he outlines in the introduction and restates in the conclusion, namely, that by abiding by the Law—inscribed by God in the cosmos but revealed to Moses—and by leading a virtuous life, one may attain a happy and blessed life (2-3; 172). Although Philo believed in some sort of retribution after death, in *De Opificio* the reward and the punishment are attained already in this life, a happy and blessed life in the first case, and a life full of distress and sufferings in the second.[121]

The "Rewritten Bible" on the Figure of Adam: Introduction

The "Rewritten Bible" is a broad group of interpretations that freely follow the biblical narrative in order to find the place and function of Israel in the world.[122] These interpretations include apocalyptic and wisdom features that express hope in a future reward on the condition that one keep God's commandments

121. Philo develops the theme of rewards and punishments in *De Praemiis et Poenis*, and may have believed in an eschatological reward or punishment of the soul after death—as did other Jews of his time. His eschatological outlook, however, is more moderated and does not advocate for the destruction of the present world in order to attain a transcendental reward. Thomas H. Tobin argues that instead of the subversive political eschatology promoted in the *Sibylline Oracles* 3 and 5, Philo proposed a nonsubversive eschatology "dependent on the observance of the Law and the practice of virtue by the Jewish nation," which the Gentiles could also share if they observe the Law and practice virtues (102-3). See Tobin, "Philo and the Sibyl: Interpreting Philo's Eschatology," *Studia Philonica Annual* 9 (1997): 84–103.

122. Citing (n. 10) G. Vermes, "The Life of Abraham," in G. Vermes, *Scripture and Tradition in Judaism. Haggadic Studies* (SPB 4; Leiden 19732), 67–126 (esp. 95), van Ruiten describes "Rewritten Bible" as "a midrashic insertion of *haggadic* additions into the biblical narrative in order to anticipate questions, and to solve problems in advance;" J. T. A. G. M. van Ruiten, *Primaeval History Interpreted: The Rewriting of Genesis 1–11 in the Book of Jubilees* (JSJSup 66; Leiden: Brill, 2000), 3.

contained in the Law. In these interpretations Adam's sin is characterized as disobedience to God's commandment and functions as the prototype of the historical transgressions of Israel and the nations that brought into the world all sorts of misfortunes for humankind, especially untimely death. The story of the fall also explains the misfortunes of Israel, typically the destruction of the temple and Jerusalem. In this context, the righteous are exhorted to adhere to the Law in order to attain the promised restoration in the eschaton.

The Book of Jubilees

The book of *Jubilees* seeks to explain the place of Israel among the nations.[123] The book was originally written in Hebrew between 161 and 152 b.c.e. probably in Palestine.[124] The author, who possibly belonged to the Hasidim or a stream of thought that preceded the Essenes,[125] reinterpreted the narrative from Genesis to the first part of Exodus, using a text "more in line with the wording

123. See James C. VanderKam, *The Book of Jubilees* (Guides to the Apocrypha and Pseudepigrapha; Sheffield: Sheffield Academic Press, 2001), 135; John C. Endres, S.J., *Biblical Interpretation in the Book of Jubilees* (CBQMS 18; Washington, DC: Catholic Biblical Association of America, 1987), 245; Michael Segal, *The Book of Jubilees: Rewritten Bible, Redaction, Ideology and Theology* (JSJSup 117; Leiden: Brill, 2007), 4; van Ruiten, *Primaeval History Interpreted*, 3. *Jubilees* contains testaments, ritual laws, chronologies, blessings, apocalypses, and curses; seeEndres, 197–98; and O. S. Wintermute, "Jubliees," in *The Old Testament Pseudepigrapha*, ed. James H. Charlesworth (2 vols.; New York: Doubleday, 1983–85), 2:36–41.

124. *Jubilees* underwent a complex textual history. Earlier studies on the book relied mostly on the Ethiopic version, but the discovery of the Dead Sea Scrolls provided invaluable information for the study of this work as well as other documents. VanderKam traced the history of the text and concluded that, from the original text in Hebrew (written between 163 and 140 b.c.e.), it was translated into Greek (ca. 200 c.e.?) and Syriac (ca. 500 c.e.?). From the Greek it was also translated into Latin (ca. 450 c.e.?) and Ethiopic (ca. 500 c.e.?); see James C. VanderKam, *Textual and Historical Studies in the Book of Jubilees* (HSM 14; Missoula, Mont.: Scholars Press, 1977), 15, 283–84. See also his *Book of Jubilees*, 17-21. For similar dating, see Wintermute, "Jubilees," 44. Endres likewise locates *Jubilees* "in Palestine, before the Hasmonean era" (*Biblical Interpretation*, 236).

125. See Wintermute, "Jubilees," 45; VanderKam, *Book of Jubilees*, 141–43. According to VanderKam, there have been found about fourteen fragmentary manuscripts of *Jubilees* at Qumran, CD 16.2-4; 4Q225-28; 4Q217; 4Q252; 1QapGen Apocryphon; 4Q265; *Temple Scroll*, pp. 143–46. According to Joseph A. Fitzmyer (*The Genesis Apocryphon of Qumran Cave I*: A *Commentary* (2nd rev. ed.; BibOr 18A; Rome: Biblical Institute Press, 1971), 11, J. T. Milik reported about ten fragmentary manuscripts of *Jubilees* in caves 1, 2, and 4 (Milik, *Ten Years of Discovery in the Wilderness of Judaea* [SBT 26; Naperville, Ill.: Allenson, 1959], 32). The author of the work was concerned with cultic and priestly matters: "The conclusion is consistent with his picture of scriptural heroes as priests, beginning with Adam, but it is particularly suggested in the additions which legislate priestly advantages and in the section about Levi and his ordination to the priesthood" (VanderKam, *Book of Jubilees*, 141).

now found in the Samaritan Pentateuch and the LXX than in the MT,"[126] and integrated other sources and earlier layers of redaction.[127] The title refers to the book's heptadic chronological system.[128]

The introduction presents the overall subject matter of the book: on Mount Sinai God commands Moses to write concerning the proper observance of the laws and feasts.[129] The author interprets the story of Israel from the creation of Adam until the giving of the Law to Moses on Mount Sinai to exhort his audience to keep the covenant and the laws, particularly with regard to the proper way to celebrate the feasts according the calendar.

The most significant feature in the interpretation of the story of the creation and fall is the insertion of three ritual laws.[130] First, on the sixth day of

126. VanderKam, *Book of Jubilees*, 137.

127. The author also used Enoch traditions (*Jub.* 4:15-26), possibly a *Book of Noah* (*Jub.* 7:20-39), *Aramaic Levi* (*Jub.* 21:7-20), the *Apocalypse of Abraham* 1–8 (*Jub.* 11:15—12:21), the *Testament of Judah* (*Jub.* 34:1-9), and possibly the Ionian world map (*Jubilees* 8–10) (VanderKam, *Book of Jubilees*, 136–39). Segal argues that *Jubilees* underwent a development at the redactional level: "*Jubilees* is not a homogeneous book composed by one author. It is possible to identify in it internal contradictions, doublets, tensions, and discrepancies, both in details and in references to the biblical stories in general" (*Book of Jubilees,* 34–35). Segal assigned the halakic and chronological redactions to the same editor who placed the legal material within the chronological material of the narrative, (pp. 94, 319). Gene L. Davenport identified at least three layers of redaction (*The Eschatology of the Book of Jubilees* StPB 20; Leiden: Brill, 1971], 18). The final editor is what we call the "author."

128. Segal states, "All the events from creation until the entry into the promised land are dated according to a chronological system of jubilees (49 years), weeks (7 years), and years" (*Book of Jubilees,* 7). Following Elior, 2004, Segal notes that this system is found in priestly literature (p. 7, n. 15).

129. In *Jub.* 1:27, it is the "angel of the presence" who *writes* or *dictates* the tablets to Moses. Segal states that VanderKam "Conjectured that the original Hebrew reading of 1:27, God commanded the angel of the presence 'to dictate (להכתיב)' the revelation to Moses, and not 'to write (לכתוב)' as in the Ge'ez translation. VanderKam's suggestion was subsequently confirmed in a Hebrew copy of *Jubilees* from Qumran (4Q216 IV, 6)," (Segal, *Book of Jubilees,* 16). Ultimately, the author wants to convey that the tablets were written "from [the day of creation until] the day of the new creation when the heaven and earth and all their creatures shall be renewed" (*Jub.* 1:32-34) in order to explain that the Law was preordered since eternity and that, consequently, even Adam and the patriarchs obeyed God's Law.

130. See Levison, *Portraits of Adam*, 89–97. For a detailed comparison between the narrative in Genesis 1–3 and *Jubilees,* see J. T. A. G. M. van Ruiten, "The Creation of Man and Woman in Early Jewish Literature," in *The Creation of Man and Woman: Interpretations of the Biblical Narrative in Jewish and Christian Traditions,* ed. Gerard P. Luttikhuizen (Themes in Biblical Narrative 3; Leiden: Brill, 2000), 40–48; and more extensively his *Primaeval History Interpreted,* 42-46, 72-111. As a matter of fact, this is the way the author of *Jubilees* proceeds throughout the entire rewriting of Genesis through the first part of Exodus. It is unlikely that the author distinguished between J and P in Genesis (see van Ruiten, *Primaeval History Interpreted*, 6); nevertheless, the obvious modifications that the author of *Jubilees* introduced show that he was aware of the difficulties of the double creation account.

the first week, "He made man—male and female he made them—and he gave him dominion over everything. . . . And over all this he gave him dominion" (*Jub.* 2:14-16; cf. Gen 1:26-28).[131] The author omits the motif of God's image,[132] the blessing,[133] and the command to multiply and fill the earth.[134] In its place he expands on the Sabbath and its laws (*Jub.* 2:17-33).[135] The author relates the blessing of the Sabbath to the blessing of Israel: "Just as I have sanctified and shall sanctify the Sabbath day for myself thus I shall bless them [Israel/Jacob]" (*Jub.* 2:19; cf. Sir 33:10). However, the blessing is not bestowed on all humankind but upon Israel only, and it is associated with their keeping of the Sabbath (cf. *Jub.* 2:31). In this passage, the author portrays Adam in a positive way: Adam and Jacob are blessed and sanctified (*Jub.* 2.23). Thus, the author introduces a major concern that will develop in the rest of the book—the separation of Israel from the rest of the nations by means of the observance of the Laws, particularly the keeping of the Sabbath.

The second reference to the creation of humankind is actually the description of the creation and presentation of the woman to Adam (cf. Gen 2:18-25). The author omits most of the second creation account from Gen 2:4b-17.[136] He sets the creation of woman at the end of the second week. After the angels daily brought to Adam the animals to name them, he still found himself alone (*Jub.* 3:1-3) and consequently the Lord brought Eve to Adam:

> "It is not good that man should be alone. Let us *make* for him a helper who is like him." . . . And he took one bone from the midst of his bones for the woman. And that rib was the origin of the woman

131. Translation is from Wintermute, "Jubilees."

132. This reference, however, is found in the rewriting of the covenant with Noah (Gen 8:21—9:17), "Whoever pours out the blood of a man, by man his blood shall be poured out, because in the image of the Lord he made Adam" (*Jub.* 6:8).

133. The author leaves the blessing until the context of the Sabbath (*Jub.* 2:19).

134. Van Ruiten identifies five modifications in total, noticing in particular the omission of the divine name, the use of verb "to make" instead of "to create," and the singular instead of the plural to emphasize "that God alone created the world" ("Creation of Man and Woman," 41-43).

135. Cf. also *Jubilees* 50. The author introduces the account of the creation in 2:1 with the angel of the presence commanding Moses to "write the whole account of creation, that in six days the Lord God completed all his works and all that he created. And he observed a Sabbath the seventh day, and he sanctified it for all ages. And he set it (as) a sign for all his works." In *Jub.* 2:17 and 2:25, the author summarizes the account of the creation of the world to give further instructions regarding the keeping of the Sabbath.

136. He omits the bareness of the earth (Gen 2:4b-6), the creation of man out of dust (Gen 2:7), and the description of the garden and the command not to eat from the tree (Gen 2:8-17).

> from the midst of his bones . . . and he *constructed* a woman. . . . And he *brought* her to him and he knew her (*Jub.* 3:4-7).

The author rehearses the story of Gen 2:18-25 quite literally except for the transposition of Gen 2:19-20 before the creation of woman, and the reference to their innocent nakedness after the laws of purification (*Jub.* 3:16). He also tries to ease the tension found in Genesis: since male and female had already been created during the first week (*Jub.* 2:14), he suggests that the woman was actually in Adam's rib, but not until the second week is she shown to him (*Jub.* 3:8).[137] Then the author inserts the legislation on purification after childbirth (*Jub.* 3:8-14; cf. Lev 12:2-5). The creation of man and woman and their sexual intercourse occurred while they were still outside the garden, in the land of 'Elda (*Jub.* 3:6, 32). The author portrays the garden as the sanctuary (*Jub.* 3:12-14) to introduce the legislation that forbids a woman to enter the sanctuary or touch anything sacred until the completion of the days of her purification after childbirth (cf. Lev 12:2-5). Thus, the second reference to the creation of humankind also introduces a law that reinforces the separation between the sacred and the profane. Israel is to keep these laws to delineate Israel's distinction from other nations.

Third and last, before interpreting the story of the fall, the author inserts a passage that describes Adam and his wife tilling and guarding the garden during the first week of the first jubilee (*Jub.* 3:15-16). He resumes the narrative with a chronological marker, "At the end of seven years, . . . in the second month on the seventeenth day, the serpent drew near to the woman" (*Jub.* 3:17a). In *Jub.* 3.17b-22, the author follows most of the narrative of Gen 3:1-7 but introduces several significant changes. First, he solves the apparently unfulfilled sentence of death (*Jub.* 3:18; cf. 3:25; Gen 2:17; 3:3, 19) by describing that Adam died "at the end of the nineteenth jubilee in the seventh week, in the sixth year (*Jub.* 4:29)."[138] Second, he omits the description of the serpent as the most cunning

137. "On the basis of paleographical grounds" that date 4Q216 (col. VII) between 125 and 100 b.c.e. and further structural analysis, van Ruiten rejects the theses of Michel Testuz (*Les Idées religieuses du Livre des Jubilés* [Paris, 1960], 45) and John R. Levison (*Portraits of Adam, in Early Judaism,* 1988, 90–91, 214–15) that deems *Jub.* 2:14 a later scribal interpolation and considers "the text of Jubilees with regard to the creation of man and woman as a (perhaps not completely successful) attempt to solve the tensions within the biblical text of Genesis 1-2" (van Ruiten, "Creation of Man and Woman," 46–47).

138. The author explains that "he lacked seventy years from one thousand years, for a thousand years are like one day in the testimony of heaven and therefore it was written concerning the tree of knowledge, 'In the day you eat from it you will die.' Therefore he did not complete the years of this day because he died in it" (*Jub.* 4:29-30).

of all the animals (Gen 3:3) and that the tree was desirable for gaining wisdom (Gen 3:6)—perhaps to prevent associating the first act of disobedience with getting any wisdom from this tree. He also omits the hiding from God (Gen 3:8–13)[139] and abbreviates the curse upon the serpent and the sentence upon the woman and Adam (cf. Gen 3:14–19). Third and most important, the author relates the shame of Adam and his wife (*Jub.* 3:21–22; cf. Gen 2:25), inserting the law regarding covering their nakedness for the sacrifice (*Jub.* 3:26–31; cf. Exod 20:26; 28:42). Thus, on the day of his expulsion from the garden, Adam "offered a sweet-smelling sacrifice . . . from the day he covered his shame" (*Jub.* 3:27).[140] He concludes that the commandment to cover their shame was written "in the heavenly tablets . . . that they should not be uncovered as the gentiles are uncovered" (*Jub.* 3:31). In this way, he antedates the laws found later in Exod 20:26; 28:42 to suggest that they were kept even since Adam's generation. Therefore, the author portrays Adam in priestly fashion, who offers a sacrifice purportedly to cover his and his wife's "shame." This law is another instance of the author's concerns to keep the laws and the "sacredness" of Israel in a Gentile cultural context.[141]

In sum, the author of *Jubilees* inserts into the narrative of the creation and fall of Adam ritual laws regarding the Sabbath (*Jub.* 2:17–33), the purification after childbirth (*Jub.* 3:8–14), and covering nakedness for the sacrifice (*Jub.* 3:26–31). His main concern is not the primeval story per se but the introduction of the laws since the beginning of the creation of the world and humankind. Adam is portrayed in a positive fashion as the first patriarch and priest who kept the Law, and as an example to follow for the author's generation. Thus, the story of the creation and fall of Adam is to be interpreted in the context of the introduction of *Jubilees*, when God predicts to Moses that Israel will rebel against God and will forget his commandments, covenant, and Sabbaths "and will walk after the gentiles and after their defilement and shame" (*Jub.* 1:7–10) and that God will "remove them from the midst of the land" (*Jub.* 1:13). However, they will turn to God and his commandments, and he will restore them as his people (*Jub.* 1:15–25). Therefore, the story of the creation and fall

139. The author also reduces the narrative of Gen 3:20–24 to the clothing of Adam and his wife and their expulsion from the Garden of Eden. In this way the author connects the shame because of Adam and his wife's nakedness and the law regarding the sacrifice Adam offers the day of his expulsion from the garden.

140. The author also points out, "On that day the beasts stopped from speaking," and were expelled from the garden (*Jub.* 3:28–29).

141. This law was also possibly a response to the Gentiles' nakedness while they were in the gymnasium (cf. *Jub.* 3:31).

of humankind functions as a prediction of Israel's unfaithfulness to the covenant and Israel's future restoration as a new creation, on the condition that they return to God and God's Law and celebrate the Jewish feasts accordingly.

Josephus's Jewish Antiquities

Josephus's works are marked by the turmoil of the Jewish revolt against the Romans toward the end of the first century.[142] The *Jewish Antiquities*, written ca. 93 c.e.[143] is an "apologetic historiography" that interprets the story of the Jewish people in order to explain their place among the nations (see *Ant.* 20.266).[144]

The temple occupies a central place in *Antiquities:* the first half ends with the fall of the First Temple (*Ant.* 10.276–81), and the second half concludes on the eve of the fall of the Second Temple.[145] In the proem, Josephus explains that he wrote "in the belief that the whole Greek-speaking world will find it worthy of attention; for it will embrace our entire ancient history (ἀρχαιλογίαν) and political constitution (διάταξιν τοῦ πολιτεύματος), translated from the Hebrew records" (*Ant.* 1.5).[146] Of course Diaspora Jews would also have benefited from his work.[147] Purportedly his source was the Hebrew Scriptures,[148] but scholars

142. For an introduction to Josephus's biography and works (*Jewish War, Jewish Antiquities, Life,* and *Against Apion*), see Steve Mason, *Josephus and the New Testament* (Peabody, Mass.: Hendrickson, 1992).

143. See H. St. J. Thackeray, *Josephus,* vol. 4 (LCL; Cambridge, Mass.: Harvard University Press, 1937), x.

144. Louis H. Feldman quotes Gregory Sterling who defines "apologetic historiography" as "the story of a subgroup of people in an extended prose narrative written by a member of the group who follows the group's own traditions but Hellenizes them in an effort to establish the identity of the group within the setting of the larger group (Gregory E. Sterling, 1992, 17)," Feldman, *Josephus's Interpretation of the Bible* (Hellenistic Culture and Society 27; Berkeley: University of California Press, 1998), 132.

145. Mason identifies a concentric structure around the temple (*Josephus and the New Testament*, 99). Josephus places further chronological markers around the temple, "and from the creation of Adam the first man to the time when Solomon built the temple there elapsed altogether three thousand one hundred and two years" (*Ant.* 8.62), and also "from the birth of Adam to the time when these things [destruction of the temple] happened to the temple it was an interval of four thousand five hundred and thirteen years, six months, and ten days" (*Ant.* 10.148). This emphasis on the temple shows Josephus's priestly allegiance.

146. Translations from Thackeray, *Josephus,* LCL. Josephus mentions the support he received from a Greco-Roman patron, Epaphroditus (*Ant.* 1.8; cf. 1.9), and throughout *Antiquities* he explains Jewish traditions in Greco-Roman conventions.

147. Particularly Jews who leaned toward assimilation into their Gentile milieu; see Feldman, *Josephus's Interpretation,* 46–50.

148. Josephus claims to undertake and improve the translation of the Hebrew Scriptures into Greek launched by Eleazar, which included only the Law, "For even he failed to obtain all our records" (see *Ant.* 1.10–13), and claims that he would not add nor omit anything (*Ant.* 1.17).

have noted that Josephus used different texts and translations of the Scriptures as well as other Jewish and Greco-Roman sources.[149] *Antiquities*' purpose is twofold: first, "to refute those who in their writings were doing outrage to the truth" (*Ant.* 1.4), that is, to dispel false charges against the Jews during the war against the Romans (cf. *Life* 336-39), and to counter the charge that the Jews did not produce honorable men (*Ant.* 1.6; cf. 1.18-23).[150] Thus, Josephus praises the virtues and deeds of the Jewish leaders from the past—especially Moses their lawgiver—for their piety, wisdom, character, and other virtues, against whom Josephus compares other legislators. For the most part, Josephus will omit or excuse the failures of the Jewish leaders, and whenever they are found at fault, the audience ought to learn from their mistakes.[151] The second and more important purpose of *Antiquities* is to draw moral lessons:

> The main lesson to be learnt from this history by anyone who cares to peruse it is that men who conform to the will of God, and do not venture to transgress laws that have been exceedingly laid down, prosper in all things beyond belief, and for their reward are offered by God felicity (εὐδαιμονία); whereas, in proportion as they depart

149. Harold W. Attridge (*The Interpretation of Biblical History in the Antiquitates Judaicae of Flavius Josephus* [HDR 7; Missoula, Mont.: Scholars Press, 1976]) summarizes the scholarly consensus and concludes that "Josephus used a combination of the Hebrew text, the LXX, and perhaps an Aramaic targum as well, with a different primary source in different sections of the work" (p. 30). See also Feldman, *Josephus's Interpretation,* 23–46. Mason claims that Josephus may also have used oral traditions (*Josephus and the New Testament*, 119-21). The important and detailed study by Thomas W. Franxman, *Genesis and the "Jewish Antiquities" of Flavius Josephus* (BibOr 35; Rome: Biblical Institute Press, 1979), unfortunately limits the extent of its analysis mostly to the MT. In regard to the sources, most scholars have noted the similarities between Josephus, Dionysius of Halicarnassus, and Thucydides (Feldman, *Josephus's Interpretation,* 7-8, 23). Feldman argues that, for his rewriting of the Bible, Josephus "had at his disposal both Jewish sources—notably the Bible itself, the Septuagint, the Pseudepigrapha, Philo, Pseudo-Philo's *Biblical Antiquities*, rabbinic midrashim, and targumin—and non-Jewish works—notably Hecataeus of Abdera, Berossus, Megasthenes, and Manetho. In addition, he may have consulted a number of historians whose Jewish identity has been questioned—namely, Demetrius, Philo the Elder, Eupolemus, Pseudo-Eupolemus, and Artapanus" (p. 14; see also 51–56).

150. See Feldman, *Josephus's Interpretation,* 133.

151. Josephus imitated contemporary works such as Plutarch's *Lives,* which compared individuals rhetorically (*synkrisis*) to instill ethical consequences into the narrative. In the first part of *Antiquities,* Josephus seems to turn historiography into biography, "which permits him to draw moral lessons, of virtue and vice, from each life he sketches (e.g., *Ant.* 1.53, 60-61, 66, 72)" (Mason, *Josephus and the New Testament,* 116–17). Attridge analyzes the virtues and vices of the Jewish leaders that Josephus describes in the narrative (*Interpretation of Biblical History*, 109–40). A similar approach was undertaken by Feldman in *Josephus's Interpretation;* and in *Studies in Josephus' Rewritten Bible* (JSJSup 58; Leiden: Brill, 1998).

> from the strict observance of these laws, things (else) practicable become impracticable, and whatever imaginary good thing they strive to do ends in irretrievable disasters (συμφορὰς) (*Ant.* 1.14).[152]

Josephus integrates Stoic ethical principles into the Deuteronomistic axiom of divine retribution (see Deuteronomy 28). Thus, living according to *reason* (νοῦς) and *nature* means keeping God's Law (see *Ant.* 1.19).[153] Josephus also discusses divine retribution and divine providence (πρόνοια) (*Ant.* 1.46; 10.277-80; 16.395-404).[154] In this respect, the history of Israel exemplifies God's providence, which "consists primarily in the rewarding of virtue and the punishing of vice."[155] Finally, divine retribution and providence freed one from concerns (ἀπάθεια) (*Ant.* 1.46, 276).[156] Consequently, God rewards the one

152. The concept of divine retribution is found also in the proem, "God . . . grants to such as follow him a life of bliss (εὐδαίμονα βίον), but involves in dire calamities (συμφοραῖς) those who step outside the path of virtue" (*Ant.* 1.20; cf. 1.23; 3.84; Philo, *Opif.* 61.172). Feldman notices "the striking resemblance between the preface to the *Antiquities* 1.1-21 and Philo's introduction to *De Opificio Mundi* 1.1—2.12, in that both offer substantially the same reason why the account of Creation precedes that of the giving of the commandments of the Torah—namely, to mold to obedience the minds of those who were to receive the laws" (*Josephus's Interpretation of the Bible*, 52–53. It is very likely that Josephus knew of Philo; see *Ant.*18.259-60.

153. The Stoics believed that reason is the natural life for rational beings. Zeno identified "as the end 'life in agreement with nature' which is the same as a virtuous life, virtue being the goal towards which nature guides us [Thus] the end may be defined as life in accordance with nature, or, in other words, in accordance with our own human nature as well as that of the universe [i.e. according to] right reason which pervades all things, and is identical with this Zeus, lord and ruler of all that is. And this very thing constitutes the virtue of the happy man and the smooth current of life, when all actions promote the harmony of the spirit dwelling in the individual man with the will of him who orders the universe" (Diogenes Laertius, *Lives* 7.86-88 [LCL]). However, Attridge rightly notes that Josephus used the concept "nature" differently (as in *Ant* 4.193, where human nature is a negative inclination), and that he may have relied on other sources, such as Philo, *Opif.* 140-43. Josephus identifies himself with the Pharisees, a sect that he says has "points of resemblance" with the "Stoic school" (*Life* 12).

154. For instance, in his paraphrase of Moses' speech before the crossing of the Red Sea (*Ant.* 2.330-33), Josephus recalls God's special providence for Israel in miraculous ways and exhorts his audience to "have faith in such a defender" and to be "not dismayed at the Egyptians' array." According to Feldman, "the Stoic term πρόνοια appears no fewer than seventy-four times in the first half of the Antiquities" (*Josephus's Interpretation*, 193–94). Attridge points to the connection between God's πρόνοια and the moralizing tendency of *Antiquities* (*Interpretation of Biblical History*, 71-144).

155. Attridge, *Interpretation of Biblical History*, 107.

156. Feldman points out that "the term ἀπαθής . . . as well as the corresponding noun ἀπάθεια (freedom from emotional disturbance) are common Stoic terms denoting freedom from emotion" (*Josephus's Interpretation of the Bible*, 193). He contends that "Josephus's picture of the decline from this primitive age (*Ant.* 1.60-62) is within Stoic tradition (Pseudo-Seneca, *Octavia* 427-28)" (p. 193).

who keeps the Law and leads a virtuous life with freedom from concerns in this life. It seems that, for Josephus, God's providence and retribution are to be found in this life; he does not envision any sort of afterlife divine retribution or resurrection. In sum, in the proem Josephus sets the premises to interpret the *Antiquities*, which seeks both to explain the uniqueness of Israel among the nations and to convey the ethical implications to the biblical narrative.

Josephus interprets the story of the creation and fall of humankind (Genesis 1–3) by reorganizing, omitting awkwardnesses, and explaining the biblical narrative. He distinguishes between the first and second creation accounts. He regards the former as "what Moses has said concerning the creation of the world" (*Ant.* 1.26) and the latter as Moses' own interpretation, "And here, after the seventh day, Moses begins to interpret nature (φυσιολογεῖν)" (*Ant.* 1.34a).[157] Thus, Josephus first paraphrases the creation of humankind (Gen 1:27), "On the sixth day He created the race of four-footed creatures, making them male and female: on this day also He formed man" (*Ant.* 1.32)[158] and explains the etiology of Jewish traditions, names, and laws, particularly concerning the Sabbath (*Ant.* 1.33). Then he explains separately Moses' interpretation of the creation of man (*Ant.* 1.34)[159] and of woman (*Ant.* 1.35–36; cf. Gen 2:18–25).[160]

Furthermore, discussing Abraham's story, Feldman points out, "In this primeval Utopia, all things that contribute to enjoyment and pleasure spring up spontaneously through G-d's providence (πρόνοιαν, a standard Stoic term), men have long lives, and old age does not soon overtake them" (p. 271). Cf. *Opif.* 81.

157. Josephus says that before presenting the laws by which people should abide, he needs to start with "the nature of the universe," that the lawgiver would present in "enigmas," "allegory," "plain speech," or even in philosophical language (*Ant.* 1.24-25; see Levison, *Portraits of Adam*, 102).

158. Josephus changes the verb and the number ποιήσομεν (first person plural) into ἔπλασε (third person singular) and omits the creation of man in the divine image, the command to rule over the creatures, the blessing, the command to multiply, the giving of food, and the concluding phrase about the goodness of creation.

159. Josephus inserts the participle λαβών (cf. *Ant.* 1.34; Philo, *Opif.* 12.31), and substitutes the verb ἐνῆκεν for ἐνεφύσησεν. He also omits εἰς τὸ πρόσωπον and ἐγένετο ὁ ἄνθρωπος, and ζωῆς/ζῶσαν but preserves the pair πνεῦμα/ψυχήν (cf. Wis 15:10b–11). He also explains the etymology of Adam from the Hebrew "red" (1.34b; cf. Franxman, *Genesis*, 49) and instead of Adam, it is God who names the animals (cf. Gen 2:20; *Jub.* 3:4–7).

160. Instead of a "helper like him," βοηθὸς ὅμοιος αὐτῷ (Gen 2:20), Adam realizes that he is "without female partner and consort," θῆλυ καὶ συνδιαίτησιν, and looks "with astonishment at the other creatures who had their mates" (*Ant.* 1.35). So woman was created from one of Adam's ribs and was brought to him; Adam recognized that "she was made from himself." Afterwards Josephus explains that in Hebrew woman is called ἔσσα (*Ant.* 1.36), an incorrect transliteration from אִשָּׁה (Gen 2:23), along with the

In the next section, Josephus briefly interprets the story of paradise (*Ant.* 1.37-39; cf. Gen 2:8-17). He explains that by the tree of wisdom (φρονήσεως) "might be distinguished what was good and what evil" and describes the etymologies of the rivers.[161] He postpones to the next section God's forbidding eating from the tree of knowledge of good and bad, and the threat of dying in the event of failing to obey.

Josephus devotes a major section to the interpretation of the story of the fall and expulsion from paradise (*Ant.* 1.40-51). He modifies substantially the narrative of Genesis 3 in order to expand on the moral lessons he set earlier in the proem. He begins with God's prohibition against eating from the tree of wisdom (φρονήσεως), "warning them that, if they touched it, it would prove their destruction (ὄλεθρον)" (*Ant.* 1.40), not "death" as in Gen 2:16-17. Then he describes the serpent's deceitful speech and his motivation, jealousy (φθονερῶς), to persuade the "woman to taste of the tree of wisdom" (*Ant.* 1.41-42; cf. Gen 3:1-5).[162] This is in accordance with the "main lesson" that Josephus set in the proem—that disobedience to God's commands would cause disasters (συμφοράς), whereas obedience would propitiate felicity (εὐδαιμονία) (*Ant.* 1.14). The serpent's deceit was not that by tasting of the tree of wisdom they would acquire discernment between what was good and what was evil (τἀγαθοῦ καὶ τοῦ κακοῦ διάγνωσιν), but that this would bring her "a blissful existence (μακάριον βίον) no whit behind that of a god" (*Ant.* 1.42). Paradoxically, after she tasted of the tree and persuaded Adam to do likewise, "they became aware they were naked and, ashamed . . . bethought them of a covering; for the tree served to quicken their intelligence" (*Ant.* 1.43-44).[163] After covering themselves with fig-leaves, they falsely "believed themselves the happier for having found what they lacked before" (*Ant.* 1.44).[164] However, when God entered into the garden, Adam became conscious (συνειδὼς, *sic*) of his crime (not of his nakedness, as in Gen 3:7, 10) and withdrew from God's presence (*Ant.* 1.45). Adam's silence prompts God's discourse:

explanation of Eve as "mother of all living" (Gen 3:20). Josephus leaves out the explanation for the unity between man and woman (Gen 2:24) and their nakedness and shamelessness (Gen 2:25).

161. Philo gives an ethical interpretation to the meaning of the rivers (*Leg. All.* 1.63-87).

162. Josephus explains the serpent's and other characters' evil motivation (*Ant.* 1.259; 2.10, 27, 201, 255; 4:14; 6.193; 10.256; 13.288; 18.240-41, 255; 20.29; see Levison, *Portraits of Adam,* 104–5).

163. Philo interprets the nakedness allegorically in ethical terms: "The mind that is clothed neither in vice nor in virtue, but absolutely stripped of either, is naked" (*Leg. All.* 2.53).

164. In the proem, Josephus points to the "imaginary good thing" that the wicked do that "ends in irretrievable disasters" (*Ant.* 1.14).

> Nay, I had decreed for you to live a life of bliss (βίον εὐδαίμονα), unmolested (ἀπαθῆ) by all ill, with no care to fret your souls; all things that contribute to enjoyment and pleasure were, through my providence (πρόνοιαν), to spring up for you spontaneously, without toil or distress of yours; blessed with these gifts, old age would not soon have overtaken you and your life would have been long. But now thou hast flouted this my purpose by disobeying my commands; for it is through no virtue that thou keepest silence but through an evil conscience (συνειδότι πονηρῷ) (*Ant.* 1.46–47).

After tasting of the tree, Adam and his wife indeed gained consciousness, but consciousness of their nakedness (see *Ant.* 1.43) and of their crime (1.45–47) rather than any positive insight.[165] Consequently, humankind lost a long life of bliss, not immortality. Josephus here ties the theme of divine providence and ἀπάθεια (see *Ant.* 1.46; 10.276–80; 16.395–404) and implies that divine retribution is a matter circumscribed to this life. Josephus integrates stoic concepts into his interpretation of the story of the fall in order to exhort his audience to obey God's commands, who would provide a blissful life, free of concerns in this life, and a long life to those who obey his commands. Conversely, God will chastise with turmoil those who disobey him and his commands. This is the most important contribution Josephus provides to the story of the fall of humankind that shows the moralizing implications that he draws from the narrative.

In *Ant.* 1.47–51, after Adam and Eve offer excuses, the former blaming his wife and the latter the serpent, Josephus reverses the order of the punishments that God imposed on them as found in Gen 3:14–19. He paraphrases the penalties against Adam, Eve, and the serpent, adding that Eve was chastised because she "brought calamity" upon Adam, and that the serpent lost his capacity for speech (*Ant.* 1.41; cf. *L.A.E.* 7:1; 14:2). Most important are the omissions that Adam would return to the ground (Gen 3:19) and that they are banishment from the tree of life (Gen 3:22), since, according to Josephus, they were never granted immortality,[166] but simply a life of bliss, free of concerns, and long life, had they obeyed God's commandments. Afterwards "God removed Adam and Eve from the garden to another place" (*Ant.* 1.51).

In sum, Josephus devotes relatively little space to the interpretation of the creation of Adam. Instead, he expands on his interpretation of the fall in order

165. *Pace* Levison, *Portraits of Adam*, 104, who claims that "the tree itself actually improved the quality of life."

166. Indeed, Josephus tells of Adam's death at the age of 930 years! (*Ant.* 1.67).

to respond to the moral lesson he sets in the proem (*Ant.* 1.14). He modifies the biblical narrative by omitting repetitions or tensions and, more importantly, by introducing into his commentary Stoic terminology in order to convey an ethical message to the narrative. Additionally, according to Josephus, divine retribution is established in this age with a long and blissful life, free of concerns for those who obey God's commands, and with catastrophes in this life for those who disobey God.

Pseudo-Philo's Liber Antiquitatum Biblicarum

Liber Antiquitatum Biblicarum (*L.A.B.*) creatively reinterprets the biblical narrative from Adam to the death of Saul.[167] Its title in Latin comes from the Sichardus's text printed in 1552, but the text was actually translated from the Greek, which was translated from an original Hebrew, written between 135 b.c.e. and 70 c.e. in Palestine.[168] The author may have belonged to a priestly circle that followed the Deuteronomistic pattern of sin, divine punishment, repentance, and salvation through a divinely appointed leader in order to reassure his audience of God's covenantal faithfulness with Israel.[169] He presents

167. Daniel J. Harrington ("Pseudo-Philo," in Charlesworth, *Old Testament Pseudepigrapha*, 2:297–377) avers, "Rather than making a clear distinction between the biblical text and its interpretation, Pseudo-Philo interweaves the two" (p. 301). Nevertheless, he also notes that "[i]n matters of apocalyptic language it stands closest to *4 Ezra* and *2 Baruch*" (p. 302). *L.A.B.* is part of a rich history of biblical interpretation that stems from the biblical text itself. *L.A.B.*'s relationship with other Jewish interpretations of the Scriptures, particularly with *Jubilees, 2 Baruch* and *4 Ezra*, is evident. See M. R. James, *The Biblical Antiquities of Philo* (New York: Ktav, 1971), 42–60, revisited by Feldman's Prolegomenon, LI–LXX.

168. For the text, date, and provenance, see Harrington, "Pseudo-Philo," 298–300; Howard Jacobson, *A Commentary on Pseudo-Philo's Liber Antiquitatum Biblicarum* (2 vols.; AGJU 31; LeidenBrill, 1996), 1:195–211, 254–81; Feldman's Prolegomenon to James, *Biblical Antiquities of Philo*, XVI–XXXI; Frederick J. Murphy, *Pseudo-Philo: Rewriting the Bible* (New York: Oxford University Press, 1993), 3–7, 262–70. George W. E. Nickelsburg ("Good and Bad Leaders in Pseudo-Philo's *Liber Antiquitatum Biblicarum*," in *Ideal Figures in Ancient Judaism: Profiles and Paradigms*, ed. George W. E. Nickelsburg and John J. Collins [SBLSCS 12; Missoula, Mont.: Scholars Press, 1980], 63–64) presses his case for a pre-70 date. See also Bruce Norman Fisk, *Do You Not Remember? Scripture, Story and Exegesis in the Rewritten Bible of Pseudo-Philo* (JSPSup 37; Sheffield: Sheffield Academic Press, 2001), 41-45, 265, 327-31.

169. Mary Therese DesCamp ("Why Are These Women Here? An Examination of the Sociological Setting of Pseudo-Philo through Comparative Reading," *JSP* 16 [1997]: 53–80) contends that the author of *L.A.B.* was a Jewish woman. Cf. Nickelsburg, "Good and Bad Leaders," 50, 59-60. Frederick J. Murphy ("The Eternal Covenant in Pseudo-Philo," *JSP* 3 [1988]: 43-57) identifies the same pattern but points out the "reduced emphasis on repentance and the increased attention to the promises of God," in order to "reassure and give hope to a beleaguered people rather than to call readers to confession and repentance" (p. 44). Murphy notes that the author of *L.A.B.* emphasizes God's faithfulness to his covenant; God would forgive his people despite their sins and quite often their lack of repentance. For Pseudo-

the historical leaders of Israel as examples who call their people to keep the covenant and the Law.[170] In this respect the figure of Adam plays only a secondary and tangential role in the narrative.

The first Adamic passage simply introduces the genealogies from Adam to Noah, "In the beginning of the whole world Adam became the father of three sons and one daughter: Cain, Noaba, Abel, and Seth" (1:1).[171] In addition to the unique mention of Adam's daughter, the author introduces the names of his twelve sons and eight daughters as well as Adam's age when he died, seven hundred years (1:2–4). The author omits the two creation accounts and the story of the fall and modifies the subsequent genealogies from Cain to Abram, including the story of the flood, as compared with Genesis 4–10.[172] In this passage, Adam simply stands as the father of the human race and prepares the stage for Abram as the father of Israel. Pseudo-Philo leaves the story of the fall for later (ch. 13) and continues with the story of Cain and the flood in the following chapter.

The second passage is set in the context of the instructions God gave to Moses concerning the cult and the festivals in chapter 13. The cultic prescriptions convey a restoration of the order of creation and particularly of the covenant with the fathers of Israel after the flood (13:6–7). After God gave Moses "the command regarding the year of the lifetime of Noah" (cf. Gen 6:3), God showed men "the place of creation and the serpent":[173]

> And he said, "This is the place concerning which I taught *the first man,* saying, 'If you do not transgress what I have commanded you, all things will be subject to you.' But that man transgressed my ways and was persuaded by his wife; and she was deceived by the serpent.

Philo's literary technique, see also Murphy, *Pseudo-Philo*, 20–25, 244–46. That the covenant and idolatry are central themes in *L.A.B.* is defended also by Fisk, *Do You Not Remember?* 45–53; and Feldman, "Prolegomenon," XXXIII–XLVII.

170. See Nickelsburg, "Good and Bad Leaders," 59–60.

171. Translations are from Harrington, "Pseudo-Philo." The Latin is taken from Jacobson, *Commentary on Pseudo-Philo's Liber Antiquitatum Biblicarum.*

172. The author's interest in the genealogies and the unique description of the census of Noah's descendants (*L.A.B.* 5) suggests that he was probably associated with the priestly class in Jerusalem. Murphy notes that "Pseudo-Philo reverses the order of the genealogies from Genesis 4–5. *L.A.B.* 1 recapitulates Genesis 5 and *L.A.B.* 2 does the same for Genesis 4. . . . By presenting humanity's positive side first, Pseudo-Philo suggests humanity's potential before dealing with its failures" (*Pseudo-Philo*, 29).

173. Harrington emends *colorem,* as attested in most manuscripts, to *colubrum* (13:8), according to the context ("Pseudo-Philo," 322). Jacobson, keeps *colorem* but acknowledges that it "surely makes no sense" (*Commentary,* 520).

> And death was ordained for the generations of men." And the Lord continued to show him the ways of paradise and said to him, "These are the ways that men have lost by not walking in them, because they have sinned against me" (*L.A.B.* 13:8-9).

"The place of creation and the serpent" clearly refers to Eden, which Adam lost because of his disobedience. Pseudo-Philo summarizes the story of the creation of the *protoplastum* (Gen 2:7),[174] his dominion (Gen 1:26-28), his transgression of God's commandment (Gen 2:17), and the punishment God appointed for him and his wife (cf. Genesis 3), but he adds that death was declared also for Adam's descendants.[175] Then God showed Moses "the ways of paradise that men have lost because they sinned against me."[176] According to the immediate context, "The ways to paradise" suggests righteous conduct.[177] With the plural *homines*, Pseudo-Philo explains to his generation that their misfortunes and loss are due to their own transgressions. It also explains that God foreknew that his people would disobey him as Adam did and that they would forget the covenants. What is more significant is that Pseudo-Philo inserts the allusion to Adam's disobedience and his punishment in the context of cultic ordinances and festivals to convey that the cult may symbolize and lead to the restoration of "the ways of paradise" that Adam lost with his transgression.[178] Furthermore, after the allusion to Adam's transgression and punishment, God assures Moses that "if they walk in my ways, I will not abandon them but will have mercy on them" (13.10). Pseudo-Philo sets a parallelism between Adam, "if you do not transgress my commandment," and the people, "if they walk in my ways," to

174. From the Greek πρωτοπλάστου; cf. Wis 7:1 and 10:1.

175. Jacobson argues, "The notion that death was introduced into the world as a result of Adam's sin was a minority Jewish opinion." Since this sentence is missing in the manuscript π he suggests that it "could have been a Christian addition, or could have been removed from the text by a Jew who did not hold this view and felt the sentiment sounded too Christian" (*Commentary*, 521). But see *L.A.B.* 26:6, where the death penalty is decreed upon the *protoplastum*.

176. Although it is not clear who the *ei* is referring to, the context suggests it is Moses; so Jacobson (*Commentary*, 519–23), who sees a parallel between this text and *L.A.B.* 19:10. See also *2 Bar.* 4:3-6.

177. See also 13:10, "by not walking in them," and "if they will walk in my ways."

178. Contra Levison, C. T. R. Hayward ("The Figure of Adam in Pseudo-Philo's Biblical Antiquities," *JSJ* 23 [1992]:1-20) argues that "the evidence of *L.A.B.* suggests that it is legitimate to speak of a continuous 'Adam tradition' that extends from the book of *Jubilees* (second century BCE) to the rabbinic period, at any rate in respect of Adam as priest, sacrificer, and Patriarch of Israel" (p. 20). Cf. *Jub.* 8:19; 3:27. However, Pseudo-Philo does not present Adam in priestly fashion nor does he speaks of the garden as the temple. Instead, the cultic laws are meant to undo the chaos that Adam's transgression brought into the world.

elicit ethical implications from the story of the fall. Thus, Pseudo-Philo inserts the Adam story between the cultic ordinances (13:1-7) and God's conditional promise to not abandon Israel if they keep God's commandments to convey that God may restore for them the original blessings of paradise that Adam lost because of his transgression. For Pseudo-Philo, the cultic prescriptions are related to the ethical demands to "walk" in God's ways. Nonetheless, the story of Adam explains that ultimately God is in charge of history and God's promises will be kept if people keep God's commandments.

The third passage is set in the context of "the Kenaz cycle" (chs. 25–29; cf. Josh 15:17; Judg 1:13; 3:9, 11).[179] Unable to destroy the precious stones, Kenaz extols God,

> Blessed be God, who has done so many mighty deeds for the sons of men, and he made Adam as the first created one and showed him everything so that when Adam sinned thereby, then he might refuse him all these things (for if he showed them to the whole human race, they might have mastery over them) (*L.A.B.* 26:6).

This passage also is set in a cultic context. It echoes the second creation account (*protoplastum Adam*) and presents Adam negatively, indicating that when he sinned he lost the things that God revealed to him in paradise. The context of the precious or magic stones which provided foreknowledge may imply that Adam lost esoteric knowledge to which he had access before his transgression,[180] which was restored later in the giving of the Torah to Moses at Mount Sinai.[181] The context also shows that Pseudo-Philo links Adam's sin and punishment to Israel's sins and the destruction of the temple. Furthermore,

179. After the tribe of Asher confesses that they stole and hid the Amorites' sacred nymphs with the precious stones (25:10-12), Kenaz burns the men with their goods, except the stones, which he unsuccessfully attempts to destroy. After the seven stones disappear in the heart of the sea, they are replaced by twelve other precious stones, each representing a tribe, which Kenaz put in the ark of the covenant (26:8-15).

180. So Murphy, *Pseudo-Philo,* 123–24.

181. The Law is presented as the light or wisdom revealed since paradise, lost and revealed again to Moses at Sinai; see *L.A.B.* 11:1; 19;6; 32;7; 33;3; 53;8; see also *2 Bar.* 17;4. Hayward notes that it is not only Moses who receives the Torah at Sinai but also Kenaz before he dies (*L.A.B.* 28:8-9, 13-14). Although the people as a whole also receive the light through the cult and the Law, "[f]ull restoration of Adam's privileges, however, will not be possible until the end of this present world which effectively takes its beginning from Noah. Then, with a new heaven and a new earth, the righteous will rejoice in the light of the precious stones of Paradise" (Hayward, "Figure of Adam," 14). Murphy argues, "In this passage the stones symbolize preternatural blessings lost by humanity" (*Pseudo-Philo,* 124).

the author implies that the stones and the tablets should return to their original place, paradise, in the eschaton, when God will return to judge the human race (26:13-14).[182] Thus, Pseudo-Philo introduces the Adam motif to elucidate that, as Adam's transgression led to the loss of heavenly secrets, so the sins of God's people (as confessed by each of the tribes, including Asher's) prevent them from the wisdom that is attained only in the Law.

The fourth passage is part of Deborah's hymn after the defeat of Sisera,

> Rejoice, earth, over those dwelling in you, because the knowledge of the Lord that builds a tower among you is present. Not unjustly did God take from you the rib of the first-formed, knowing that from his rib Israel would be born. Your forming will be a testimony of what the Lord has done for his people (*L.A.B.* 32:15).[183]

Pseudo-Philo reworks Judges 5 and expands it considerably, giving prominence to the stories of Abraham and Moses. Deborah's hymn exhorts the cosmos to celebrate and to witness the defeat of Sisera and God's wonderful deeds, and to offer assurance that God has not forgotten his covenant (cf. 32:13, 15). Thus, the creation of the protoplast from which Israel is formed is a testimony of God's fidelity and plans for his people. The expression "God did take from *you* [the earth] the rib of the first formed" may be an awkward conflation of Gen 2:7 (ἀπὸ τῆς γῆς) and Gen 2:21-22 (μίαν τῶν πλευρῶν αὐτου, that is, of the protoplast). It should be noted that the passing allusion to the creation of Adam here does not mention his transgression or his punishment but simply presents him as the ancestor of Israel. "Your forming" also refers to the creation of the earth, which "will be a testimony of what the Lord has done for his people."[184]

182. *L.A.B.* 26:13: "And when the sins of my people have reached full measure and enemies begin to have power of my house, I will take those stones and the former stones along with the tablets, and I will store them in the place from which they were taken in the beginning."

183. The textual evidence and translation present several difficulties. Jacobson prefers the π manuscript group's version of *concio* ("congregation") over Δ's *conscientia* ("knowledge") and *turrificat* ("to burn incense") over *thurificat* ("to build a tower"). That is, "The congregation of the Lord, that burns incense, is present." However, he also recognizes that it is not clear why *L.A.B.* emphasized the offering of incense. Indeed, it is the forming of the protoplast as the rib from which Israel is formed (cf. 32:1) that better supports Harrington's emendation. On the other hand, Jacobson (*Commentary*, 890–91) correctly rejects Hayward's hypothesis that *L.A.B.* is reacting "against a portrait of Adam as incense-offering priest." Although the context mentions the sacrifices and holocausts, they are offered by Deborah and the people (32:18), but nothing suggests that the author reacts against a portrayal of Adam as a priest.

184. The context makes clear that it refers to the earth, "rejoice, earth . . . God took from you [earth] the rib"; contra Jacobson (*Commentary*, 892), who interprets *plasmatio tua* as referring to "mankind."

Thus, the creation of the cosmos and humankind witnesses to the wonders God has made in favor of Israel. Thus, Deborah's song recalls God's creation, including Adam, and rehearses the history of salvation in favor of Israel in order to assure that God will keep his promises in favor of his people Israel, whose ultimate salvation will entail cosmic relevance in the eschaton as a "renewal of creation" itself (cf. 32:17).

The fifth and last passage is part of the tale about Abimelech, who, wishing to be the leader of the people, killed all his brothers (*L.A.B.* 37; cf. Judg 9:7-15).[185] When the trees ask the thornbush to reign over them, it replies,

> When the thorn was born, truth shone forth in the form of a thorn. And when *the first-formed* was condemned to death, the earth was condemned to bring forth thorns and thistles. And when the truth enlightened Moses, it enlightened him by means of a thicket of thorns. And now it will be that the truth may be heard by you from me (*L.A.B.* 37:3).

There are other Jewish traditions that speak of the burning bush as a thornbush, suggesting *L.A.B.* as their source.[186] Pseudo-Philo transforms the thornbush's answer, paradoxically conflating the stories of Adam's condemnation to death and the curse of the earth that was to yield "thorns and thistles" (Gen 3:18-19), and the theophany to Moses in the burning bush (Exod 3:2-3). It may also be the case that the fire that consumed the other trees (Judg 9:15; *L.A.B.* 37:4) induced the overlap of earlier independent traditions. The irony is that the thornbush, the product of the curse resulting from Adam's sin, becomes the source of knowledge and truth, found in the Law, so that this unsuitable plant becomes a king who speaks the truth to the other trees (37:3-4). This parenthetical allusion to Adam's condemnation to death and the curse of the earth to yield thorns makes no sense in this context, for it would have been easier to omit it than to insert it.[187] In any case, Pseudo-Philo may have seen in

185. Pseudo-Philo takes Jotham out of the story, reverses the order of the trees, and presents the apple tree instead of the olive tree as the one asked to be king.

186. Hayward ("Figure of Adam," 17–18) notes that the Septuagint translates the Hebrew *snh* as *batos* ("bramble-bush" or "wild raspberry"). Philo also explains that this *batos* was composed of thorns (*Mos.* 1.65, 68). Likewise rabbinic traditions spoke of the burning bush as a thornbush (*Exodus Rabbah* 2, 7; *Tanhuma Shemot* 14). Jacobson also avers that "L.A.B. may be the earliest example of *sentix* used generically as 'thorn-bush'" (*Commentary,* 935).

187. Jacobson (*Commentary,* 934), following James, considers this passage "problematic," "unclear," and a "mystery."

the thorns and thistles an antecedent of the burning bush of Exodus to convey that the revelation of the Law was issued in primeval times. Another possibility is that Pseudo-Philo also saw in Adam and Moses a fitting contrast of the curse and blessings they respectively brought to Israel.

In sum, the allusions to Adam in Pseudo-Philo are parenthetical and usually related to his transgression and condemnation to death and his loss of paradisiacal blessings. Pseudo-Philo does not draw explicit ethical consequences from the Adam motif itself; instead he often locates the story in the context of cultic motifs that may suggest that through rituals and festivities God may forgive the sins and remember his covenant with Israel.[188] On the other hand, Pseudo-Philo also relates the cultic ordinances and rituals to the conduct of the people, assuring them that God's blessings will be granted to them on the condition that they "walk in His ways," that is, on the condition that they keep His commandments. Thus, *L.A.B.* opens the biblical narrative to an eschatological horizon, common to apocalyptic works such as *4 Ezra* and *2 Baruch*, and leaves to God the judgment of the righteous and the wicked at the time of the visitation, when he will reward them according to their deeds (3:9-10; 19:12; 25:7).

Sibylline Oracles

The *Sibylline Oracles* is a collection of oracles written between the second century BCE and the seventh centuryCE in Babylon, Syria, Egypt, Asia Minor, and Rome.[189] These oracles were eventually integrated into Jewish and Christian traditions, especially those of the prophets and apocalypses, to call for

188. Following Charles Perrot, Murphy asserts that "Pseudo-Philo is less concerned to convey ideas about the afterlife than to engender obedience" (*Pseudo-Philo*, 266).

189. See John J. Collins, "Sibylline Oracles," in Charlesworth, *Old Testament Pseudepigrapha*, 1: 317–20. According to Collins, "The most famous collection of Sibylline oracles in antiquity was the official one at Rome. Legend places the origin of these oracles in the time of Tarquinius Priscus. This probably indicates that the Romans had acquired a collection of oracles in Greek hexameters before the fall of the monarchy" (p. 319). See also John J. Collins, *The Sibylline Oracles of Egyptian Judaism* (SBLDS 13; Missoula, Mont.: Society of Biblical Literature, 1972). Although the oracles flourished "even in the most remote localities . . . [m]ost lists of sibyls give the number ten. So Varro lists Persian Libyan, Delphic, Cimmerian, Erythrean, Samian, Cumean, Hellespontian, Phrygian, and Tiburtine sibyls" (*Sibylline Oracles*, 1).

a new social order.[190] The stories of the creation and fall of humankind also advocate for the coming of a new creation manifested in a new social order.

The prologue summarizes the story of the creation and fall, "the fashioning of man and the expulsion from the garden and again the new formation" (24–26).[191] Thus, the final word is not destruction but a new creation.

Book 1 integrates Hellenistic motifs into the story of the creation of the cosmos (1:5-21), man and woman (1:22-37), the story of the fall (1:38-64), and of the first seven generations.[192] *Sib. Or.* 1:22-37 inverts the two creation accounts, first the fashioning of man (Gen 2:7) as an "animate object," and then as "a *copy* from his own [God's] image" (Gen 1:27). Additionally man is portrayed as "youthful, beautiful, wonderful," who was placed in the garden "so that he might be concerned with beautiful works."[193] Likewise woman is "a wonderful maidenly spouse." They also "were far removed from evil heart" (1:36), as opposed to "the heart's evil desire" (cf. Gen 6:5; 8:21). *Sib. Or.* 1:38-58 changes the order of the story of the fall as found in Genesis 3. First, after God commanded them "not to touch the tree," the serpent deceived the woman, who subsequently persuaded the man; consequently, "instead of good they received evil" (46) and were expelled "from the place of immortals" (51). Then God commanded them to "increase, multiply" (cf. Gen 1:28), and to "work on earth with skill, so that by sweat you may have your fill of food" (cf. Gen 3:19). Finally, the serpent also was punished and became a foe of humankind (cf. Gen 3:14). After the fall, the first seven generations continue to decline and their sins to increase, and like Adam (1:80-82), they also died (1:100, 107,

190. According to Collins, "The political interest of apocalyptic shows both continuity with biblical prophecy and parallelism with the Hellenistic oracles. . . . While there were important differences between Jewish apocalyptic and Hellenistic oracles, they shared the basic expectation of a time of distress followed by a radical transformation which would be accompanied by a future ideal kingdom" (*Sibylline Oracles,* 18). Unlike apocalypses that mark "a clean break between this world-order and the next . . . [t]his is not expressed in the sibylline" (p. 110). Collins explains that the oracles "usually addressed crisis in the state and often spoke of political transformation" (p. 4).

191. Translation is from Collins. The prologue was written no earlier than the sixth century; see Collins, "Sibylline Oracles," 327. After introductory remarks about the meaning of the name "Sibyl" and the origins of the oracles, the editor presents what the Sibyl "expounded about the God who had no beginning" (*Sib. Or.* 94) and inserts a creedal formula of the "one God" creator of heaven and earth, including humans, "He himself established the shape of the form of mortals" (*Sib. Or.* 99).

192. For a detailed comparison between Genesis 1–3 and Sib. Or. 1.5-64, see van Ruiten, "Creation of Man and Woman," 48-54.

193. Contra Louis Ginzberg, *Legends of the Jews* (Philadelphia: Jewish Publication Society of America, 1909–38), 1:59-62; 6:78-80. Ginzberg explains that the positive portrayal of Adam was due to Jewish influences; van Ruiten claims that it was due to Hellenistic influences ("Creation of Man and Woman," 53).

115-19), until total annihilation came with the flood (1:125-282). Only the sixth generation is exalted and called "heavenly" (1:286), which will be ruled by three righteous kings, descendants of Noah (1:293-95), who will bring back the original glorious status of the first creation (1:297-98). However, they will also die and "will go away to Acheron in the halls of Hades," but they will have there a place of honor (1:301-6). But their descendants, the Titans, "will have a proud heart" and will be destroyed (1:307-23). Thus, the primary author of book 1 of the *Sibyllines* freely rewrote the story of the creation and fall of humankind, inserting Hellenistic motifs to explain that the sufferings in the world came "through the impiety of men" (1:3-4). Nevertheless, he also looked for a restoration of creation into a golden age, possibly with the aid of a messianic agent or agents, where justice and "fair deeds" would be practiced (1:4, 295-96).

Book 5 integrates Hellenistic motifs and apocalyptic traits into the creation motif, "the beginning and great end of toil for men, when creation is damaged and saved again by the Fates" (5:238-85).[194] It predicts earlier the destruction of the nations, Egypt, Ethiopia, and Corinth, and the return of Nero, the archenemy of God and the Jews (5.214-27). The reason for their destruction is their vices, idolatry, sexual offenses, and homosexuality, especially idolatry (5.278-80).[195] Conversely, it foretells the coming of a messianic figure, "one exceptional man from the sky" (5.256-63; see also 5:108-9, 155-61, 414-25; cf. Num 24:7, 17), and the restoration of the Jews and their city. Thus, the pious and righteous will enjoy the fruits of the holy land because of their faith in the one God (5.281-86). Therefore, book 5 of the *Sibyllines* predicts the destruction of the wicked nations because of their vices and anticipates the restoration of Israel as a nation because of their faithfulness to the Law.[196]

In sum, the *Sibylline Oracles* use the story of the creation and fall as an example to persuade the audience to keep God's commandments in order to enjoy bliss in this life, and to condemn the impious whether Gentile or renegade Jew. Thus, the destruction of this world would prompt the coming of a new

194. Collins locates book 5 "in Egypt after the destruction of the temple, but probably before the Bar Kochba revolt" (*Sibylline Oracles*, 94), except for 5:257, which is a Christian interpolation (see Collins, "Sibylline Oracles," 399). For the overall structure of *Sib. Or.* 5, see Collins, *Sibylline Oracles*, 73–76.

195. See Collins, "Sibylline Oracles," 392.

196. See Tobin, "Philo and the Sibyl," 84–103. Tobin compares Philo's eschatology in *De Praemiis et Poenis* 93-97 and 163-72 and *Sib. Or.* 3 and 5. He observes that, instead of the subversive political eschatology promoted in the *Sib. Or.*3 and 5, Philo proposed a nonsubversive eschatology "dependent on the observance of the Law and the practice of virtue by the Jewish nation," which the Gentiles could also share if they observe the Law (Leviticus 26; Deuteronomy 28; 30) and practice virtues (pp. 102–3).

age and a new social order where the righteous will enjoy the original blessings that God bestowed upon humankind.

THE GREEK LIFE OF ADAM AND EVE (L.A.E.)

The richness and complexity of Adam traditions are epitomized in the *Life of Adam and Eve.* This document was translated into different languages which preserve several traditions attested in numerous manuscripts.[197] Although some have suggested an original Hebrew or Aramaic text,[198] most agree that the Greek version represents "the oldest retraceable stages of this process, accounting for all other versions."[199] The earliest version of *L.A.E.* may be

197. Michael E. Stone distinguishes between "primary 'Jewish' Adam literature" and "secondary Adam literature." The former has been preserved in the *Greek Apocalypse of Moses*, the Latin *Vita Adam et Evae*, the Slavonic *Vita Adam et Evae*, the Armenian *Penitence of Adam*, and the Georgian *Book of Adam*, in addition to a fragmentary Coptic version, all of which were apparently translated independently from the Greek (Stone, *A History of the Literature of Adam and Eve* [SBLEJL 3; Atlanta: Scholars Press, 1992], 6, 42). This distinction was taken up by Marinus de Jonge and Johannes Tromp, *The Life of Adam and Eve and Related Literature* (Guides to Apocrypha and Pseudepigrapha; Sheffield: Sheffield Academic Press, 1997), 7. See also Johannes Tromp, "Introduction," in *Literature on Adam and Eve: Collected Essays,* ed. Gary Anderson, Michael Stone, and Johannes Tromp (SVTP 15; Leiden: Brill, 2000), 235–37. For a synopsis of the books of Adam and Eve, see *A Synopsis of the Books of Adam and Eve,* ed. Gary A. Anderson and Michael E. Stone (2nd rev. ed.; SBLEJL 17; Atlanta: Scholars Press, 1999).

198. M. D. Johnson ("Life of Adam and Eve," in J. H. Charlesworth, *Old Testament Pseudepigrapha,* 2:249-295) suggests that "the Greek [was translated] directly from the Hebrew and the Latin directly either from the Hebrew or from the Greek" (p. 251).

199. De Jonge and Tromp, *Life of Adam and Eve,* 30. They claim that "the Greek of *L.A.E.* may be bad Greek, measured by classical standards, but it is genuine Greek, containing, for instance, many syntactical constructions that are typical of that language" (p. 67). See also Marinus de Jonge "The Literary Development of the *Life of Adam and Eve,"* in Anderson et al., *Literature on Adam and Eve,* 239–49. More specifically, de Jonge and Tromp claim that "the 'short' text-form, that is, the text-form represented by DSV (K) PG B, contains the oldest form of the *Life of Adam and Eve* known to us" (*Life of Adam and Eve,* 34). For the history of the text-forms and manuscripts, see de Jonge and Tromp, *Life of Adam and Eve,* 30–44; Stone, *History of the Literature,* 6–14. Nevertheless, even in the Greek there are a variety of text-forms that should "be preserved and studied rather than neglected in favor of an eclectic text or translation that obviates significant differences among them" (John R. Levison, *Texts in Transition: The Greek Life of Adam and Eve* (SBLEJL 16; Atlanta: Scholars Press, 2000), 4. He classifies and dates different text-forms of the *L.A.E.* in four forms: I (mss D and S), IA (mss A and T), II (mss R and M), and III (mss N and K) (pp. 21-46), and concludes that "there is no pristine, static ancient text known as the Greek *Life of Adam and Eve.* The Greek *Life* exists in various text forms that exhibit distinctive editorial and thematic features, divergent uses of the Bible, and varying characterizations of its central figure [Eve]" (p. 46).

located in Palestine to respond to the crisis in the aftermath of the fall of the second Temple.[200]

The preface that presents *L.A.E.* as a "narrative" (διήγησις) revealed to Moses is a later addition that has erroneously led to the title *Apocalypse of Moses*.[201] Thus, *L.A.E.*'s interpretation of the story of the protoplasts is better located among the "Rewritten Bible" group.[202] The author starts off at Adam's deathbed explaining retrospectively first according to Adam (7-8) and then according to Eve (15-30) what led them to their expulsion from paradise, to sickness, and to death. Nevertheless, the emphasis is not on the dire situation of the protoplasts but on the hope of resurrection they may be granted after their death. Thus, the perspective of *L.A.E.* is not etiological but eschatological. *L.A.E.* portrays Adam as a suffering and repentant sinner in order to explain to the audience their dire situation after the events of 70 c.e., and most importantly to offer them the assurance of an eschatological vindication.[203] In order to

200. *Pace* de Jonge and Tromp, who argue that "*L.A.E.* was first composed by Christian authors" (*Life of Adam and Eve,* 74). They claim that the antithesis between Adam and Christ as found in Rom 5:12-21 and 1 Cor 15:21-22, though not necessarily introduced by Paul, was introduced by Christians who "used traditional material available to them, much of which was already of Jewish origin, but had never been written down before" (p. 74). See also Marinus de Jonge, "The Christian Origin of the *Greek Life of Adam and* Eve," in Anderson et al., *Literature on Adam and Eve,* 347–63. However, although the antithesis is evidently Christian, it does not imply that the author(s) of *L.A.E.* is Christian. On the contrary, the portrayal of Adam and Eve in the New Testament is rather negative and stands in contrast to Christ (1 Cor 15:21; 2 Cor 11:3; Rom 5:12-21, and 1 Tim 2:13-14). Furthermore, salvation is envisioned not after Adam and Eve but after Christ. Therefore, the Christian elements found in *L.A.E.* are better explained as later interpolations.

201. See M. D. Johnson, "Life of Adam and Eve," 259. Text-form I renders Διήγησις καὶ πολιτεία ἀδὰμ; text form IA, Διήγησις καὶ πολιτεῖα ἀδὰμ καὶ εὖας; text-form II renders Αυτη ἡ διήγησις ἀδὰμ καὶ εὖας; and text-form III, Βίος καὶ πολιτεία ἀδὰμ καὶ εὖας. Thus, the supplements πολιτεία and βίος show the redactors' awareness that the content of the *Life* was not simply an account but also a narrative that conveyed a "way of life" or "conduct" (see BAG, 686, s.v. πολιτεία 686). Except for variations in the accents, *L.A.E.* 1:1 introduces the narrative as text form II, Αυτη ἡ διήγησις ἀδὰμ καὶ εὖας in all its text forms except in text form III, ἀδὰμ καὶ εὖας τῶν πρωτοπλάστων. Furthermore, Moses' name never appears again in *L.A.E.* nor does *L.A.E.* portray any significant apocalyptic feature.

202. See de Jonge and Tromp, *Life of Adam and Eve,* 47–49.

203. Levison distinguishes between Greek *Apocalypse of Moses* and Latin *Vita* (*Portraits of Adam,* 163–90) and concludes: "The dominant purpose of *ApMos* is to provide hope for its readers by presenting Adam as a forgiven sinner who endures the pain of existence, faces death with uncertainty, but receives mercy after death. In contrast, the dominant purpose of Vita is to exonerate Adam and to denigrate Eve, thus presenting the readers with a perfect penitent, a righteous figure who receives mercy during life and after death" (p. 164). In his "The Exoneration and Denigration of Eve in the *Greek Life of Adam and Eve*," in *Literature on Adam and Eve: Collected Essays*, 251–75, Levison analyzes mss DSV, ATLC, RM, and

receive the reward at the end-time, the audience is exhorted to repent and turn to God. Thus, at the end of her account Eve tells her children that she has shown the way she and her husband were deceived in order to warn her children to "watch yourselves so that you do not forsake the good" (30:1).

After the introduction (1:1—4:2),[204] *L.A.E.* could be divided into four sections: (1) Adam's account of the fall (5:1—8:2); (2) Eve and Seth's unsuccessful quest for the oil from the tree of paradise (9:1—14:3); (3) Eve's account of the fall (15.1—30.1); and (4) Adam and Eve's death and burial (31:1—43:4).[205]

In the first section, Adam tells his account of the fall (5:1—8:2). On his deathbed Adam summoned his progeny (cf. Genesis 5), who "came to the door of the house in which he used to enter to pray to God" (5:1).[206] Seth inquires about Adam and his illness and offers to bring him "fruit from Paradise" and to intercede for him. Then Adam relates his account of the fall: "When God made (εποίησεν) us, me and your mother, through whom I am dying (δι εἶς καὶ ἀπόθνίσκω), he gave us every plant in Paradise, but concerning one he commanded us not to eat of it, (for) we would die by it (δι εις καὶ ἀποθνίσκομεν)" (7:1; cf. Gen 2:16-17).[207] Initially Adam blames Eve for his distress, but then he excuses Eve, explaining that the enemy persuaded her because "he knew that neither I nor the holy angels were near her. Then he gave also to me to eat" (7:2; cf. Gen 3:1-7).[208] Thus, both Adam and Eve take

NIK of the *L.A.E.* In this essay he modifies his previous thesis ("The Exoneration of Eve in the Apocalypse of Moses 15-30," *JSJ* 20 [1989]: 135-50), which claimed that Eve was exonerated in the Testament of Eve (*L.A.E.* 15-30) and now argues that further distinctions should be made also in *L.A.E.*15-30. Thus, he concludes that "the first and the third text forms, represented by ATLC and NIK, tend to denigrate Eve throughout the *Greek Life of Adam and Eve*, including Eve's testament. . . . The second text form, represented principally by M, tends to incorporate substantial elements of exoneration, even in *L.A.E.* 1-14 and 31-43" (p. 275).

204. After the heading "this is the account of Adam and Eve" (1:1), the author introduces the leading characters, Eve and Seth (cf. Genesis 3–5), assigning to Adam only a secondary and passive role. It is divided by the preposition μετά ("after") in three parts: "after they had come out from paradise . . ." (1:2-3; cf. Gen 3:24); "and after these things . . ." Adam and Eve find out that Cain killed his brother Abel (2:1-3; cf. Genesis 4); and "after these things . . ." Adam and Eve begat Seth (4:1; cf. Gen 4:25; 5:3).

205. J. Levison provides useful parallels to the account in Genesis 1-5 (*Texts in Transition*, 34–36).

206. Translations are from M. D. Johnson, "Life of Adam and Eve," with slight emendations when I translate text-form I.

207. For the variants in the manuscripts, consult Levison, *Texts in Transition*, 45-123. For consistency, I follow the Greek text form I. In 7:1 text-forms IA, II, and III change the first pronoun εἶς into ἧς, αὐτῆς, and ἧς, respectively. Then the second pronoun εις is modified into οὗ (text form IA), and οὗ (text forms II and III).

208. M. D. Johnson, translates "she," that is, Eve, who gave Adam to eat, but he also acknowledges the alternative reading "he" or "that one." Since the precedent subject is the enemy, "he" should be preferred.

an active part in the transgression; the blaming of Eve is not as evident as previously presumed. Then the author resumes and substantially modifies the narrative of Gen 3:8-19. Disappointed, God questions Adam, "Where are you? And why do you hide from my face? Can the house hide from its builder?" (8:1).[209] The author omits the dialogue between God and the fearful protoplasts as well as the indictments against the serpent and Eve. He explains that the cause of the indictment against Adam is that he forsook God's covenant and listened to the enemy.[210] The chastisements (cf. Gen 3:17b-19) are replaced by seventy plagues inflicted on Adam's body, of which only the first two are described.[211] Thus, the author summarizes the story of the fall and explains that Adam's present distress, the plagues, is because of his infringement of the covenant. At this point of the narrative, the author simply points to the origins and causes of the dire present situation of Adam.

In the second section, Eve and Seth unsuccessfully search for the oil from the tree of paradise (9:1—14:3).[212] This section is divided into two parts, the encounter with the beast (10.1—12.2) and the encounter with the (arch)angel (13.1—14:3). In the first part, on their way to paradise Seth and Eve encounter an evil beast (θηρίον πονηρόν), who attacked Seth. Eve exclaims, "Woe is me! For when I come to the day of resurrection, all who have sinned will curse me saying that Eve did not keep the command of God" (10:1-2).[213] The author

It seems that the author attributes the death of Adam and Eve to both Eve's transgression (7:1) and the enemy (8:2). Text-form I in 8:2 points out that it was because Adam "forsook the covenant and listened to the enemy" that he was inflicted with seventy plagues in his body.

209. The serpent (16:4) and the protoplasts (Eve, 18:2-3, 6; Adam, 21:4) are aware and afraid that God may become angry if they disobey his command.

210. Only text-form I includes both the covenant (διαθήκην) and the enemy (ἐχθρός); the other text forms mention only the covenant.

211. "The pain of the first plague is affliction of the eyes; the pain of the second plague is of the hearing; and so one after the other all the plagues shall pursue you" (8:2).

212. *L.A.E.* 9:1-3 is a transition between the previous section¨, where Adam had replied to Seth's question (cf. 7:1), and this section, where Adam cries out, "What shall I do? I am in great distress" (9:1). So Eve asks Adam to give her half of his illness "because this has happened to you through me; because of me you suffer troubles and pains" (Text-form I adds δι εμὲ εν ηδρώτιτη τοῦ προσώπου σου· τὸν ἄρτον εσθιεις· δι εμὲ πάντα· υπομαίνεις) (9:2). Subsequently, Adam sends her and their son Seth for the oil from the tree from paradise, "and I will anoint myself and rest" (Text-form I adds ἐκ τοῦ νόσου μου; and text-form III renders ἀπὸ τῆς νόσου μου. A Christian interpolation in 4 Ezra 2:12 identifies this tree with the tree of life (9:3).

213. Eve accuses the "evil beast" of attacking *the image of God.* Then the beast reproves Eve, "neither your greed nor your weeping are due to us, but to you, since the rule of the beasts has happened because of you. How is it that your mouth was opened to eat from the tree concerning which God commanded you not to eat from it? Through this also our nature was changed" (10:1—11:3).

combines the *imago Dei* (εἰκόνα τοῦ θεοῦ) and the dominion bestowed on man and woman (Gen 1:26-27) with the story of the fall (Gen 3:1-6). Ironically, the beast accuses Eve of "opening your mouth" (cf. 21:3) and eating from the tree that God commanded "you" not to eat, introducing also the rule (ἀρχή) of the beasts and the change of their nature (αἱ φύσεις ἡμῶν μετηλάγισαν). Subsequently, Seth commands the beast, "Shut your mouth and be silent, and keep away from the image of God until the Day of Judgment." Leaving Seth wounded, the beast went away from "the image of God" (12:1-2). Thus, the author puts the blame on Eve not only for Adam's illness but also for Seth's perils and the disruption of the order in nature. In the second part (13:1—14:3) the archangel Michael comes out to meet Seth and Eve near paradise and tells Seth that he will now not obtain the oil to anoint Adam (13:1-3a). Instead, he sends Seth out to his father Adam, who would die in three days, "And as his soul departs, you are sure to witness its fearful upward journey" (13:6).[214] Thus, Seth and Eve return to "the tent where Adam was lying" (cf. 5:3), and Adam questions Eve again, "Why have you wrought destruction among us and brought great wrath, which is death gaining rule over all our race?" (14:1). He commands Eve to call their children so she may tell them her own story (14:2).

In this section the author interprets the story of the fall in an eschatological perspective, looking forward to "the day of resurrection" (ἡμέραν τῆς ἀναστάσεως, 10:2).[215] The emphasis is not so much on the origins of the present dire situation as it is on the eschaton, when the glory of paradise will be fully restored. Despite the protoplasts' disobedience, which led them and their descendants to the loss of paradise, they still possess the *imago Dei,* which assures them of a future restoration.

The third is the longest and the central section, Eve's account of the fall (15:1—30:1). It follows Adam's command to Eve to tell their children how they transgressed (14:1). This section begins with Eve summoning her children to listen (15:1) and concludes with her exhortation, "But you watch yourselves so that you do not forsake the good" (30:1). This section is divided into three parts: first, the temptation (16:1—21:6); second, God's judgment and Adam's pleadings (22:1—29:6); and, third, the protoplasts' mourning and

214. Text-form I omits the eschatological and universalistic turn, "but at the end of times. Then all flesh from Adam up to that great day shall be raised, such as be the holy people; then to them shall be given every joy of Paradise and God shall be in their midst, and there shall not be any more sinners before him, for the evil heart shall be removed from them, and they shall be given a heart that understands the good and worships God alone" (13:3b-5).

215. Cf. "the day of judgment" (ἡμέρας τῆς κρίσεως, 12:1). Text-forms IA and II render "the end of the times" (13:2) and the "great day" (13:3).

penance (29:7-17), which concludes with Eve's exhortation to her children (30:1).

In the first part (16:1—21:6), the author significantly supplements the account of the temptation from Gen 3:1-7 to warn the audience against the devil's temptations. The devil (διάβολος)[216] tempts first the serpent in order to deceive Adam and "make him be cast out of Paradise through his wife, just as we were cast out through him" (16:4). Then Satan (Ζατανᾶς) came into paradise to tempt Eve through the serpent's mouth to eat from the plant/tree of life (17:1—20:5; cf. 7:2; Gen 3:1b-6a).[217] The author inverts the order of Gen 3:5.[218] He omits the serpent's exclamation, "you certainly will not die" (Gen 3:4), for Adam was about to die. The "glory" of the tree is paradoxically related to the glory that Adam and Eve eventually lose (18:1).[219] Even though Eve was afraid of the Lord (cf. 18:2, 6), she gives up and the devil makes her swear to him that she will give of the tree also to her husband (19:1-2). The serpent "sprinkled his evil poison on the fruit,[220] which is the covetousness (ἐπιθυμία); for the covetousness is every sin" (19:3).[221] After the woman ate the fruit, her eyes were opened and she discovered that she was "naked of righteousness with which I had been clothed" and "estranged from my glory."[222] Then Eve looked for leaves to cover her "shame" (αἰσχύνην) (20:1-5). Finally, the devil tempts Adam through Eve, "Do not fear; for as soon as you eat, you

216. In text-form I, the devil calls the serpent "wiser than all the beasts" who "associate with you"; text-forms IA and II add that the devil calls the serpent "greater than all the beasts," only to point out, "yet you are prostrate to the very least." For further textual variants see Levison, *Texts in Transition,* 67–68.

217. "Which is in the middle of Paradise, concerning which God commanded us not to eat of it, else you shall most surely die" (17:5; cf. Gen 3:1b-3).

218. "Your eyes will be opened and you will be like gods, knowing good and evil. But since God knew this, that you would be like him, he begrudged you and said, 'Do not eat of it'" (18:3).

219. *L.A.E.* 18:1: τὴν τιμὴν τοῦ ξύλου; so text-forms I, IA, and III. In 18:5 text-forms I and III render δόξαν μεγάλην, and text-form IA adds περὶ αὐτοῦ; text-form II ἐν ἑαυθτῶ. Text-form IA further adds ἐγὼ δὲ πρόσἔσχον τῶ φυτῶ· ἴδον δόξαν μεγάλην περὶ αὐτοῦ. εἶπον δὲ αὐτῶ ὅτι ὅρεον ἐστὶν τοῖς ὀφταλμοῖς κατάνοῆσαι·

220. Text-form IA adds ὅν ἔδωκέν μοι φαγῆν; and the slightly different text-form III renders ὅν ἔδωκέ μοι φαγεῖν.

221. Text-form IA adds that ἐπιθυμίας was the serpent's desire. Text-from IA also adds that ἐπιθυμία was the beginning, κεφαλῆ—and with text-form I—of every sin, πάσης ἁμαρτίας. "In Jewish Greek ἐπιθυμία and ἐπιθυμεῖν can denote sin. This usage is plainly dependent in part on the Stoic usage, and in part a result of the above development in Judaism [i.e. condemnation of both evil act and evil will or desire]" (F. Büchsel, ἐπιθυμία, *TDNT* 3:170. Cf. Rom 7:7; 13:9. For the meaning of ἐπιθυμία in Philo, see Hans Richard Svebakken, "Philo of Alexandria's Exposition of the Tenth Commandment" (Ph.D. diss., Loyola University Chicago, 2009), 40–99.

222. Text-form IA adds "with which I was clothed."

shall know good and evil (21:3–4). After he ate "his eyes were opened, and he also realized his nakedness." Then he exclaimed, "O evil woman! Why have you wrought destruction among us? You have estranged me from the glory of God'" (21:5–6). Thus, the author continued to put the shame on Eve while Adam plays a passive, almost naïve role. He identified righteousness and glory, the same glory that paradoxically attracted Eve to eat from the tree and that now they lost (cf. 21:3, 6). Without their clothes, they realize their nakedness and are ashamed; the loss of their glory is their loss of righteousness. The author also introduced covetousness or desire to explain that eating the fruit was the beginning of sin.

The second part (22:1—29:6; cf. 8:1-2; Gen 3:8–19) corresponds to God's judgment and Adam's pleadings. God comes into paradise in his chariot and sits on his throne by the tree of life to judge Adam and Eve (22:1—23:5; cf. 8:1).[223] Adam's sentence is framed with the charge, "because you transgressed my commandment" (24:1) and "because you did not keep my commandment" (24:4b). In addition to the charges found in Gen 3:17–19,[224] the author emphasizes Adam's hardships.[225] The charge against Eve is the same (25:1). In addition to the pangs of birth (cf. Gen 3:16), she could also lose her life when she gives birth but "you shall come and confess and say, Lord, Lord, save me and I will never again turn to the sin of flesh."[226] The author also mentions the hostility between the woman and the enemy (cf. Gen 3:15a) and her turning again to her husband, who will rule over her (25:4). The serpent is chastised "because you become an ungrateful vessel (cf. 16:4–5), so far as to lead astray the careless of heart" (26:1–2). In addition to the punishments related in Gen 3:14, the serpent loses "the food which you used to eat" and the serpent is deprived of her feet, ears, wing, and limbs,[227] "all of that with which you enticed (them) in your depravity and caused them to be cast out of Paradise" (cf. 16:3). Finally, the author mentions the hostility between the serpent and Adam's seed "until the day of judgment" (26:3–4). Thus, the judgment of the protoplasts anticipates

223. The author changes the order of the punishments as found in Gen 3:14–19, serpent–woman–Adam, to Adam–woman–serpent (24:1—26:4).

224. "Because you transgressed my *commandment* and listened to your wife, cursed be the ground (ἡ γῆ; following the LXX; text-form IA adds ἐν τοῖς ἔργοις σου) in your labors. For when you work it, it will not give you strength"; then *L.A.E.* paraphrases Gen 3:18.

225. "You shall suffer many a hardship: you will grow weary (text-form IA adds κάμῃ καὶ μὴ ἀναπαύου); be afflicted with bitterness and not taste sweetness; be afflicted by heat and burdened by cold (text-form IA adds καὶ κοπïάσῃς πολλὰ· καὶ μὴ πλουτήσῃς· καὶ εἰς τέλος ὑπάρξῃς)," and will lose dominion over the animals, who "will rise against you in disorder" (24:4a; cf. 11:1).

226. Text-form IA adds ἀλλὰ καὶ πάλιν ἐπιστρέψῃς.

227. Text-form IA adds χειρῶν.

the judgment of their descendants in the eschaton. The author emphasized and developed the narrative of the punishments of the protoplasts in order to show the consequences of the fall and to warn the audience against disobeying God's commands. After Adam's expulsion from paradise, the author introduces Adam's three pleas for God's mercy (27:1—29:6). First, Adam asks the angels to let him stay a little longer in paradise "so that I may beseech God that he might have compassion and pity me, for I alone have sinned" (27;2). But the Lord admonished the angels, saying, "is the guilt mine, or did I judge badly?" to which they replied, "You are righteous, Lord, and you judge uprightly" (27:3-5). Thus, the author emphasizes Adam's culpability and repentance, on the one hand, and God's righteousness, on the other. Second, Adam pleaded for the tree of life, which God refuses to give him "now" and appoints the cherubim and the flaming sword to guard it (cf. Gen 3:22-24). Instead, God leaves Adam with "the strife (πόλεμον) which the enemy has placed in you" (28:3).[228] Most importantly, the author introduces an exhortation and a promise, "But when you come out of Paradise, if you guard yourself from all evil, preferring death to it (ὡς βουλόμενος ἀποθανεῖν), at the time of the resurrection I will raise you again, and then there shall be given to you from the tree of life, and you shall be immortal forever" (28:4). Once more the author introduced an eschatological twist into the narrative with evident ethical implications. Thus, righteousness in the present is the condition to take part in the resurrection in the eschaton. Third, after Adam was expelled from paradise, he beseeched the angels, "let me take fragrances (εὐωδίας) from Paradise, so that after I have gone out, I might bring an offering (θυσίαν) to God so that God will hear me" (29:3). Then God granted him the "aromatic fragrances and seeds for his sustenance,"[229] and "other seeds for his food" (29:5-6). Thus, what Adam gets are the means for his sustenance while outside Paradise, the seeds (cf. Gen 1:29) for his physical sustenance, and the fragrances for the sacrifice to appease God.[230] Afterwards Eve concludes, "And so we came to be on the earth" (29:6).

In the third part, the protoplasts mourn and do penance (29:7-17).[231] This takes place at the Jordan and the Tigris rivers, respectively, but the devil

228. This expression was probably meant to counter the idea that God has placed in man the "evil heart" (cf. 4 Ezra 3:20-21).

229. Text-form IA adds ἐκ τοῦ παραδδείσου but omits the repetitious καὶ σπέρματα in 29:5, which is later found in 29:6.

230. *Jubilees* 3:27 also describes Adam offering a "sweet-smelling sacrifice" on the day he was expelled from paradise.

231. Extant only in text-form II. Then text-forms I, IA, and III join text-form II with Eve's paraenetic conclusion.

deceives Eve for a second time making her cease her penance beforehand. Then Eve concludes, "Now then, my children, I have shown you the way (τρόπον) in which we were deceived. But you watch yourselves so that you do not forsake the good" (30:1). Thus, the author closes Eve's account of the fall with an emphatic exhortation, which reflects the paraenetic character of the account.

The fourth and last section of the book (31:1—43:4) is divided into three parts: first, Adam's death (31:1—37:7); second, the burial of his body (38:1—41:3); and, third, Eve's death and burial (42:1—43:4).

In the first part (31:1—37:7), after Eve describes the fall, she asks Adam, "Why are you dying and I live?" (31:2; cf. 14:1-3). Adam assures her that both will die and will be buried together, but that "God will not forget me, but will seek his own vessel which he has formed (τὸ ἴδιον σκεύος ὅ ἔπλασεν)" (cf. Gen 2:7), and he exhorts her to rise and pray to God while they await to meet their maker, "whether he shall be angry with us or turn to have mercy on us" (31:3-4). Then Eve and Seth see the seven heavens open and the angels pleading with God to forgive (συγχώροσον αὐτῷ) Adam "for he is your image (ὅτι εἰκόν σου ἐστίν)" (33:5; 35:2), while the opaque sun and moon also pray for Adam (36.1-3). Afterwards the angels bless the Lord because "he had mercy on Adam, the work of his hands" (37:2). After Adam was washed in the lake Acheron, the Lord took him and handed him to Michael to "take him up into Paradise, to the third heaven" until the day of judgment, "and all the angels sang an angelic hymn being amazed at the pardoning of Adam" ([ἐπ]ι [τῇ συγ]κορίσει τοῦ ἀδάμ) (37:3-6).[232] Thus, the author resumes Adam's first plea for mercy (cf. 27:2) and introduces Eve's repentance; she confesses her sin while Adam dies (32:1-4). God finally answered Adam's pleading for mercy, listened to Eve's prayer of repentance, and responded to the prayer of the angels and of the whole creation, forgiving Adam for his sin because he was the image of God.

In the second part, after Adam was forgiven and taken into the third heaven of paradise, his body and Abel's body were buried (38:1—41:3).[233] The

232. The origins of the lake Acheron are attested in Homer (see *Iliad* 23.71-74; *Odyssey* 10.508-15) and in Plato's *Phaedos* 107-15. Plato describes the geography of Hades and the survival of the soul in the afterlife. This tradition was eventually adapted in Jewish and Christian literature (*Apocalypse of Peter* 14; *Sib. Or.* 2:330-38; *Apocalypse of Paul* 22-23; and the *Book of the Resurrection of Christ* 21-22. These texts, including *L.A.E.* 37 "represent early *Christian* appropriations of the Greek traditions about the Acherusian Lake" (Marinus de Jonge and L. Michael White, "The Washing of Adam in the Acherusian Lake (Greek *Life of Adam and Eve* 37.3) in the Context of Early Christian Notions of the Afterlife," in *Early Christianity and Classical Culture: Comparative Studies in Honor of Abraham J. Malherbe*, ed. John T. Fitzgerald, Thomas H. Olbricht, and L. Michael White (NovTSup 110; Leiden: Brill, 2003), 621.

author summarizes why Adam lost his dominion and died,[234] the quest for the oil from paradise,[235] and Adam's origins from the dust to which he is about to return.[236] However, at the climax of the narrative the author reintroduces the promise of resurrection for Adam and his descendants, "Now I promise you the resurrection (ἀνάστασιν); I shall raise you on the last day in the resurrection with every man of your seed" (41:3; cf. 10:2; 28:4). Afterwards God sealed Adam's tomb until Eve was reunited to him, and God and his angels went back to their place (42:1-2).

In the third and last part (42:1—43:4), Eve prays and also dies. Then Michael instructs Seth how to prepare Eve's burial—procedures that should be followed for "every man that dies until the day of the resurrection (ἕως ἡμέρας τῆς ἀναστάσεως)" (42:3—43:4).[237] The angel also commanded Seth not to mourn beyond six days but to rest and rejoice on the seventh day with God and his angels, for they also rejoice on that day "with the righteous soul, who has passed away from the earth." Afterwards the angel "ascended into heaven glorifying (God) and saying 'Alleluia, to whom the glory and power forever and ever'" (43:4). Thus, in addition to the instructions for the burial, the author reiterates and concludes with the assurance of the resurrection.

In sum, the author of *L.A.E.* summarized his interpretation of the story of the fall, correlating Adam and Eve's burial also with their origins from the earth and dust, and reintroduced the hope of the resurrection. He does not elaborate on the nature of this event, but claims that it will happen in the eschaton and should be a reason to rejoice. Thus, his interpretation of the transgression explicates the dire situation of humankind in the present and introduces the hope of the resurrection at the end of the times. Therefore, the story of the fall is a warning of the consequences of transgressing God's commands, and concomitantly it exhorts the audience to keep God's commandment in order to

233. Abel's body had been unburied since the time when Cain slew him because the earth would not take another body (ἕτερον πλάσμα) until the first body (πρῶτον πλάσμα), "the dust from the earth (τ[ὸν χοῦν] ἐξ γῆς), is returned to me" (40:5). Then they were buried "in the regions of Paradise, in the place where God had found dust and made Adam" (40:6; cf. Gen 3:19).

234. "'Adam, why did you do this? If you had kept my commandment those who brought you down into this place would not have rejoiced.'" Adam is assured that he will be restored "in your dominion on the throne of your seducer," who will be cast out into this place (39:1-3).

235. God commands the archangels to cover Adam's body with cloths of linen and silk and to "bring the oil from the oil of fragrance and pour it into him" (40:2; cf. 9:2; 13:2).

236. God called Adam and "the body answered from the ground (σῶμα ἐκ τῆς γῆς), 'Here I am Lord,' and God said 'I told you that you are dust and to dust you shall return'" (41:1-2).

237. She prayed that, as she was united to her husband in the garden as well as in the transgression, so she also might be buried with him (42:3-8).

participate in the future resurrection. Ultimately, the story of the fall was framed within the larger motif of restoration of the creation on behalf of Adam as the image of God.

Apocalyptic Interpretations on the Figure of Adam: Introduction

Apocalyptic interpretations emphasize the story of the fall over the story of the creation of humankind to explain the hardships and the destruction of Jerusalem and its temple. It is interpreted as an example and an effect of the protoplasts' disobedience to God's commandment on their descendants as well as their own unfaithfulness to the covenant. In these interpretations, heavenly beings typically reveal the destruction of the wicked—Israel's enemies or sinners— and the salvation of the righteous in the eschaton. The destruction of this world anticipates the coming of a new creation.[238]

4 Ezra

4 Ezra is an apocalypse written originally in Hebrew to give voice to the anxious questions of the Jews after the fall of the Second Temple.[239] The author draws on earlier material and ventures an answer by means of his reinterpretation of the Scriptures.[240] He interprets the story of the creation and

238. See John J. Collins, ed. *Apocalypse: The Morphology of a Genre* (Semeia 14; Missoula, Mont.: Scholars Press, 1979), 9; William Adler, "Introduction," in *The Jewish Apocalyptic Heritage in Early Christianity,* ed. James C. VanderKam and William Adler (CRINT, Section 3, Jewish Traditions in Early Christian Literature 4; Minneapolis: Fortress Press, 1996), 9; Nickelsburg, "Wisdom and Apocalypticism," 17-37.

239. For the history of scholarship on *4 Ezra,* see Michael E. Stone, *Fourth Ezra: A Commentary on the Book of Fourth Ezra* (Hermeneia; Minneapolis: Fortress Press, 1990), 10–28. He asserts that *4 Ezra* was originally written in Hebrew, perhaps with some Aramaic influences, arguably in Palestine, and then translated into Greek, Latin, Syriac, Ethiopic, Georgian, Arabic, Armenian, and Coptic (pp. 1-9). See also Bruce M. Metzger, "The Fourth Book of Ezra," in Charlesworth, *Old Testament Pseudepigrapha,* 1:518–20; cf. Bruce W. Longenecker, *2 Esdras* (Guides to Apocrypha and Pseudepigrapha; Sheffield: Sheffield Academic Press, 1995), 13–16. For the literary genre of *4 Ezra,* see Stone, 36–42; Collins, 33–34; Longenecker, 16–17. The pseudonym Ezra and his interest in the right interpretation of the Torah point to an official interpreter of the Scripture; see *4 Ezra* 14:48. For *4 Ezra* and wisdom literature, see Tom W. Willett, *Eschatology in the Theodicies of 2 Baruch and 4 Ezra* (JSPSup 4; Sheffield: JSOT Press, 1989), 49.

240. See Stone, *Fourth Ezra,* 23. Most scholars acknowledge that the book is framed by two Christian additions, the introduction (1:1—2:48), which describes Ezra's vocation and mission (2:42-48), and the appendix (chs. 15–16, extant only in Latin), which indicts the enemies of God's people and exhorts the chosen ones to trust in God (see Metzger, "Fourth Book of Ezra," 517). See also Theodore A. Bergen,

fall as an example of destruction and death caused by the "evil heart" of the human being but also envisions an eschatological salvation for the righteous.

The introduction sets the context and tone for the entire book, that is, why the righteous suffer while the ungodly prosper.[241] The book is divided into seven episodes or visions given by the angel Uriel to Ezra: (1) 3:1—5:20; (2) 5:21—6:34; (3) 6:35—9:26; (4) 9:27—10:59; (5) 11:1—12:51; (6) 13:1-58; (7) 14:1-48. Ezra's thought evolves from an initial reluctance as he discusses with the angel the problem of evil in the world, human freedom, and God's justice, until he envisions a solution at the eschaton with the end of the present wicked age and the coming of transcendent salvation for the righteous.[242]

"Christian Influence on the Transmission History of 4, 5, and 6 Ezra," in VanderKam and Adler, *Jewish Apocalyptic Heritage,* 102–27.

241. *4 Ezra* 3:1-4: "In the thirtieth year after the destruction of our city, I Salathiel, who am also called Ezra, was in Babylon. I was troubled as I lay on my bed, and my thoughts welled up in my heart, because I saw the destruction of Zion and the wealth of those who living Babylon. My spirit was greatly agitated, and I began to speak anxious words to the Most High, and I said . . . ." Translations are from Metzger, "Fourth Book of Ezra."

242. In the first three episodes the author grieves, complains, and demands "understanding" (cf. *4 Ezra* 4:10-11, 20-21; 5:31, 37-38). After his questions are unsatisfactorily answered (cf. 7:46-61), Ezra appeals to God's mercy (7:62—8.36) and seeks a new kind of understanding: "Then, drink your fill of understanding, O my soul, and drink wisdom" (8:4). And yet, in his prayer (8:19b-36) Ezra still makes his case before the one "whose throne is beyond measure and whose glory is beyond comprehension" (8:22). "For as long as I live I will speak, and as long as I have understanding I will answer" (8.26). The third episode ends with the angel's exhortation "not to continue to be curious as to how the ungodly will be punished; but inquire how the righteous will be saved, those to whom the age belongs and for whose sake the age was made" (9:13). The fourth episode (9:26-58) is a turning point, where Ezra becomes the consoler and instructor of a mourning woman who grieves the lost of her son and who eventually becomes the heavenly Jerusalem. This episode begins with Ezra's rehearsal of the giving of the Law to the forefathers and their failure to keep it, and compares them with the present generation (9:37). The fifth (11:1—12.39) and sixth (13:1-58) episodes are symbolic dreams followed by their interpretations (cf. Daniel 7). The seventh and last episode (14:10-48) compares Ezra with Moses as the lawgiver and leader of Israel (cf. 5:17; 14:6; 15:13; 14:27-36). After Ezra drank from the cup he was offered, his "heart poured forth understanding, and wisdom increased" in his heart; and the Most High gave the five men understanding (14:40-42). *4 Ezra* concludes with the command "Make public the twenty four books that you wrote first and let the worthy and the unworthy read them; but keep the seventy that were written last, in order to give them to the wise among your people. For in them is the spring of understanding, the fountain of wisdom, and the river of knowledge" (14:45-48). In this way, Ezra's quest to understand why the pious suffer while the ungodly prosper is tentatively answered with a private revelation reserved to Ezra and to a few wise ones with the promise of an eschatological and otherworldly salvation. Ezra admonishes his people, "If you, then, will rule over your minds and discipline your hearts, you shall be kept alive, and after death you shall obtain mercy. For after death the judgment will come, when we shall live again; and then the names of the righteous will become manifest, and the deeds of the ungodly will

The Adam motif is found in the first and third episodes only and is to be interpreted within this dynamic, as the angel corrects Ezra's misconception of Adam until he leads Ezra to an appropriate understanding.

In the first episode (3:1—5:20) Adam is found in the first part of Ezra's discourse (3:4-27),[243] and also in the angel's response (4:26-32). The first part of Ezra's discourse contains four cycles in which each generation is related to the story of Adam as the paradigm of transgression and punishment. However, the main problem is not the punishment inflicted because of their disobedience to God's commands—already elucidated by the Deuteronomist (Deut 30:15-20)—but that the ungodly, Babylon, also transgresses and yet rules over Zion (3:28-36).

In the first cycle, the author substantially modifies the story of the creation of humankind and the fall, as compared to Genesis 1–3 and presents Adam as the head of all generations after whom all transgress and are punished with death:

> O sovereign Lord, did you not speak at the beginning, when you formed the earth [cf. Gen 2:4b]—and without help, and commanded the dust and it gave you Adam, a lifeless body. Yet he was the workmanship of your hands, and you breathed into him the breath of life, and he was made alive in your presence [cf. Gen 2:7]. And you led him into the garden which your right hand had planted before the earth appeared [cf. Gen 2:8]. And you laid upon him one commandment of yours [cf. Gen 2:16], but he transgressed it, and immediately you appointed death for him and for his descendants [cf. Gen 3:23-24] (*4 Ezra* 3:4-7).

The author omits the content of the commandment (cf. Gen 2:16b-17), the naming of the animals and the creation of woman (cf. Gen 2:18-25), and the description of the garden (cf. Gen 3:9-15)—although he mentions the tree of life in 8:52. He also summarizes the story of the fall with the clause "but he transgressed," and the punishments are reduced to the appointment of death for Adam and his descendants (cf. Gen 3:1-19). In this cycle, the author introduces his plaint against God, declaring that God alone is responsible for the creation of humankind. The kernel of his argument, however, is not the creation of humankind but the relationship between the Adam's transgression

be disclosed" (14:34-35). Ultimately, the solution to the problem of the presence of the evil in the present world is postponed until the eschaton.

243. Ezra's discourse is divided into two parts, from Adam to David (3:4-27), and the comparison between Babylon and Zion (3:28-36). See Stone, *Fourth Ezra*, 60–61.

of God's "one commandment" and the swift sentence of death upon him and his descendants (3:7a; cf. Wis 1:13; 2:23). The author does not imply that Adam and his descendants would enjoy immortality, for he does not mention the tree of life or the banishment from its fruit in this context. At this point in the narrative, Ezra is distressed because of the desolation of Zion and thinks that the ungodly and righteous face death alike—hence his plaint against God's justice. As the revelation unfolds, the author will distinguish between physical and spiritual death and will project the judgment and eventual immortality for the righteous into the future.[244]

The second cycle corresponds to the transgressions of the peoples that sprang from Adam and their punishment with the flood (3:7b–11). The author draws a parallel between Adam and his descendants, who face death as the consequence of their own wrongdoings, and not because of Adam's disobedience. He closes the second cycle with the deliverance of Noah and "all the righteous who have descended from him" (3:11). In the first two cycles, the emphasis is on the relationship between the transgressions and the death penalty for Adam and his descendants, but at this point he does not distinguish the two kinds of death that the ungodly and the righteous would face in the eschaton.

In the third cycle (3:12–22), the author describes the election of the patriarchs and the giving of the Law to the descendants of Jacob. He claims that, despite the Law, they also transgressed, "Yet you did not take away from them their evil heart, so that your Law might bring forth fruit in them. For the first Adam, burdened with an evil heart, transgressed and was overcome, as were also all who descended from him," and consequently "the evil remained" (3:20–22). The "first Adam" here functions not as the cause for the fall of his descendants but as the head of all humankind, which transgressed because of "the evil heart."

In the fourth cycle (3:23–27), the election of David and the sacrifices do not prevent the fall of the city on account of the transgressions of its inhabitants, "doing as Adam an all his descendants had done, for they also had the evil heart" (3:27). In the last two cycles, the author advances his plaint saying that God did not take away from Adam and all his descendants "the evil heart" (3:27) and therefore all have transgressed. The angel will later address this question, that is, "why the heart is evil" (4:4; 7:48). Thus, despite the Law, in the people's heart there remained "the evil root" (3:20–22); and the "grain of evil seed sown in Adam's heart from the beginning," overwhelmed the Law and produced much fruit (cf. 4:28–32; 7:92). Ultimately the angel does not provide an answer to

244. See Stone, *Fourth Ezra*, 65–67. During the third episode, the angel or God himself explains to Ezra the eschatological dimension of immortality, which is reserved for the few righteous ones only (cf. 6:35—9:25; 8:51-54; 7:13, 16; 8:37-40).

Ezra's question regarding the evil heart but envisions a solution at the eschaton. He exhorts Ezra to take notice and rejoice over the few righteous who defeat their evil desire and are saved, rather than over the many who are overcome by their evil inclination and are condemned. Their respective reward will be evident at the eschaton.[245]

The second reference to Adam in the first episode is found in the angel's response to Ezra's questions about the evil heart (4:26-32). In this context, the angel reproaches Ezra for his lack of understanding,[246] which he replaces with his revelation about the eschaton.[247] Yet Ezra still presses his case further

245. The notion of "the evil heart" or desire derives from the context of the flood, when God regretted having created man because "no desire that his heart conceived was ever anything but evil" (Gen 6:5); and afterwards, when God committed to destroy the earth never again "because of man, since the desires of man's heart are evil from the start" (Gen 8:21). The story of the flood makes clear that God is not the cause of evil in the world, but humans are, and therefore they are to be held accountable for their own actions. Further explanations of the evil in the world appeared in subsequent Jewish literature that attempted to deal with the problems of evil, sin, freedom, and responsibility, usually with an eschatological perspective. These authors attributed the presence of evil either to an external supernatural agent (such as Satan or Adam) or to each individual. One of these explanations is found in the speculations of the "evil *yetzer*," which appears in later rabbinic teachings and in Palestinian Jewish and Hellenistic Jewish sources; see Alden Lloyd Thompson, *Responsibility for Evil in the Theodicy of IV Ezra: A Study Illustrating the Significance of Form and Structure for the Meaning of the Book* (SBLDS 29; Missoula, Mont.: Scholars Press, 1977), 49–66. The author of *4 Ezra* uses different terms that refer to the same reality, that is, an evil inner inclination or desire in all humankind ("a seed of evil grain," 4:30; 8:6; 9:31; "evil thought," 7:92; see Stone, *Fourth Ezra*, 63). The author does not mention the serpent that tempted Eve (cf. Genesis 3); instead he places the cause of sin within the human being. He does so, first, to avoid attributing to God the evil tendency in the human heart, and, second, to uphold humankind's freedom, making them responsible for their actions (cf. 7:127-31; 8:56). For *4 Ezra*, all humankind struggles alike from this evil tendency or desire from the beginning, and only the righteous can overcome it (7:92). Third, and most important, the author highlights the effects of Adam's transgression upon his descendants. Ultimately the answer to the problem of the evil in the world will be solved not in its origins but in the eschaton. Accordingly, from the beginning until the present all humankind has had the evil heart or inclination that may cause humans to sin, but it is not actually sin. All humankind has to struggle against it, and the righteous can overcome it. Adam's transgression, therefore, does not cause his descendants to sin, but each one is responsible for one's own transgressions. Ezra's lament in 7:117 should be interpreted as part of the progression of thought that Ezra experiences. Ezra accuses God for not taking away the evil heart from humankind (3:20), but later he blames Adam because his transgression affected his descendants and brought them death (cf. 7:117). Although there is no mention of the evil heart in this context, the angel's response speaks of the "contest every man who is born on earth shall wage, that if he is defeated he shall suffer what you [Ezra] have said, but if he is victorious he shall receive what I have said." Then the angel upholds human freedom: "choose for yourself life, that you may live" (Deut 30:15-20).

246. Ezra does not understand "the way of the Most High" (4:2); nor does he understand the riddles (4:5-12) or the parable that the angel gave him (4:13-21).

and demands, "Why have I been endowed with the power of understanding?" (4:22; cf. 4:12; 5:34). For what he inquires is not "about the ways above, but about those things which we daily experience" (4:23a). Furthermore, he questions "why Israel has been given over to godless tribes, and the Law of our fathers has been made of no effect and the written covenants no longer exist" (4:23b).[248] The inadequacy of his previous answers makes the angel resort to an eschatological solution; that is, the "grain of seed sown in Adam's heart from the beginning" has its effects in the present and in future (4:26-32). After Ezra inquires about the end of the times (4:33-52), the angel describes the signs of the age to come (5:1-13). The first vision concludes with Ezra awakening, fastening, mourning, and weeping as the angel Uriel had urged him (5:14-20).[249]

The next reference to Adam appears in the third episode (6:35—9:26), which describes the dialogue between Ezra and the angel about the fate of Israel, raising further questions regarding the final judgment and the destiny of the righteous and the wicked (cf. 7:26-131). The theme of creation and the figure of Adam in this episode are more pervasive and are meant to elucidate this problem.

Ezra presents Adam as the forefather of Israel established "as a ruler over all the works which you had made" (6:54) and over the nations (6:55-59; cf. 4:23).[250] Yet, paradoxically, the nations, which are "nothing" and like "spittle"

247. Stone rightly points out that *4 Ezra* may reject traditional apocalypses that underscore the cosmic dimension of traditional revelations in order to emphasize the eschatological character of this knowledge. For the sources and parallels to *4 Ezra* 4:1-12 (Job 38:16-17 and *2 Apoc. Bar.* 59:5-11), see Stone, *Fourth Ezra,* 80–81.

248. Paul seems to argue in similar terms in Romans, that is, that the Law is of no avail, for despite the Law, all—Jews and Gentiles—sin alike and therefore face death as their punishment.

249. The second episode follows the pattern of the first episode and slightly develops its message. The explanations of the dynamic of transgression and punishment were partially answered in the first episode, that is, because of the evil heart. In the second episode, the author reiterates the election of Israel and the giving of the Law (5:27) but questions why Israel is punished by "the many," the Gentiles (5:29). Ezra inquires about the fate of "those who were before us, or we, or those who come after us" (5:41). The angel replies that, as creation was planned and made through him "at the beginning of the circle of the earth" (6:1), so "the end shall come through me and not through another" (6:6). Further signs will precede the coming of the end of the world, when "evil shall be blotted out . . . and truth . . . shall be revealed" (6:27-28). The second episode concludes with the angel's assurance that he will "declare to you greater things" (6:31), and the exhortation to "believe and to be not afraid" (6:33). The author recalls the creation motif, but the figure of Adam is absent in this section.

250. Cf. Gen 1:24-28; *4 Ezra* 7:62, 116; *L.A.B.* 39:7. Adam was also given to rule over the heavenly bodies (*4 Ezra* 6:45-46). The author evokes the power that was bestowed on Adam but leaves for later the mention of the *imago Dei* (*4 Ezra* 8:6, 44).

and "a drop of a bucket" (6:56),[251] rule over Israel. This section ends with Ezra's question, "How long will this be so?" (6:59), which Uriel will answer later—that is, the time has been already foreordained (7:74; cf. 9:4).

Uriel first responds with two analogies about the difficulties that Israel has to endure in order obtain her "inheritance" (7:1-10) and explains that "when Adam transgressed my statutes, what had been made was judged. And so the entrances of this world were made narrow and sorrowful and toilsome. . . . But the entrances of the greater world are broad and safe, and really yield the fruit of immortality" (7:11-13). The author evokes Adam's transgression of God's command (Gen 2:16) and the consequent punishments and banishment from Eden (Gen 3:17-24). More significant are the two shifts the author introduces in the following verses. First, the angel explains that the present world is not what Israel is to inherit—for it is corruptible and mortal—but her inheritance will be granted at the eschaton (7:15-16). Second, he rebukes Israel for not keeping the Law and the covenant. Then Ezra claims, "O sovereign Lord, behold, you have ordained in your Law that the righteous shall inherit these things" (7:17). The angel retorts that, despite Israel having received God's Law, "they scorned his Law and denied his covenants" (7:22-24; cf. Pss 14:1; 53:1). Consequently, they will perish rather than let the Law be reviled. Therefore, Israel is defined by righteousness and obedience to the Law, not by election, and their inheritance is in the world to come; the contrast is not between Israel and the Gentiles but between the righteous and the ungodly.[252]

Ezra replies that there are only a few who keep the commandments, "For an evil heart has grown up in us, which has alienated us from God, and has brought us into corruption and the ways of death, and has shown us the paths of perdition and removed us from life—and that not just a few of us but almost all who have been created" (7:48). Furthermore, "all who have been born are involved in iniquities, and are full of sins and burdened with transgressions" (7:68). Thus, the evil heart or seed comes to the fore again to explain why humankind—Israel included—failed to keep the commandments (cf. *4 Ezra* 3:20-22, 26; 4:4; 7:92).

So far the angel has still not answered why the heart is evil (cf. 4:4); instead, he replies that God will judge Adam and his descendants, who "shall be tormented, because though they had understanding they committed iniquity,

251. The description of the nations as spittle appears in other texts; see *2 Bar.* 82:5; Sir 26:22; *L.A.B.* 7:3, which may be dependent on Isa 40:15-17. See Stone, *Fourth Ezra,* 189.

252. The author will return to this idea later, when Uriel avers that paradise and immortality are prepared only for the righteous, like Ezra, whereas "thirst and torment" await for those who forsook the Law; cf. 8:37-40, 46-58; 9:13.

and although they received the commandments they did not keep them, and though they obtained the Law they dealt unfaithfully with what they received" (7:70–72). The author refers here to Israel because, like Adam, they transgressed the Law and the commandments entrusted to them. The judgment was prepared since the beginning of the creation, but will take place at the eschaton, when all will be judged (7:73).

Then Ezra inquires regarding the fate of those departed before the Day of Judgment, "when you will renew the creation" (7:75). Uriel replies that they will be judged according to their deeds when they die, but only for the righteous do blessings and immortality await (7:78–99) "because they have striven great effort to overcome the evil thought which was formed with them" (7:92; cf. 7:26–44).[253] Thus, although all have the evil heart, only the righteous overcome it and consequently will enjoy the blessings of the world to come. The eschatology of *4 Ezra* is the answer to the question regarding the fate of the righteous and the ungodly. They will be judged and receive their reward according to their deeds at the end. The author explains that the fall of the temple and Jerusalem is the consequence of the sinfulness of the people, not God's fault, and that in order to attain the reward of immortality they are to keep the commandments and the Law.

Finally, perhaps the most telling reference to Adam in the third episode, and probably in the entire book, is found in Ezra's lamentation for the lot of humankind (7:116–26).

> This is my first and last word. It would have been better if the earth had not produced Adam, or else, when it had produced him, had restrained him from sinning. For what good is it to all that they live in sorrow now and expect punishment after death? O Adam, what have you done? For though it was you who sinned, the fall was not yours alone, but ours also who are your descendants (7:116–18; cf. 3:21).[254]

Earlier the author had attributed the creation of Adam to God alone, who commanded the dust to produce Adam (3:4) and then lamented that God did not take away from Adam and his descendants the evil heart (3:20–21). Now the author moves on his way of "conversion" and blames the earth for producing

253. For a discussion on Ezra's eschatology, see Stone, *Fourth Ezra,* 204–7; Michael E. Stone, *Features of the Eschatology of IV Ezra* (HSS 35; Atlanta: Scholars Press, 1989); Willett, *Eschatology in the Theodicies of 2 Baruch and 4 Ezra,* 72–75.

254. This passage is followed by a series of questions in 7:119-25 that aim to show the human despair.

Adam (cf. 7:62) and then Adam for passing on the disgrace of his transgression to his descendants. Thus, the author now excuses God from any wrongdoing in the creation of humankind and upholds human freedom and responsibility (7:127-31; cf. Deut 30:15-20). The angel explains that the promises of paradise and immortality will be granted at the eschaton to the righteous because of God's mercy (7:132—8:3). Yet Ezra pleads for God's mercy for his people Israel (8:4-19a) and not for the nations (8:19b-36), but the angel replies that God will rejoice over the salvation of the righteous, not of the wicked (8:37-40). Ezra claims that man was formed by God's hands and called "your own image because he is made like you" (8:44). However, "man" here refers not to the entire human race but to Israel. Then the angel exhorts Ezra to align himself with the righteous, for whom paradise and immortality are promised (8:47-62). He identifies Israel with the many ungodly who have forsaken the Law (cf. 8:55-58; 9:11). Finally, Uriel describes the signs that will precede the end and the judgment and exhorts Ezra "not continue to be curious as to how the ungodly will be punished; but inquire how the righteous will be saved, those to whom the age to come belongs and those for whose sake the age was made" (9.13). Thus, the author avers that Israel is defined not by the election, the covenant, or the giving of the Law, but by the keeping of the commandments; that is, Israel is defined by righteousness, not by ethnicity, and their inheritance will be granted in the eschaton.

In sum, the figure of Adam in *4 Ezra* is marked by the literary context of the two episodes in which it is found. The angel gradually leads Ezra into a proper understanding of freedom, responsibility, and the presence of evil in the world. In the first episode, Adam represents the head of all the peoples, who transgressed the "one commandment" God gave him, for which he and his descendants are punished with death. Subsequent generations follow the same pattern of transgressions, which leads them to their death. However, Adam is not the cause of their sinning and death, but the members of each generation are responsible for their own transgressions (3:10, 21, 26). Ezra notes that not even the covenant or the Law prevents Israel from sinning. That is why he accuses God "because you did not take away from them their evil heart." Then the angel attempts to explain "why the heart is evil" (4:4) and compares the evil heart to "a grain of evil seed [that] was sown in Adam's heart from the beginning," which has produced abundant ungodliness until the present (4:30). This analogy results in the author's eschatological perspective; Ezra's pressing questions will be answered at the harvest, at the end of the times, when peoples will be judged and the righteous will be distinguished from the ungodly. The age or world where evil has prevailed is coming to an end, and a new age of immortality and bliss is about to appear and the evil heart will be removed, a theme that the author describes more extensively in the third episode, 6:35—9:25, especially in 7:26-131. In the third episode, Ezra complains that, although Adam and his descendants were endowed with power to rule over the nations—which are nothing—now they rule over Israel (6:55). The angel replies that Adam's transgression overturned the original order and introduced all misfortunes and death. Furthermore, he explains that the righteous who keep the Law—not necessarily Israel—will receive their reward in the world to come (7:16). Thus, Israel is defined not by election and ethnicity but by righteousness and piety (7:17). Ezra inquires about the few who are saved and the many who are condemned, but the angel replies that he is not to be concerned with the many godless, but with the few righteous who defeated the evil thought and will be saved in the eschaton (7:92). Then Ezra blames not God but the earth and Adam, whose trespass affected all his descendants (7:116-18), but Uriel upholds human freedom and responsibility (7:127-31). Finally, Ezra appeals to God's mercy on behalf of Israel, and the angel responds that indeed God will rejoice over the salvation of the few righteous—not necessarily Israel (8:37-40)—and exhorts Ezra to conform to the few righteous who will be rewarded in the eschaton with paradise and immortality (8:47-62).

2 Baruch

2 Baruch, written originally in Hebrew and subsequently translated into Greek and Syriac, addresses the questions about God's justice and the fate of the Jewish community in the aftermath of the events of 70 c.e.[255] The content, genre, and sevenfold structure of *2 Baruch* show a close literary association with *4 Ezra*.[256] The author was probably a scribe using the pseudonym "Baruch"

255. See A. F. J. Klijn, "2 (Syriac Apocalypse of) Baruch," in Charlesworth, *Old Testament Pseudepigrapha*, 1: 615–17.

256. There are strong elements that show the literary dependence between *4 Ezra* and *2 Baruch*: the historical context, the content (that is, questions regarding God's justice and the fate of Israel and the revelatory character of the answers by a heavenly mediator), the terminology, the apocalyptic and eschatological perspective, and the sevenfold structure. Nevertheless, *2 Baruch* believes in the human ability to keep the Law and envisions an imminent restoration of Israel, whereas *4 Ezra* believes humankind cannot keep God's commandments because of their "evil heart," and so commends humankind's salvation to God's mercy to be revealed in the eschaton. Willett compares the eschatology and theodicy of *2 Baruch* and *4 Ezra*, arriving at similar conclusions (*Eschatology in the Theodicies of 2 Baruch and 4 Ezra*, 121–25). Gwendolyn B. Sayler explains that thr relationship between these writings is due in part to the fact that both authors relied on earlier sources (*Have the Promises Failed? A Literary Analysis of 2 Baruch* [SBLDS 72; Chico, Calif.: Scholars Press, 1984], 123-34, esp. 1300. See also Klijn, "2 (Syriac Apocalypse of) Baruch," 617. Stone holds that, although the literary relationship between *4 Ezra*

who was concerned with the proper interpretation of the Law.[257] Chapters 1–77 are an apocalypse that describes the revelation given to Baruch for the proper interpretation of the Law, which is followed by an attached letter (chs. 78–87).[258]

The figure of Adam in *2 Baruch* is part of the larger creation motif that relates God's original design to the eschatological restoration of the world promised to those who keep God's commandments. In the first section (1:1—5:7) the author relates Adam's transgression and his expulsion from the garden to Israel's transgressions and the destruction of Jerusalem (4:4-7; cf. *2 Bar.* 1:2-3; *4 Ezra* 3:7; Wis 1:13; 2:23). Yet God allows the enemies to destroy the city so that they may "serve the Judge for a time" (5:3).[259]

The second section (chs. 6–20) describes God's judgments against Babylon and the nations and the fate of the few righteous and the many wicked among both Israel and the Gentiles. In this section, Baruch inquires first about the fate of the righteous, who suffer now and "await evils at that time," and the apparent success of the ungodly nations (14:13-19).[260] God explains to him that "man" will be punished because he disobeyed the Law and the instruction he had received (15:5-6). The term "man" is not general but refers to Israel, who received the instruction of the Law and yet disobeyed, as Adam did. God explains that the world and "that which is coming" were made on the account of the righteous ones, first for those who struggle in this age, the faithful Israel, and then for the nations, who eventually drew near and "mingled with the seed of the people" (15:7-8; cf. 42:3-8). Thus, the author criticizes those who relied on the covenant but did not keep the Law and includes among the righteous those who eventually joined the covenantal race and kept God's commandments and assures them of the world to come. Second, God answers Baruch's concern regarding the human life span:

and *2 Baruch* (and *Biblical Antiquities*) is unmistakable, the precise dependence is inconclusive (*Fourth Ezra*, 39-42). M. R. James argues that "the writer of *Baruch* at least was acquainted with *Philo*" (*Biblical Antiquities of Philo*, 58). For the sevenfold structure, see Sayler, 11–39, 161–62.

257. See Nickelsburg, "Wisdom and Apocalypticism," 25–26. The author's concern for the Law and its association with wisdom or right understanding is pervasive; see 14:8-9; 15:5-6; 21:18; 23:228; 32:1; 38:2-3; 41:3-4; 44:2-15; 46:1-5; 48:22-24, 36-40, 47; 51:1-10, 7[AQ: Should this be 17?]; 54:5, 13-14; 57:2; 59:2-4; 61:4; 66:5; 67:6; 75:3; 77:15-16; 84:1-2, 9; 85:3, 14; cf. *4 Ezra* 14:45-48.

258. Most scholars regard the letter as an integral part of the book; the exception is Sayler, *Have the Promises Failed*, 9, 158.

259. Translation is from Klijn, "2 (Syriac Apocalypse of) Baruch." Ultimately this is part of God's plan in order that the Diaspora Jews "may do good to the nations"; cf. 1:4; 3:5-6.

260. He realizes that "the world which was made for us, behold, it remains; but we, for whom it was made, depart" (14:19; cf. *4 Ezra* 6:55-59).

> For what did it profit Adam that he lived nine hundred and thirty years and transgressed that which he was commanded? Therefore, the multitude of time that he lived did not profit, but it brought death and cut off the years of those who were born from him. Or what did it harm Moses that he lived only one hundred and twenty years and, because he subjected himself to him who created him, he brought the Law to the descendants of Jacob and he lighted a lamp to the generation of Israel? (17:2–4)

The author shows that, regardless the span of their lives (see Gen 5:5 and Deut 34:7), Adam's transgression and Moses' obedience had opposite effects on their descendants, death (cf. *2 Bar.* 19:8; Gen 2:17) and the Law, respectively (17:5; cf. 19:3; *L.A.B.* 9:8; 15:6).[261] Third, Baruch replies, contrasting the few who imitated Moses and "took from the light," and the "many whom he illuminated [but] took from the darkness of Adam and did not rejoice in the light of the lamp" (18:2). God rejoins that, despite the covenant and the Law, the sons of Jacob sinned (19:1–3; cf. Deut 30:15). The author refers to the people of Israel as the beneficiaries of the revelation of the Law, of whom, despite their election, only a few kept the commandments but many followed after the example of Adam. Thus, the author concludes that the destruction of Jerusalem is due to their transgressions and that God's judgment is about to be revealed against both the nations and the many who trespassed against the Lord's commandments. Thus, Adam and Moses here function as opposite paradigms of disobedience and obedience, respectively.

In the third section (chs. 21–30), God responds to Baruch's anxiety for the apparent delay of the manifestation of God's power against the nations. He explains that he will reveal his power according to his predetermined plan:

> For when Adam sinned and death was decreed against those who were to be born, the multitude of those who would be born was numbered. And for that number a place was prepared where the living ones might live and where the dead might be preserved. No creature will live again unless the number that has been appointed is completed. For my spirit creates the living, and the realm of death receives the dead (23:4–5).

261. The Law is compared to a lamp that enlightens one's life: "Your word is a lamp for my feet, a light for my path" (Ps 119:105). The psalmist praises God for the Law he gave to his people, and in the immediate context the bewildered psalmist asks the Lord to give him "life in accord with your word" (Ps 119:107).

Baruch's concern is limited to those "who exist and who have passed away," but God includes "those who will come" as well (23:3). After Adam sinned, God prepared "the treasuries" for the souls of the righteous (21:23; 30:2), and the "realm of death" for the wicked (21:23; 23:5), until the coming of the Anointed One, when the souls of the righteous "will enjoy themselves," and "the souls of the wicked will the more waste away" (30:1-5; cf. 40:1-4).[262] In this way God dispels Baruch's concerns about the apparent success of the wicked who go unpunished and the righteous who suffer in the present time, for they will receive their proper reward in the appointed eschatological time.

In the fifth section (chs. 44–52), God and Baruch discuss the fate of the wicked nations and of the righteous in the eschaton. First, Baruch addresses Adam:

> O Adam, what did you do to all who were born after you? And what will be said of the first Eve who obeyed the serpent, so that this whole multitude is going to corruption? And countless are those whom the fire devours (48:42-43).

Then he addresses God:

> You, O Lord, my Lord, you know that which is in your creation, for you commanded the dust one day to produce Adam; and you knew the number of those who are born from him and how they sinned before you, those who existed and who did not recognize you as their Creator. And concerning all of those, their end will put them to shame, and your Law which they transgressed will repay them on your day (48:45-47).

In this passage, Adam represents the "inhabitants of the earth" and the many wicked, who face the judgment of God because they did not remember the Law (48:29-41; cf. 14:2; 18:2), as opposed to the few righteous who kept the Law (48:48—52:7).[263] Thus, in this passage Adam represents not the entire human race but those who disobeyed God's commands and consequently face corruption and destruction. Adam and Eve's transgression exemplifies each

262. In the context of Ezra's concern for the coming of the new age, *4 Ezra* speaks of the "chambers" where the souls of the righteous await their liberation (*4 Ezra* 4:33-43).

263. In 18:2, the "many" represent those Israelites who were illuminated by the Law and yet "took from the darkness of Adam." Thus, the distinction between the "many" and the "few" does not necessarily correspond to the distinction between the nations and Israel; rather it is set between those who keep the Law and those who ignore it (cf. chs. 41–42; 48:18-19).

person's disobedience to the Law (cf. 48:40). The earthly Adam (cf. Gen 2:7) is related to those who sinned because they "did not recognize you as their Creator" and were put to shame. The author deliberately omits any reference to the first creation account of mankind made in God's image and entrusted with power and dominion (cf. Gen 1:26-27). Thus, Adam represents those who disobey God's commandments and will be judged by God in the eschaton. He represents the wicked nations who oppressed Israel and acted corruptly and also the "many" among Israel who did not keep the Law. In this way, the author explains that the destruction of Israel is due both to the nations and to the infidelity of many in Israel. He also consoles the few faithful ones by asserting that they will be rewarded, whereas the nations and the "many" among Israel will be punished on the last day.

The sixth section (chs. 53–76) contains two Adamic passages. In the context of the first passage, the author underlines the responsibility of the individual (54:13-22). After the vision of the clouds, Baruch explains:

> Those who do not love your Law are justly perishing. And the torment of judgment will fall upon those who have not subjected to your power. For although Adam sinned first and has brought death upon all who were not in his own time, yet each of them who has been born from him has prepared for himself the coming torment. And further, each of them has chosen for himself the coming glory. For truly, the one who believes will receive reward (54:14-15).

Then he addresses the wicked:

> But now, turn yourselves to destruction, you unrighteous ones who are living now. . . . For his works have not taught you, nor has the artful work of his creation which has existed always persuaded you. Adam is, therefore, not the cause, except only for himself, but each of us has become our own Adam (54:17-19).

The author seems to refer to two groups in the community, one of Jews who received but did not love the Law (cf. 18:2), and another of Gentiles who witnessed the works of God's creation but apparently ignored God as their Creator.[264] In this context, Adam represents those who have sinned and have brought upon themselves death and destruction (cf. 56:5-10). On the one hand,

264. Paul also follows this rationale in Rom 1:18—3:20, but in the opposite order, first referring in the third person to a Gentile group and then addressing a Jewish character.

the author vindicates God's justice by explaining that the present and future destruction are due to human wickedness and to God's righteous judgment. On the other hand, he upholds the responsibility of the individual ("each of them/each of us") and emphasizes that Adam is not the cause of the transgressions of each individual (54:15-16, 19). He underlines that Adam's transgression does not hinder some from keeping the Law, subjecting themselves to the Creator, including possibly some proselytes (cf. 14:17-19; 17:1—18:2; chs. 41–42; 54:21-22), who could attain the coming glory and reward (54:16-17, 21b).

In the second passage, the angel Ramiel interprets the meaning of the vision of the first black waters as the punishments after the transgression of Adam, the first man:

> For when he transgressed, untimely death came into being, mourning was mentioned, affliction was prepared, illness was created, labor accomplished, pride began to come into existence, the realm of death began to ask to be renewed with blood, the conception of children came about, the passion of the parents was produced, the loftiness of men was humiliated, and goodness vanished. What could, therefore, have been blacker and darker than these things? This is the beginning of the black waters which you have seen (56:5–8).

The author recalls Adam's transgression and lists eleven misfortunes that his disobedience brought about (cf. Genesis 3; 6) that will disappear when the Anointed One comes.[265] The author also contrasts Adam and the Messiah and the effects they bring to humankind and to all creation—including some angels (56:10). Among the effects of Adam's disobedience are "untimely death" and corruption, whereas with the Messiah begins incorruption. This passage is followed by the explanation of the bright and black waters, which represent respectively the righteous and the wicked in the history of Israel (chs. 57–74). It culminates with the description of the last bright waters, which represent the coming of the Anointed One who will judge the nations, when joy will be revealed and all misfortunes will pass away, "And nobody will again die untimely, nor will any adversity take place suddenly" (73:3), and there will be "the end of that which is corruptible and the beginning of that which

265. For an analysis of the eleven consequences of Adam's sin, see Levison, *Portraits of Adam*, 139-42. He convincingly translates the word *nsb* as "taking away" of children, as untimely death, according to the context (p. 140). He also explains that the "mention of 'goodness' gives the entire list an ethical nuance" (p. 141).

is incorruptible" (74:2). Given the contrast between Adam and the Anointed One, and between other righteous and wicked Israelites, the author emphasizes the obedience to God's Law as the condition for participation in the joy of the future age and explains that the misfortunes are due to Adam's sin. The subsequent list of Israelites who either kept or transgressed the Law emphasizes the contrast between the righteous and the wicked.

In sum, the story of the fall explains that humankind and Israel face destruction when they disobey God. The destruction of Jerusalem is due both to the wicked among the Israelites and to the nations, which God allows to destroy the city (cf. 1:4). More importantly, the author asserts that Adam's transgression does not determine the moral character of his descendants, and consequently each individual is responsible for his or her actions. Thus, although the righteous who keep the Law still experience the hardships as a result of Adam's transgression and those who act like him, the author assures them of an eschatological reward, when the Anointed One reverses the misfortunes brought by Adam in a new age characterized by incorruption (cf. chs. 73–74).

Summary

Jewish authors interpret variously the story of the creation and fall of humankind according to their historical and cultural context. Although their interpretations have been classified in three groups for practical reasons, they all examine the paradoxical nature, freedom, and responsibility of human beings in general, and the place and function of Israel in the world in particular. Thus, on the one hand, made after God's image (Gen 1:26-27), humankind has its origins in God; on the other hand, made out of the *adamah* (Gen 2:7), Adam and his descendants are bound back to the earth and mortal by nature. The second creation account is closely related to the tale of paradise, the fall, and the expulsion from the garden. Jewish interpreters see in this story the paradigm of the loss of their land, the fall of Jerusalem and the temple, and their sufferings as due to their disobedience and failure to keep the covenant and God's commands. Thus, Adam's disobedience stands as the first—and, in some instances, as the origin of—sin and death for all humankind. Yet some interpreters anticipate the coming of a new and eschatological creation promised to those who keep God's commandments. In this context, they often elicit moral lessons to keep God's commandments in order to experience happiness in this life, and/or bliss in the eschatological life.

Hellenistic interpreters portray Adam first of all as the paradigm of all humankind. They interpret the creation of humankind after God's image (Gen 1:26-27) and "the breath of life" inbreathed into the face of the earthly man

(Gen 2:7) as the human soul or psyche, and the locus of human freedom and responsibility. The creation of the earthly man is closely related to the story of the fall. It explains, first of all, that Adam and his descendants are earthbound and mortal by nature (cf. Sir 16:30b; 17:30; 18:9; 33:10; 37:25; 40:1-11; 41:3-4; Wis 7:1-6; 15:8b; *Opif.* 134). Second, Adam's disobedience to God's command "not to eat from the tree of knowledge of good and evil" (Gen 2:16-17; 3:6) exemplifies Israel's disobedience to God's commandments and the passions and vices of all humankind that bring distress to the wicked. Therefore, they interpret the story of the creation of humankind to explain the nature and dynamics of human freedom, and the story of the fall serves as an example of the misfortunes of failing to obey God's commands. Conversely, some suggest that a virtuous life brings happiness and bliss; but in any case their retribution is confined essentially to this life. The first example that we examined was the book of Sirach. With the exception of Sir 49:16, where Adam stands as the first of Israel's ancestors bestowed with glory, the figure of Adam in Sirach represents all humankind. The author relates the giving of the Law on Mount Sinai to Israel and the command God gave humankind in the beginning of creation. The knowledge of good and evil represents for Sirach a positive quality required to praise God in his creation and to discover God's Law, but this is a gift from God that neither "the first" nor "the last man" could attain on his own. Sirach also affirms that each one is responsible for his own actions (Sir 15:14; 17:6-7; cf. Sir 40:9-10), and the Sage consequently provides an exhortation to repent and to follow God's commands (cf. 17:32b). Nevertheless, human retribution or reward remains a matter of this age; there are no repercussions after death. Similarly, for the Sage only the righteous may participate in God's immortality (ἀφθαρσία) and eternity (ἀϊδιότητος) (cf. Wis 1:15; 2:23-24; 3:4; 6:18-19; 9:5-6, 14-15; 7:1-6). Yet, he explains that, "through envy of the devil, death came into the world; and those who have part with it experience it" (Wis 2:24). Consequently, the wicked experience hardships in this life and death as punishment for their evil acts (cf. Wis 1:16; 2:23-24; 15:12). Finally, Philo develops a more extensive and complex interpretation of the creation of humankind and the fall. He relates that, on the fifth–sixth day, God created the sense-perceptible man, on whom he "bestowed mind (νοῦς) *par excellence*, life-principle of the life principle itself" (*Opif.* 66), which refers to "the Mind, the director of the soul" (*Opif.* 69). Yet the plural "let us make . . ." (Gen 1:26-27) may explain the participation of others in the fashioning of the "mixed nature" of a "creature so puny and perishable as man," who is liable to "contraries," "good and evil, fair and foul, virtue and vice." God would be credited for the good found in human beings, whereas those agents would be blamed for the vice in them (*Opif.* 72-75). Philo interprets the punishments for "these evils" and vices that "have overcome humankind," as the difficulties to obtain their proper sustenance for life (*Opif.* 79-80; cf. Gen 3:17-19). In his interpretation of the fall the characters represent the internal phenomena of the individual man: the man signifies the "mind" (νοῦς), the woman the "sense perception" (αἴσθησις), and the serpent "pleasure" (ἡδονή) (cf. *Opif* 151-170a).[266] Thus, the encounter between the first man and the woman arouses "a bodily pleasure . . . by which men bring on themselves the life of mortality and wretchedness in lieu of immortality and bliss" (*Opif.* 152). By taking from the tree that discerns what is good and evil they chose "ephemeral and mortal existence, which is not an existence but a life full of misery," and consequently they forfeited the tree of life, that is, complete virtue and a "happy and long life" (*Opif.* 156; cf. 165; Josephus, *Ant.* 1.42). Philo contrasts the serpent as "a symbol of pleasure" (157-64) and "the snake-fighter" (cf. Lev 11:22) as "self-control" (ἐγκράτεια) that fights "intemperance (ἀκρασίαν) and pleasure" (ἡδονήν) (*Opif.* 163b). He also contrasts the "austere (φιλαυστήρῳ) and honorable (σεμνῷ) life" and the "troublesome life" (χαλεπωτέραν), which is "worse than death." Finally, Philo draws two ethical lessons from the punishment God gives to man to till the ground. First, the earth ceased to yield its fruit because "wickedness has begun to abound at the expense of the virtues, and the ever-flowing fountains of God's grace have been blocked, so that they might not bring supplies to the unworthy (ἀναξίοις)" (*Opif.* 168). Second, he explains that God did not "provide food ready to hand in the same way as before, so that they might not, by indulging the twin evils of laziness and overindulgence, go astray and become insolent in their behavior" (*Opif.* 169). Therefore, Philo does not ascribe to Adam the beginning of death but concludes that every person is mortal by nature and subject to the "contraries," that is, virtue or vice, which may bring him respectively a troubled or a long and happy life (cf. *Opif.* 156, 164, 172).

The second group, classified as "Rewritten Bible," interprets the story of the creation of humankind and the fall in order to explain the place and role of Israel in the world. In these interpretations Adam stands as the ancestor of Israel, and his disobedience represents the first of the historical transgressions of Israel

266. Likewise, the fruits of the plants of paradise represent the virtues that help man to discern what is good and evil to attain incorruption: "Insight (σύνεσιν) and discernment (ἀγχίνοιαν) that never fail, by which are recognized things that are good (καλά) and evil (αἰσχαρά), and life free from disease, and incorruption (ἀφθαρσίαν), and all that is of a like nature" (*Opif.* 153b), whereas by the tree of life "he signifies reverence toward God . . . by means of which the soul attains immortality (ἀθανατίζεται); while by [the tree] that discerns between good and evil things he signifies intermediate practical insight (φρόνεσιν τὴν μέσην)" (*Opif.* 154b).

and of all the nations, which brought into the world all sort of misfortunes, including untimely death. In this context, the authors exhort their audiences to adhere to the Law in order to prevent destruction and misfortunes so as to be restored either in this life or in the eschaton. In the book of *Jubilees,* Adam is portrayed in positive terms as the first patriarch and priest who kept the ritual laws regarding the Sabbath (*Jub.* 2:17–33), the purification after childbirth (*Jub.* 3:8–14), and covering nakedness for the sacrifice (*Jub.* 3:26–31). Although, Israel fails to keep these laws (*Jub.* 1:7–13), God will restore them if they return to him and celebrate the Jewish feasts according to his Law (*Jub.* 1:15–25). Similarly, Pseudo-Philo's *Liber Antiquitatum Biblicarum* relates the story of the fall to cultic motifs, suggesting that through rituals and festivities God may forgive the sins and remember his covenant with Israel. Yet the people should also walk "in his ways" and keep his commandments. Ultimately *L.A.B.* opens the biblical narrative to an eschatological horizon and leaves to God the judgment of the righteous and the wicked at the time of the visitation, when he will reward them according to their deeds (3:9–10; 19:12; 25:7). In his *Antiquities,* Josephus interprets the Jewish Scriptures so that those who obey God's commands may attain a long and blissful life, free of concerns (*Ant.* 1.14; 1.20). Thus, God commands Adam and Eve not to eat from the tree of knowledge of good and evil so they are not destroyed (*Ant.* 1.40; cf. Gen 2:16–17). However, the serpent persuaded them to taste from the tree (1.42), and consequently they lost "a life of bliss (βίον εὐδαίμονα), unmolested (ἀπαθῆ) by all ill" (1.46–47; cf. *Opif.* 152, 156, 165). Likewise, those who break God's commands lose the benefits of a blissful life, free of concerns. Pseudo-Philo also affirms that, after the transgression, humankind lost the Law contained in the "ways of paradise"; though it was revealed again to Moses at Sinai (see *L.A.B.* 11:1; 19:6; 26:6; 28:8–9, 13–14; 32:7; 33:3; 53:8; cf. *2 Bar.* 17:4). The *protoplastum's* transgression brought about death to all (*L.A.B.* 13:8; 37:3), but at the time of the visitation in the eschaton God will judge humans and reward them according to their deeds (3:9–10; 19:12; 25:7). Finally, the most extensive interpretation of the fall, *Life of Adam and Eve,* explains that the expulsion from paradise of Adam and Eve, their sickness, and their death were part of the "seventy plagues" because they disobeyed God's command not to eat from one "plant" in paradise (7:1), and because they forsook God's covenant and listened to the enemy (8:2). Thus, Adam rebukes Eve, for she brought destruction and "death gaining rule over all our race" (14:1; cf. 21:5–6). The author interprets the evil poison that the serpent sprinkled on the fruit as "covetousness (ἐπιθυμία), which is every sin" (19:3). After their transgression, their eyes were opened and they discovered that they were naked of righteousness and estranged from the glory of God (20:1—21:6). Consequently, God punishes the protoplasts (22:1—29:6). But after Adam pleads guilty and implores God's mercy,[267] God promises to raise him at the time of the resurrection and to give him the tree of life or immortality, only "if you guard yourself from all evil, preferring death to it" (28:4; cf. 10:2; 41:3; 28:4). Thus, Adam is forgiven and taken into "Paradise, to the third heaven" until the Day of Judgment and the day of resurrection (37:2-6; cf. 42:3—43:4), while Abel and Adam's bodies are buried "in the regions of Paradise, in the place where God had found dust and made Adam" (38:1—41:2). Apparently, when the righteous die, their souls ascend to a place in paradise while their bodies wait until the Day of Judgment and the day of the resurrection (cf. 37:3-6; 43:4). Overall, therefore, the narrative explains that the actual cause of misfortunes and death of humankind is not Eve but humans' "desires" and God's righteous judgment. Thus, the author warns Adam's children against all evil (28:4) and exhorts them not to "forsake the good" (30:1) but to plead for God's mercy so that God may reward the righteous in the future, at the time of the resurrection, with immortal life.[268]

The third and last group represents apocalyptic interpretations that anticipate a new creation and the restoration of the righteous in the eschaton. They discuss questions about the problem of evil in the world, human freedom, and God's justice, especially with regard to the sufferings of the righteous and the prosperity of the wicked (cf. *4 Ezra* 3:1-4; *2 Bar.* 14:13-19). *4 Ezra* explains that Adam's disobedience and the transgressions of subsequent generations brought death "for him and for his descendants" (3:4-11). Thus, despite the election of the patriarchs and the Law (3:12-22; cf. 7:70-72), and despite David's election and the sacrifices (3:23-27), they transgressed because, like Adam, they were burned with "the evil heart," or the "evil root" (cf. 3:22-27; 4:28-32; 7:92). However, the few righteous who defeat their evil heart will be saved in the eschaton (cf. 7:15-16, 92). Ezra blames Adam: "For though it was you who sinned, the fall was not yours alone, but ours also who are your

267. Before Adam dies, he exhorts Eve to pray for God's mercy while they wait to meet their maker (31:3-4). The angels, the sun, and the moon also pray for God's mercy (33:2—36:3).

268. Other documents suggest that the righteous would be vindicated in this life or in the future. Thus, for instance, book 1 of *Sibyllines* says that, after the fall, the forefathers were expelled "from the place of immortals" (*Sib. Or.* 1:51) and went to "Hades," along with subsequent generations—except the Titans—although "Hades" is understood as a place of "honor" where they await their restoration (1:80-323). Then book 5 predicts the destruction of the nations because of their vices (5:214-80) and foretells the coming of a messianic figure (5:256-86) and the restoration of the righteous Jews and their city.

descendants" (7:116-18). *4 Ezra* upholds human freedom and responsibility (7:127-31), and explains that the righteous who defeat the "evil heart" and keep God's commands will be acquitted in the eschaton because of God's mercy (7:132—8:3; cf. 6:35—9:25; 8:51-54; 7:13, 16; 8:37-40). Finally, *2 Baruch* relates Adam's disobedience and his expulsion from the garden with Israel's transgressions of the Law and the destruction of Jerusalem (1:1—5:7; cf. *4 Ezra* 3:7; Wis 1:13; 2:23). He also believes that some among the Gentiles would be "mingled with the seed of the people" (15:7-8; cf. 42:3-8) and consequently would receive the eschatological salvation with the few righteous among Israel. The author contrasts Adam's disobedience and the death he brought to "those who were born from him" (*2 Bar.* 17:2; cf. 19:8; 56:5-10) with Moses' submission to God and the Law he brought to "the descendants of Jacob" (17:5; cf. 19:3; *L.A.B.* 9:8; 15:6) Yet, despite their election and covenant, the sons of Jacob followed after the example of Adam, and only a few kept the Law (19:1-3). *2 Baruch* believes that the souls of the righteous go to a temporary stage, "the treasuries" (21:23; 30:2), while the wicked go to the "realm of death" (21:23; 23:5), until the coming of the Anointed One. Then the souls of the righteous "will enjoy themselves" and "the souls of the wicked will the more waste away" (30:1-5; cf. *2 Bar.* 40:1-4; 73:3; cf. *4 Ezra* 4:33-43), and there will be "the end of that which is corruptible and the beginning of that which is incorruptible" (*2 Bar.* 74:2). Finally, *2 Baruch* clearly upholds human responsibility, so that "each of them who has been born from him has prepared for himself the coming torment. And further, each of them has chosen for himself the coming glory. For truly, the one who believes will receive reward" (54:14-15). "Adam is, therefore, not the cause, except only for himself, but each of us has become our own Adam" (54:19). Therefore, although Adam is credited with introducing sin and death into the world, each one is responsible for his or her own actions and will be judged accordingly in the eschaton.

For Jewish interpreters, Adam represents the paradigm of humankind and of Israel in particular. Made after God's image, humankind has its origins in God; made also out of clay, humankind is bound to the earth, mortal. The story of the fall represents Israel's failure to keep God's commands and human sinfulness, which bring misfortunes to all. Although Adam's disobedience may have an effect on his descendants, Jewish interpreters maintain that Israel, and each generation and each person is responsible for his or her actions. Therefore, in order to prevent destruction and misfortunes, they are to keep God's commands and walk in his ways. For the most part, retribution is confined to this life, to happiness and bliss. However, in those instances where the righteous still suffer, some anticipate an eschatological retribution, a Day of Judgment, when the wicked who seem to prosper will be punished. Paul's contrast between the first and the last Adam exemplifies also that their opposite actions, disobedience and obedience, bring either death or life to those who belong to them. Consequently, those who belong to the last Adam, Christ, will also walk in the newness of life now in order to attain the eschatological resurrection.

3

The Figure of Adam in 1 Corinthians 15:21-22, 45-49 and Romans 5:12-21

Introduction

As we surveyed in chapter 2, Jewish interpreters often used the story of the creation and fall of Adam to explain that the crises they faced were a consequence of their own disobedience to God's commands and their disloyalty to the covenant. Consequently they exhorted their audience to abide by God's commandments in order to avoid punishments and to be rewarded either in this life or in the future. Paul's letters reflect this trend of Jewish interpretation of the story of the creation and fall of Adam, which inferred ethical implications from it. This does not imply literary dependence but rather common traits of interpretation. Paul interprets the Scriptures through the prism of the eschatological event of Christ as the fulfillment of the promises found in the Jewish Scriptures, promises made also to those who believe in Christ and in his resurrection. Yet, as his Jewish contemporaries did, Paul also draws ethical implications from the narrative of Genesis 1–3. He introduced the figure of Adam explicitly at least twice in his letters, 1 Cor 15:21-22, 45-49, and Rom 5:12-21.[1] In both passages, Paul contrasts Adam and Christ and the effects on those who belong to each. In the context of the first passage, Paul responds to those who claim that there is no bodily resurrection of the dead. In the context of the second passage, Paul discusses the transformation of believers from sin and death into God's grace and eternal life through Christ's expiatory death. In 1 Corinthians 15 Paul exhorts the believers "to sin no more" (15:34), "to put on the imperishable," and "to stand firm abounding in the work of the Lord" (15:53, 58). Likewise, in Romans 5 Paul concludes that Christ's grace abounded all the more "so that grace may also reign through righteousness to eternal life

1. James D. G. Dunn, among others, includes Phil 2:6-11, which may possibly have some reference to Adam but not explicitly.

through Jesus Christ our Lord" (Rom 5:20-21). Therefore, in these passages Paul introduces the Adam typology in order to illustrate the antithesis between the first and the last Adam, and between the death and life that their deeds introduced into the world. In order to participate in the eschatological victory over sin and death, believers must clothe themselves "with the imperishable, and the mortal with immortality" (1 Cor 15:53) and must die to sin so that God's grace may reign through righteousness into eternal life (Rom 5:21).

Part One: Adam and the Resurrection of the Dead: 1 Corinthians 15

Literary Structure of 1 Corinthians 15

In his correspondence[2] with the Christian community in Corinth, Paul addresses several issues concerning the identity of the community in the midst of a cosmopolitan society.[3] In 1 Corinthians 15, Paul discusses the question of

2. For a synthesis of the scholarship and a bibliography of 1 Corinthians 15, see Anthony C. Thiselton, *The First Epistle to the Corinthians: A Commentary on the Greek Text* (NIGTC; Grand Rapids: Eerdmans, 2000), 1169–82. Most scholars identify a tripartite structure in 1 Corinthians 15; see Gordon D. Fee, *The First Epistle to the Corinthians* (NICNT; Grand Rapids: Eerdmans, 1987), 713–17. Duane F. Watson divides 1 Corinthians 15 into three parts: (1) *Exordium* (vv. 1-2); (2) *Narratio* (vv. 3-11); (3) *Confirmatio* (*Probatio*) and *Refutatio* (vv. 12-57): (a) First Unit of *Refutatio* and *Confirmatio* (vv. 12-34), and (b) Second Unit of *Refutatio* and *Confirmatio* (vv. 35-57); (4) *Peroratio* (v. 58). See Watson, "Paul's Rhetorical Strategy in 1 Corinthians 15," in *Rhetoric and the New Testament: Essays from the 1992 Heidelberg Conference*, ed. Stanley E. Porter and Thomas H. Olbricht (JSNTSup 90; Sheffield: Sheffield Academic Press, 1993), 231–49.

3. The scholarly consensus is that 1 Corinthians is a single work written by Paul. For a recent discussion on the Corinthian correspondence, see Margaret M. Mitchell, "Paul's Letters to Corinth: The Interpretive Intertwining of Literary and Historical Reconstruction," in *Urban Religion in Roman Corinth: Interdisciplinary Approaches*, ed. Daniel N. Schowalter and Steven J. Friesen (HTS 53; Cambridge, Mass.: Harvard University Press, 2003), 307–38, especially 324. In this letter, Paul addresses several issues that affected the identity and unity of the Christian community in Corinth; see Raymond F. Collins, *First Corinthians* (Sacra Pagina 7; Collegeville, Minn.: Liturgical Press, 1999), 1–29. For 1 Corinthians as "Deliberative Speech," see Elisabeth Schüssler Fiorenza, "Rhetorical Situation and Historical Reconstruction," in *Christianity at Corinth: The Quest for the Pauline Church*, ed. Edward Adams and David G. Horrell (Louisville: Westminster John Knox, 2004), 145–60. She claims that Paul tries to convince his audience "to make the right decision for the future" (pp. 150, 159), given their new "baptismal self-understanding" of being in Christ as a new creation (p. 160). See also Elisabeth Schüssler Fiorenza, *Rhetoric and Ethics: The Politics of Biblical Studies* (Minneapolis: Fortress Press, 1999), 105–28; Margaret M. Mitchell, *Paul and the Rhetoric of Reconciliation: An Exegetical Investigation of the Language and Composition of 1 Corinthians* (Louisville: Westminster John Knox, 1991). Watson ("Paul's Rhetorical Strategy," 232) claims that 1 Corinthians 15 is "deliberative rhetoric." Finally, James D. G. Dunn regards

the resurrection of Christ and of believers and how their faith or lack of it may affect their conduct and their future participation in the resurrection from the dead.[4] Most scholars recognize that Paul builds his argument on traditional material with which the Corinthians were probably familiar, either through Paul himself or through another Jewish Christian missionary (cf. 1:12; 3:5). First, he introduces the creedal formula about Christ's resurrection and his victory over death. Second, he also incorporates two sets of Jewish traditions of the creation of the world, Adam, and the fall.[5] The first is an apocalyptic

1 Corinthians 15 as "the most sustained theological section in the whole letter—almost as though Paul had decided that before he closed the letter he would move on from seemingly endless practical issues to a major theological discourse" (*1 Corinthians* [New Testament Guides; Sheffield: Sheffield Academic Press, 1995], 84).

4. Joost Holleman argues that Paul inconsistently combined two different concepts of Christ's resurrection: the martyrological (cf. 2 Maccabees 7) "which took place in heaven soon after his death," and "the eschatological resurrection which was expected to take place on earth on the last day" ("Jesus' Resurrection as the Beginning of the Eschatological Resurrection (1 Cor 15,20)," in *The Corinthian Correspondence,* ed. R. Bieringer (BETL 125; Leuven: Leuven University Press; Peeters, 1996), 659–60; cf. 655. However, this distinction is untenable, for Paul interpreted Christ's resurrection in cosmic dimensions that encompassed both heaven and earth; he did not view the resurrection as an eschatological event that took place in heaven only. Even more problematic is Holleman's claim that Paul depicted Jesus' resurrection in heaven, "while the resurrection of his followers [took] place on earth" (p. 656).

5. Scholars recognize that Paul and his audience were familiar with the Scriptures and Jewish interpretations, but they still debate the extent of their knowledge and the interplay of the Scriptures, Jewish traditions and interpretations of the Scriptures, and early Christian traditions in Paul's letters. See the essays in the collection edited by Stanley E. Porter and Christopher D. Stanley, *As It Is Written: Studying Paul's Use of Scripture* (SBLSymS 50 (Atlanta: Society of Biblical Literature, 2008). In part 2, Steve Moyise, Stanley E. Porter, Roy E. Ciampa, and Steven DiMattei discuss Paul's use of Scripture. In part 3, Christopher D. Stanley, Stanley E. Porter, and Bruce N. Fisk analyze the acquaintance with the Jewish Scriptures that Paul's audiences (mostly Gentile) had. See also Richard B. Hays, *Echoes of Scripture in the Letters of Paul* (New Haven: Yale University Press, 1989), and, more recently, Hays, *The Conversion of the Imagination: Paul as Interpreter of Israel's Scripture* (Grand Rapids: Eerdmans, 2005). Hays explores "what Scripture looks like from within Paul's imaginative narrative world" in order to "discover a way of reading that summons the reader to an epistemological transformation, a *conversion of the imagination*," (*Conversion of the Imagination,* x). See also Christopher D. Stanley, *Arguing with Scripture: The Rhetoric of Quotations in the Letters of Paul* (New York: T&T Clark International, 2004). Stanley distinguishes three levels of biblical literacy among Paul's audience, "informed," "competent," and "minimal." On the other hand, John Paul Heil, applying both historical-critical and literary-critical approaches, analyzes the way Paul rhetorically integrated the biblical references in 1 Corinthians (*The Rhetorical Role of Scripture in 1 Corinthians.* Studies in Biblical Literature 15; Atlanta: Society of Biblical Literature, 2005). He argues that, in order for Paul's rhetorical strategy to work, the members of his audience were expected to be acquainted with the Jewish Scriptures that they received during the Jewish liturgies before Paul arrived in Corinth, and then through Paul's instructions when he preached his gospel to them (pp. 5-10).

interpretation that attributes to Adam the beginning of death; the second interpretation contrasts the earthly and the heavenly man. In this context, Paul contrasts Adam and Christ as paradigms of the old and new creations who respectively brought death and life to all (1 Cor 15:21-22, 45-49). Paul conveys that the audience's faith and life would be vain *if* there is no resurrection of the dead, and he exhorts his audience to live and behave according to what they believe—"come to your right mind, sin no more" (15:34), "stand firm (ἑδραῖοι γίνεσθε)[6] [in this faith] immovable, always abounding in the work of the Lord, knowing that in the Lord your labor is not in vain" (15:58).

In order to rediscover the transformative power of Paul's gospel, which impels a transformation of the individual and the community, we need to identify the traditional material Paul used, the rhetorical comparison between Adam and Christ in the context of chapter 15, and the ethical implications for the believer in the present in order to participate in the future resurrection.[7]

After Paul discusses the spiritual gifts in the Christian community, exhorting them to behave properly in the assembly (12:1—14:40), he addresses the question of the resurrection of believers. Apparently this matter also caused divisions among them that affected their conduct.[8] The overall structure of chapter 15 is divided into three sections:

A. Christ's resurrection as the foundation of the believers' resurrection (15:1-11). Paul recalls the gospel that he preached and that the Corinthians received, which contained a pre-Pauline creedal formula concerning Christ's resurrection and his appearances to Cephas and the Twelve (vv. 3-5).[9] Then

6. According to Raymond Collins, "In Hellenistic Judaism the verb 'to stand fast' (*histemi*) was used to describe steadfast faithfulness to the law and covenant" (*First Corinthians,* 533). Here Paul refers to his gospel and the traditions he received and passed on to the Corinthians; cf. 1:22-23; 15:2, 58; 11:2

7. This study is an effort to respond partially to what Elisabeth Schüssler Fiorenza calls "ethics of interpretation" (*Rhetoric and Ethics*. especially appendix 1, pp. 195–98). Her emphasis is on the actual rhetorical function of the biblical texts and the ethical implications for the contemporary reader and scholar. It helps to make of the biblical texts a meaningful message that transforms the individual and the community, an objective that Paul certainly had in his correspondence to his Christian communities.

8. Mitchell emphasizes that the issue at stake is again the divisions in the community, caused now by the question of the resurrection (*Rhetoric of Reconciliation*, 283-91). "United in the common ancestor (Adam) and the common savior (Christ), all Christians will share in the same fate [i.e. the eschatological resurrection] without distinctions (15:21-22)" (p. 288).

9. For discussion and bibliography on the creedal formula, see Hans Conzelmann, *1 Corinthians: A Commentary on the First Epistle to the Corinthians* (Hermeneia, electronic version), 251; Fee, *Corinthians,* 722–29. Citing Vernon H. Neufeld, *The Earliest Christian Confessions* (New Testament Tools and Studies 5; Leiden: Brill, 1963), 42–51, Thiselton concludes that "1 Cor 15:3-5 clearly demonstrates its early 'primitiveness' but embodies qualifying descriptive phrases which place Christ's death and resurrection

he adds a list of further appearances (vv. 6-7) that culminates with Christ's appearance to Paul himself, which by the grace of God, makes him an official and authorized apostle of the gospel (vv. 8-10; cf. 9:1). The creedal formula asserts that Christ's death and resurrection occurred "according to the Scriptures" (vv. 3b-4).[10] Christ's burial emphasizes his death, and his appearances underlie his resurrection. Paul asserts that his proclamation of the gospel and the Corinthians' faith would be *vain* (εἰκῇ, 15:2) if there were no resurrection from the dead, a theme he develops further in vv. 12-19.[11] Thus, this section validates Paul's apostleship, and, more importantly, it lays the foundation for the belief of the Christians in bodily resurrection, which Paul develops in the following two sections.

B. Paul retorts to "some" (τινες) who deny the resurrection of the dead (15:12-34). The structure of this section forms the following chiasm:[12]

a. 15:12-19: Through seven conditionals clauses (εἰ δέ) Paul demonstrates *ad absurdum* how futile (κενός, ματαία) his preaching and the Corinthians' faith would be *if* there is not resurrection from the dead. Consequently, Christ has not been raised from the dead either and those who are alive "are still in your sins," and "those who have fallen asleep in Christ are lost (ἀπώλοντο)" with no hope at all (vv. 17-19).

b. 15:20-28: These verses constitute the kernel of the argument, where Paul emphatically states, "but indeed (νυνὶ δέ) that Christ has been raised from the dead" (v. 20a).[13] This section stands in

within a scriptural, salvific, and self-involving frame of reference" (*First Epistle,* 1187; see also 1189-1204).

10. Cf. Isa 53:3-5; Hos 6:2. But this expression is broadly descriptive and therefore may refer to the Scriptures in general, probably more in line with sacrificial atonement of the lamb in the exodus tradition and the suffering servant in Isaiah. Furthermore, Christ's resurrection could be viewed in the context of God's creating and making things anew, hence the figure of the new Adam.

11. Cf. κενή, 15:10; ματαία, 15:17; and κενός, 15:58.

12. For the chiastic structure of vv. 12-19, see Fee, *Corinthians,* 739.

13. R. Collins views vv. 20-28 as "the nub of Paul's argument" (*First Corinthians,* 547). *Pace* C. E. Hill ("Paul's Understanding of Christ's Kingdom in 1 Corinthians 15:20-28," *Novum Testamentum* 30 [1988]: 279–320), Jan Lambrecht divides vv. 20-28 into two units: first, Christ as the first fruits (v. 20), explained with the Adamic typology (vv. 21-22); second, Christ as the first fruits (vv. 23-24), explained with a midrash on Psalms 8 and 110 (vv. 25-28) ("Structure and Line of Thought in 1 Cor. 15,23-28," *Novum Testamentum* 32 [1990]: 143–51; see also his "Paul's Christological Use of Scripture in 1 Cor,20-28," *NTS* 28 [1982]: 502–27).

sharp contrast to sections a (15:12-19) and a′ (15:29-34), where Paul describes what would be "*if* there is no resurrection of the dead."

a′. 15:29-34: Paul questions those who practice baptism "on account of the dead" (15:29),[14] and asks, "why are we put in danger every day . . . *if* there is no resurrection of the dead at all (ὅλως)?" (15:29-32a). He ironically concludes that "*if* (εἰ) the dead are not raised, 'let us drink and eat for tomorrow we die'" (v. 32b), possibly referring to the attitude and practice of those who did not believe in the resurrection of the dead.[15] Thus, disbelief in the resurrection apparently led some into a dissolute lifestyle.

Paul concludes section B (15:12-34), exhorting the audience: "Do not be misled (μὴ πλανᾶσθε), 'bad company corrupts good character.'[16] Come back to your right senses (ἐκνήψατε δικαίως), and to sin no more (μὴ ἁμαρτάνετε). For there are *some* who are ignorant of God—I say this to your shame" (15:33-34). Paul turns from the argumentative style to a direct exhortation with three imperatives in the second person plural, μὴ πλανᾶσθε, ἐκνήψατε, and μὴ ἁμαρτάνετε.[17] He addresses "*some* who ignore God (ἀγνωσίαν γὰρ θεοῦ τινες ἔχουσιν)," that is, those who deny the resurrection of the dead (vv. 12-34; cf. v. 12).[18]

14. See Fee, *Corinthians,* 762–67; R. Collins, *First Corinthians,* 556–62; Thiselton, *First Epistle,* 1240–44. For a recent comprehensive discussion of this question, see Michael F. Hull, *Baptism on Account of the Dead (1 Cor 15:29): An Act of Faith in the Resurrection* (SBLDS 22; Atlanta: Society of Biblical Literature, 2005).

15. Cf. Isa 22:13; however, the saying "As long as you are alive, be happy, eat, drink, live high, embrace others. For this was the end," was commonly found on tombs in the Hellenistic world. See M. Eugene Boring, Klaus Berger, Carsten Colpe, eds, *Hellenistic Commentary to the New Testament* (Nashville: Abingdon, 1995), 439–40. This saying may reflect the Epicurean thought of the time; see Heil, *Rhetorical Role,* 221–29; Fee, *Corinthians,* 772.

16. This phrase was a popular maxim, probably from Menander's *Thais*; see Conzelmann, *Corinthians,* electronic source, 278 n. 139. Fee argues that the whole thrust of chapter 15 "is integrally tied to the matters of behavior that have preceded"; to the extent "that both major sections of this argument conclude with an exhortation to proper behavior [vv. 33-34, and v. 58]" (*Corinthians,* 716; see also 762, 772–75). As a matter of fact, Paul mentions the resurrection of Christ and of the believers (6:14) in the context of his exhortation to proper behavior relating to abuses involving food and sexual immorality (6:12-20).

17. Fee notices the rhetorical shift: "In typical diatribe style, the *argumentum ad absurdum* turns truly *ad hominem*, and becomes a word of exhortation for the Corinthians to mend their ways" (*Corinthians,* 772). R. Collins identifies vv. 33-34 as a paraenesis (*First Corinthians,* 560–61). However, they assess these verses as the conclusion of vv. 29-34, and not as the conclusion of the whole section B (15:12-34).

C. In the third section (15:35-58) Paul responds to "someone" (τις) who questions the bodily resurrection from the dead. This *one* can be identified with the *some* (τινες) in 15:12, and also with those whom Paul calls "bad company who corrupt good character" and have a dissolute lifestyle (15:32-33).[19] This section contains three subunits. First, Paul describes different kinds of bodies found in creation (15:35-44). Second, he contrasts the first and the last Adam as two paradigms of humankind, earthly and heavenly, respectively (vv. 45-49). Third, Paul concludes this section—and the entire chapter 15—by describing the eschatological events, when the perishable and the mortal will be transformed into imperishable and immortal, and "death will be swallowed up in victory" (v. 54; cf. 15:26); by praising God for Christ's victory; and by exhorting the audience to "stand firm abounding in the work of the Lord" (15:58).

The Adam and Christ Antithesis: 1 Corinthians 15: 21-22, 45-49

In sections B (15:12-34) and C (15:35-58), Paul introduces the figure of Adam in contrast to Christ to explain the future and bodily resurrection of believers. The figure of Adam is part of the larger creation motifs that Paul uses to explain the resurrection of the dead. In the first section, Paul contrasts the coming of death and resurrection through Adam and Christ that affects all (15:21-22; cf. Rom 5:12-21). In the second section, he contrasts the earthly and the heavenly

18. The "some" here may be identified with those who claimed to have "knowledge" (1 Cor 6:9-10); see Fee, *Corinthians*, 773; R. Collins, *First Corinthians,* 561; and Thiselton, *First Epistle,* 1256.

19. The "some" in chapter 15 are probably the same ones found in the rest of the letter and possibly in 2 Corinthians too. They were some who contested Paul's apostleship and authority in different regards, possibly boasting in their own wisdom and in a higher social status. Theyclaimed to be *pneumatikoi* (2:6, 14-15; 3:1). See Birger A. Pearson, *The Pneumatikos-Psychikos Terminology in 1 Corinthians: A Study in the Theology of the Corinthian Opponents of Paul and Its Relation to Gnosticism* (SBLDS 12; Missoula, Mont.: Society of Biblical Literature, 1973), 26. In chapter 15 they deny the bodily resurrection of the believers, which leads them to a dissolute lifestyle. Christopher M. Tuckett claims that the "some" in 1 Corinthians 15 held that the resurrection was a "present reality," and that consequently Paul stressed the futurity, albeit also bodily, resurrection ("The Corinthians Who Say 'There is no resurrection of the Dead' (1 Cor 15,12)," in Bieringer, *Corinthian Correspondence*, 247-75). However, his contention that Paul stresses the present reality of death rather than the future resurrection is hardly defensible. See Ben Witherington III, *Conflict & Community in Corinth: A Socio-Rhetorical Commentary on 1 and 2 Corinthians* (Grand Rapids: Eerdmans, 1995). He claims that the "some" are wealthy Gentile Christians in Corinth who held a realized eschatology and "were not counting on a future reckoning or resurrection, so they could eat, drink, and be merry, since only death was on the horizon. Their ethics were negatively affected by this lack of future eschatology" (pp. 292, 295). Witherington identifies "a social component" in Paul (15:23-24), who "seeks to replace the present imperial eschatology of some Corinthians with his own brand of Christian 'already . . . not yet' eschatology" (p. 298; cf. also 304-6).

man as paradigms for those who are like them (15:45-49). The references to the story of the creation and fall are evident in both sections. However, since death did not figure among the punishments explicitly declared against Adam and Eve, let alone against their descendants, nor is the distinction between the earthly and heavenly man evident in the narrative of the creation of humankind, it has been suggested that Paul relied on earlier Jewish interpretations of the narrative of Genesis 1–3. Thus, on the one hand, some Jewish apocalyptic interpreters attributed to Adam and/or Eve the introduction of sin and death. On the other hand, Alexandrian Jewish interpreters distinguished between the earthly and heavenly man.[20] The presence of at least two Jewish trends of interpretations in the same passage should prevent one-sided approaches to the question of Paul's exegetical backgrounds; yet his emphasis on the eschatological events locates him closer to apocalyptic interpreters. For Paul, Adam represents the old creation, the earthly man dominated by sin, corruption, and death, whereas Christ, the "last Adam," represents the new creation, heavenly, incorruptible, and immortal. Since Christ and Adam are representative figures, those who belong to either one or the other share their ethical and ontological qualities. Thus, those who belong to Adam are of dust and "perishable," and consequently they cannot inherit the kingdom of God (cf. 15:50), whereas those who belong to Christ are spiritual, heavenly, and "imperishable." Yet, for Paul, the distinction between the earthly and spiritual entails a transformation from the earthly and perishable into the heavenly and immortal (cf. 15:37-44), not a rupture with the physical as *some* in Corinth claimed.[21] Thus, Paul called those who denied the bodily resurrection of the dead "bad company" (ὁμιλίαι κακαί) who "corrupt (φθείρουσιν) good character (ἤθη χρηστά)" (v. 33). Consequently Paul urges them, "come to your own senses (ἐκνήψατε δικαίως) and sin no more" (μὴ ἁμαρτάνετε) (15:34).[22] He also exhorts them to "clothe with the imperishable and immortality"

20. See Gregory E. Sterling, "'Wisdom among the Perfect': Creation Traditions in Alexandrian Judaism and Corinthian Christianity," *Novum Testamentum* 37 (1995): 355–84, esp. 366–67. Sterling suggests (pp. 357–67) that the Corinthians' position reflected in 1 Cor 15:44-49 resembles Alexandrian exegetical traditions on the creation of humankind like those found in Philo (*Opif.* 134-35; *Leg. All.* 1.31-32). See also Gregory E. Sterling, "The Place of Philo of Alexandria in the Study of Christian Origins," in *Philo und das Neue Testament: Wechselseitige Wahrnehmungen. 1. Internationales Symposium zum Corpus Judaeo-Hellenisticum. 1.–4. Mai 2003, Eisenach, Jena,* ed. Roland Deines and Karl-Wilhelm Niebuhr (WUNT 172; Tübingen: Mohr Siebeck, 2004), 21–52.

21. Apparently, those in Corinth who denied the bodily resurrection were among those who claimed to be spiritual and to be wise (cf. 1 Cor 3:10-18), which provoked divisions in the community.

22. Disregard for the physical apparently led *some* to think that whatever they did with their bodies or in the physical realm did not have any moral implication: "The body is not meant for immorality, but for

(ἀφθαρσίαν καὶ ἀθανασίαν) (15:50-53). The final exhortation to "be steadfast, immovable, always abounding in the work of God" (15:58) also suggests that their faith in Christ's resurrection and their hope in their own should imprint in them the character and faithfulness of Christ.[23]

Christ's Resurrection as the 'ΑΠΑΡΧΗ of the Dead, and Head of the New Humankind: 1 Corinthians 15:20-23

Between the two sections where Paul argues *ad absurdum*, "if there is no resurrection of the dead . . ." (vv. 13-19 and 29-32), he emphatically reiterates Christ's resurrection, "indeed Christ has been raised from the dead" (v. 20a), and that of believers. He describes the resurrection of the dead as a series of eschatological events that began with Christ's resurrection as "the first fruits (ἀπαρχή) of those who have fallen asleep (τῶν κεκοιμημένων)" (v. 20), and also as "the ἀπαρχή those who belong to Christ (οἱ τοῦ Χριστοῦ)" (15:23c). In the LXX, ἀπαρχή represents the first fruits of the harvest offered to God, which would anticipate the fullness as well as the consecration of the rest of the crop (Exod 23:16, 19a; Lev 23:10-14; Num 18:8-12; Deut 18:4; 26:2, 10; 2 Chr 31:5; Neh 10:37; Ezek 45:13-16).[24] Three out of six times in Paul, ἀπαρχή refers to those who first accepted the gospel and were consecrated to Christ (Rom 11:16; 16:5; 1 Cor 16:15).[25] In Rom 8:23, Paul describes the Spirit as the ἀπαρχή of the believers, who anticipate with all creation the redemption of their bodies (Rom 8:18-23).[26] These events will take place "in an orderly way" (ἐν τῷ ἰδίῳ

the Lord, and the Lord for the body. And God raised the Lord and will also raise us up by his power" (6:13-14).

23. According to Witherington, "For Paul resurrection, both Christ's and the Christian's, is the basis for a new moral order. . . . [T]here is one place where the new life and God's agenda should be manifest on earth: in the behavior of Christians, in particular in the Christian community as it gathers for worship and fellowship" (*Conflict & Community*, 311). Luke Timothy Johnson, argues that, for Paul, human prudence (φρόνησις) is affected by the faith of Jesus Christ (Rom 12:3; cf. 2:21-26; 5:12-21) ("Transformation of the Mind and Moral Discernment in Paul," in *Early Christianity and Classical Culture: Comparative Studies in Honor of Abraham J. Malherbe*, ed. John T. Fitzgerald, Thomas H. Olbricht, and L. Michael White [NovTSup 110; Leiden: Brill, 2003], 225–27). Thus, "The transformation of the believers 'in the renewal of mind' means therefore their 'putting on' the mind of Christ, so that the process of φρόνησις is aligned with the ἀρχαί, apprehended by their νοῦς thus renewed and informed" (p. 229).

24. See G. Delling, ἀπαρχή, κτλ, *TDNT* 1:484-86; R. Collins, *First Corinthians*, 548, 551.

25. Romans 11:16 refers to Israel as the ἀπαρχή, and to the Gentiles as the φύραμα of those who are holy. Here ἀπαρχή may refer to those among Israel who have accepted Christ; see Joseph A. Fitzmyer, *Romans: A New Translation with Introduction and Commentary* (AB 33; New York: Doubleday, 1993), 614.

26. David E. Aune, "Distinct Lexical Meanings of ἀπαρχή in Hellenistic Judaism and Early Christianity," in Fitzgerald et al., *Early Christianity and Classical Culture*, 103–29. He revises previous

τάγματι, v. 23a; cf. the sequence ἔπειτα and εἶτα), which will culminate with the annihilation of death and the submission of all (τὰ πάντα) to God the Father (15:26–28).[27]

Between the double assertions of Christ's resurrection as the ἀπαρχή of the dead (vv. 20b and 23b), Paul incorporates the figure of Adam in contrast to Christ to explain how death and resurrection came into the world (15:21–22). In a sense, they stand as opposite ἀπαρχαί or heads of humankind, who respectively brought death and resurrection to all. Evidently Paul alludes to the story of the fall (Genesis 3); yet in the narrative of Genesis death does not explicitly figure among the punishments God appointed for Adam, let alone that death befell all his descendants. Indeed, some Jewish authors believed that death was connatural to humankind and was not the result of Adam's transgression (see Sir 16:30b; 17:30; 18:9; 33:10; 37:25; 40:1–11; 41:3–4; Wis 7:1–6; 15:8b; *Opif.* 134). Nevertheless, it is very likely that Paul and the Corinthians were acquainted with other Jewish traditions that attributed to Adam the introduction of sin and death upon all his descendants.[28] As we

definitions of ἀπαρχή and argues that, unlike the agricultural use of the LXX, in all the New Testament passages (nine times, with the exception of Rom 11:16) ἀπαρχή refers to human beings and is used literally rather than metaphorically. "This is particularly striking in 1 Cor 15:20, 23 and *1 Clem.* 24:1, where the identification of Christ as ἀπαρχή from the dead is not a metaphorical use of a cultic term from the LXX in which the ἀπαρχή ('first-fruits') guarantees the rest of the harvest, but rather is a common use of ἀπαρχή with the distinctive meaning 'first of a set'" (p. 129). This meaning is closely related to Christ as the "first born of the dead" (cf. Col 1:18; Rev 1:5; Acts 26:23) (p. 129; cf. 121–24).

27. It is not clear if Paul thinks of two separate eschatological events: first, Christ's parousia (15:23c), when "those who belong to him" will be raised; and, second, the end (τὸ τέλος), when he will destroy all his enemies and will hand over the kingdom to God the Father (15:24-28). In any case, Paul does not envision a universal resurrection; it is assured only for those who belong to Christ. For τάγμα, see BAGD, 802–3. For Fee, τάγμα conveys the military order of the troops in various numbers, and he sees in the series ἔπειτα and εἶτα a logical rather than a chronological sequence (*Corinthians,* 753). However, the sequence of events of the "parousia" in v. 23b, and "the end" in v. 24a suggests that τάγμα means the order pre-established by God, in which Christ occupies the first "rank" as "first fruits" of the resurrection, followed by those "who belong to him" (v. 23); cf. Delling, τασσω, κτλ, *TDNT* 8:27-31. Thiselton explains, "This ordered sequence [τάγμα] of temporality, representation, and promise or pledge of what is to come [ἀπαρχή] begins *Paul's demonstration of a divine purposive order*" *First Epistle*, 1224 (italics in original). Thus, "Paul expressly defines 'the end' not as the time of another resurrection but as the time when the Son submits himself and his pacified kingdom to the Father and when God becomes 'all in all'" (Hill "Paul's Understanding of Christ's Kingdom," 309).

28. Thomas Tobin argues that Paul used a "traditional early Christian creedal statement that contrasted Adam and Christ and used it to substantiate his argument that there is an order to the resurrection" (*Paul's Rhetoric in Its Contexts: The Arguments of Romans* [Peabody, Mass.: Hendrickson, 2004], 177). It seems that Paul introduced this contrast using two sets of traditions, the early tradition of Christ's expiatory death for all/many, on the one hand, and the Jewish tradition about Adam's introduction of

analyzed in chapter 2, several Jewish authors interpreted the story of the fall as the beginning of death for all humankind, and they typically infer that disobedience to God's commands brings corruption and death. For instance, Pseudo-Philo affirms that the transgression of the *protoplastum* brought death to all (*L.A.B.* 13:8; 37:3). In addition to death, the *protoplastum* lost also the "ways of paradise," that is, the righteousness that comes from keeping the Law (see *L.A.B.* 11:1; 19:6; 26:6; 28:8-9, 13-14; 32:7; 33:3; 53:8; cf. Bar 17:4). Similarly, the Greek *Life of Adam and Eve* (*L.A.E.*) explains that the expulsion of Adam and Eve from paradise, their sickness, and their death were the result of their disobedience to God's command not to eat from one "plant" in paradise (7:1). Although at first Eve is blamed for the introduction of death upon all (14:1; cf. 21:5-6), the author later interprets the evil poison that the serpent sprinkled on the fruit as "covetousness" or desire (ἐπιθυμία) (19.3).[29] He also explains the expulsion from paradise as their loss of "righteousness" and of the "glory of God" (20:1-21:6).[30] Since humankind is sinful and God's judgment is righteous (22:1-29:6), humankind must rely on God's mercy after all.[31] God promises to raise Adam and his descendants "at the time of the resurrection," only "if you guard yourself from all evil, preferring death to it" (28:4; cf. 41:3).[32] In the end, Adam is forgiven and taken into "paradise, to the third heaven," until the Day of Judgment and the day of resurrection (37:2-6; cf. 42:3—43:4).[33] The *Sibyllines* also explain that, after the fall, the forefathers were expelled "from the place of immortals" (*Sib. Or.* 1:51) and went to "Hades," where they await their restoration (*Sib. Or.* 1:80-323). Finally, *4 Ezra* and *2 Baruch* address the problem of evil in the world, human freedom, and God's justice, especially with regard to the sufferings of the righteous and the prosperity of the wicked. They find

death upon all, on the other. Stanley E. Porter argues that in v. 21 Paul makes "a general statement that death came through (διά), or by way of, humankind itself and that resurrection from the dead (νεκρῶν is used again) came through (διά) humankind as well" ("The Pauline Concept of Original Sin, in Light of Rabbinic Background," *Tyndale Bulletin* 41.1 [1990]: 14). Paul actually meant to contrast Adam and Christ as historical individuals whose actions impacted those who are either *in* Adam or *in* Christ.

29. This "desire" is what *4 Ezra* and *2 Baruch* call "evil heart" or "evil root."

30. The *Rule of the Community* (1QS) foretells that at the time of the visitation God will renew the covenant with them and "the glory of Adam will be theirs" (4:23). For the translation, see Michael Wise, Martin Abegg Jr., and Edward Cook, *The Dead Sea Scrolls* (San Francisco: Harper, 1996), 131.

31. Before Adam dies, he exhorts Eve to pray for God's mercy while they wait to meet their maker (31:3-4). The angels, the sun, and the moon also pray for God's mercy (33:2—36:3).

32. "I will raise you again, and then there shall be given to you from the tree of life, and you shall be immortal forever" (28:4).

33. In the meantime his body and Abel's body are buried "in the regions of Paradise, in the place where God had found dust and made Adam" (38:1—41:2).

that the answer is not found in the origins but in the eschaton (cf. *4 Ezra* 3:1-4; *2 Bar.* 14:13-19). *4 Ezra* explains that Adam's transgression brought death "for him and for his descendants" (3:4-11). Even the patriarchs, despite the election and the Law (3:12-22; cf. 7:70-72), and David, despite his election and the sacrifices (3.23-27), all transgressed like Adam because they also were burned with "the evil heart" (cf. 3:22-27; 4:28-32; 7:92).[34] Thus, Adam's transgression is not seen as the cause but as the first of the transgressions of Israel and humankind, "For though it was you who sinned, the fall was not yours alone, but ours also who are your descendants" (7:116-18; cf. 7:127-31).[35] *2 Baruch* also explains that Adam's disobedience brought the destruction of Jerusalem (1:1—5:7; cf. Wis 1:13; 2:23), and death to "those who were born from him" (*2 Bar.* 17:2; cf. 19:8; 56:5-10).[36] Despite their election, the covenant, and the Law that Moses brought to "the descendants of Jacob," they followed after the example of Adam, and only a few kept the Law (*2 Bar.* 17:5; cf. 19:1-3; cf. *L.A.B.* 9:8; 15:6). Among the righteous, Baruch includes some Gentiles who would "mingle with the seed of the people" and receive the eschatological salvation with the few righteous among Israel (15:7-8; cf. 42:3-8). He believes that there is a temporary stage where the souls go: the righteous to "the treasuries" (21:23; 30:2; cf. *L.A.E.* 37:2-6; 42:3—43:4), and the wicked to "the realm of death" (21:23; 23:5). They will wait there until the coming of the Anointed One, when the souls of the righteous "will enjoy themselves" and "the souls of the wicked will the more waste away" (30:1-5; cf. *2 Bar.* 40:1-4; 50:1—51:3; 73:3; cf. *4 Ezra* 4:33-43). Then there will be "the end of that which is corruptible and the beginning of that which is incorruptible" (*2 Bar.* 74:2). *2 Baruch* realizes that although "Adam sinned first and has brought death upon all who were not in his own time, yet each of them who has been born from him has prepared for himself the coming torment. And further, each of them has chosen for himself the coming glory, for truly, the one who believes will receive reward" (54:14-15). Addressing the wicked, the author says, "Adam is, therefore, not the cause, except only for himself, but each of us has become our own Adam" (54:19). Thus, the author clearly maintains that each person is free and will receive the proper reward in the eschaton.

34. The author explains that the "evil heart" is like an evil seed found in the heart of every person, which inclines them to evil.

35. "For when Adam sinned and death was decreed against those who were to be born, the multitude of those who would be born was numbered. . . . For my spirit creates the living, and the realm of death receives the dead" (*2 Baruch* 23:4-5).

36. "For when he transgressed, untimely death came into being . . . the realm of death began to ask to be renewed with blood" (56:5-8; cf. *2 Bar.* 48:42-43).

Within this etiological-eschatological framework these authors exhort their audiences to walk according to God's commands and not to disobey as Adam did, so they may attain immortality and incorruption in the eschaton. Thus, Pseudo-Philo foretells that only the righteous will be vindicated at the time of the visitation (3:9-10; 19:12; 25:7).[37] Similarly, in *L.A.E.* 28:4 (cf. 41:3) God promises Adam to raise him at the time of resurrection "if you guard yourself from all evil;" and after Eve tells her story of the fall she exhorts her children, "watch yourselves so that you do not forsake the good" (*L.A.E.* 30:1). The *Sibyllines* foretell the destruction of the nations because of their vices, and the restoration of the righteous Jews and their city at the coming of a messianic figure (*Sib. Or.* 5:214-86).[38] In another case, the angel exhorts Ezra to conform his life to the few righteous who will be rewarded in the eschaton with paradise and immortality (*4 Ezra* 8:44-62). As for the few righteous who defeat their evil heart and still suffer, they will receive their inheritance in the eschaton (cf. 7:13-16, 92; cf. 6:35—9:25). Baruch also emphasizes obedience to God's Law as the condition for participation in the joy of the future age (*2 Bar.* 14:2; 18:2; 48:40). Even some among the Gentiles who keep the Law will be rewarded (15:7-8; 42:3-8). Consequently, although Adam as the head of humankind affects all his descendants, his disobedience does not preclude each individual and the members of each generation from being liable for their actions (*4 Ezra* 7:127-31; *2 Bar.* 54:13-22).[39] Each one follows after the example of Adam's disobedience, but he is ultimately not the cause, only the first who transgressed God's command and started a process of corruption and decay that affects Adam's descendants.

Paul's outlook resembles particularly the apocalyptic Jewish interpretations that contrast the primordial and the eschatological creation.[40] This perspective is also evident in 1 Cor 15:45-49, where Paul contrasts the first and earthly man to the last and heavenly man, correcting the Corinthians' view that contrasted

37. Other interpreters also conclude that only the righteous would participate in God's incorruptibility (ἀφθαρσία) (cf. Wis 1:15; 2:23-24; 3:4; 6:18-19; 9:5-6, 14-15; 7:1-6), whereas the wicked experience hardships in life and death as punishment for their acts (Wis 1:16; 2:23-24; 15:12; cf. Sir 40:9-10; Philo, *Opif.* 164).

38. Daniel 12:2-4 describes the eschatological events, when "the many who sleep on the ground of the earth (אַדְמַת־עָפָר) will awake for eternal life (לְחַיֵּי עוֹלָם), but many others for reproach and eternal abhorrence (לְדִרְאוֹן עוֹלָם)." In the context of this passage the author is referring to the restoration of Israel and the destruction of the Israel's enemies (Antiochus IV Epiphanes).

39. Paul also sustains human freedom and responsibility; see 1 Cor 7:24, 39, 21-22; 10:29.

40. The motif of the new creation is prevalent in both the Old Testament and the New Testament (see Isa 65:17; 66:22; Rev 21:1).

the heavenly and earthly men. Thus, Adam represents the primordial times dominated by sin and death, standing at the opposite end of the eschatological times of the new creation.

In 1 Cor 15:21-22, Paul succinctly introduces this Jewish tradition, which attributed to Adam the beginning of death in a double antithesis,

> For since death [came] through a man (δι' ἀνθρώπου), the resurrection of the dead [comes] also through a man (δι' ἀνθρώπου). For as in Adam all die, so in Christ all will be made alive. (15:21-22)

The first antithesis emphasizes the contrast between death (θάνατος) and resurrection (ἀνάστασις) as opposite entities that came through a man (δι' ἀνθρώπου). The second antithesis emphasizes the opposite effects that all undergo by their participation in Adam (ἐν Ἀδάμ) and in Christ (ἐν τῷ Χριστῷ), respectively. Whereas the preposition διά denotes human agency,[41] the preposition ἐν indicates the participation of all in Adam and in Christ, respectively. The contrast between ἐν τῷ Ἀδάμ and ἐν τῷ Χριστῷ "implies a whole world, an order of life and death. Each includes his adherents in and under himself."[42] There is also a contrast between the present mortal condition (ἀποθνῄσκουσιν) and the future resurrected status (ζῳοποιηθήσονται) of *all* (πάντες). That is, whereas those who are in Adam actually die, those who are in Christ will be made alive at the eschaton (cf. vv. 23-28). Furthermore, while in Adam all actively die, in Christ all are objects of God's agency; as God raised Christ from the dead (cf. 15:20), he will also raise those who belong to him (15:23). Notably, Paul and *2 Baruch* contrast Adam "the first man" and the Messiah, the "last man" who will bring incorruption and immortality to all (cf. 1 Cor 15:21-22; 15:45; *2 Bar.* 54:16-17, 21b; 73:3; 74:2).

Like other apocalyptic interpreters, Paul also significantly elicits a moral lesson within this etiological-eschatological frame. First of all, Adam and Christ stand as two opposite ἀπαρχαί through which death and life came upon all. Second, they represent opposite moral orders, one dominated by sin and death, and the other by life and incorruption. This contrast will be further developed later between the earthly and the heavenly man and those who are from the earth and from heaven (1 Cor 15:45-49), and between the perishable and imperishable (1 Cor 15:50-54). "Being in Christ" is a typical Pauline expression

41. See BAGD, 180, s.v. διά.

42. A. Oepke, ἐν, *TDNT* 2:542. See BAGD, 259–60, s.v. ἐν. Quite frequently Paul uses the expression "in Christ" or "in Jesus Christ," and with the pronoun ἐν αὐτῷ (at least fifty-two times) to signify that one belongs to Christ.

that indicates the relationship between Christ and those who belong to him. "Being in Christ" also entails belonging to a new creation, "if anyone is in Christ, he is a new creation, the old has gone, the new has come" (2 Cor 5:17),[43] which is expressed in a new way of life (cf. Gal 6:15; Rom 6:2-4; Eph 4:22-24). The literary context provides further interpretative clues to the moral lessons that Paul instills in 1 Corinthians 15. In the previous subunit (15:12-19), he reasons that if there were no resurrection of the dead their faith would be vain, they would remain in their sins, and those who have fallen asleep would be lost (ἀπώλοντο) (15:17-19). In the following subunit, Paul concludes that if the dead are not raised we should "eat and drink, for tomorrow we die" (15:32), and he calls those who presumably deny the resurrection of the dead "bad company who corrupt good character" (15:33). Thus Paul exhorts them to "come back to your own senses, and stop sinning" (15:34).

After Paul contrasts Adam and Christ's resurrection as the ἀπαρχή of those who belong to him (vv. 20 and 23), he proceeds to explain the events that will occur in Christ's parousia: "Then (ἔπειτα), in his parousia (ἐν τῇ παρουσίᾳ αὐτοῦ), those who belong to him . . ." (v. 23b). The term "parousia" refers to the coming of the Lord at the end of time and the salvation of "those who belong to him," that is, believers. It referred originally to the arrival of rulers as liberators or benefactors.[44] Thus, Christ's coming as savior or liberator is further illustrated by the language of Christ's kingship, ruling over "all dominion, authority, and power," a topic Paul develops in the following section.[45] "Then (εἶτα) the end (τὸ τέλος) will come." In vv. 24-28 Paul describes Christ's resurrection in terms of a cosmic and eschatological victory over "all dominion, authority and power," until he hands over the kingdom, and even himself to God the Father. Paul illustrates Christ's eschatological victory with an earlier tradition that interpreted Pss 110:1 (15:25) and 8:6b (15:27), which joined the words "under you/under his feet."[46] He adds that "death" will be the last enemy among

43. This passage is preceded by the contrast between "the earthly tent" and the "building from God, an eternal house in heaven" (2 Cor 5:1; cf. 1 Cor 15:44-48). Williams S. Campbell explains that in Romans 11 Paul's goal was to redefine the relations between Jews and Gentiles in a new social order expressed in terms of a new creation in opposition to the order defined by the Roman Empire (*Paul and the Creation of Christian Identity* (Library of New Testament Studies 322; London: T&T Clark, 2008), 143, especially 163–65.

44. Cf. 1 Thess 2:19; 3:13; 4:15; 5:23; 2 Thess 2:1, 8, 9. As an official term παρουσία refers to "the visit of a person of high rank, esp. of kings and emperors visiting a province," and of Christ it refers to "his Messianic Advent in glory to judge the world at the end of this age," BAGD, 629–30. See also R. Collins, *First Corinthians*, 552; Thiselton, *First Epistle*, 1229–30; Fee, *Corinthians*, 753 n. 33.

45. In Rom 14:9, Paul asserts that Christ died and rose, "so that he may rule the dead and the living" (ἵνα καὶ νεκρῶν καὶ ζώντων κυριεύσῃ).

"all the enemies" that Christ will subdue (v. 26; cf. Pss 8:7; 109:1). The inclusion of "death" (θάνατος) as the last enemy to be destroyed may point to the notion of death as a hypostatized power (cf. 15:26 and 15:55-56).[47] It also brings back the antithesis established earlier between the death that Adam brought and the resurrection that Christ brought to all (vv. 21-22).[48]

In sum, in 1 Cor 15:20-28 Paul incorporates earlier traditions of the story of Adam's fall and the death that befell him and his descendants, and traditions of Christ's victory over all his enemies, including death (15:26). Since the narrative of Genesis does not explicitly convey that Adam's disobedience brought death upon his descendants, it is presumed that Paul incorporated apocalyptic interpretations that saw in Adam a representative figure whose disobedience brought death upon his descendants. These interpreters also contrasted the primeval times with the restoration of the righteous at the eschaton, which Paul saw fulfilled in Christ's death and resurrection as the "first fruits" of a new creation. For these authors Adam is also a paradigm of disobedience, although this does not prevent his descendants from being responsible of their actions. Furthermore, it is the salvation envisioned by these apocalyptic authors that motivates them to exhort their audiences to obey God's commands and to conform to the righteous. They envisioned in the coming of the Messiah (awaited in *2 Baruch* and fulfilled in Paul) the coming of a new creation characterized by incorruption and immortality. For Paul, to be in Christ and to belong to Christ assured the believer of the future resurrection, but also required of the believer to be conformed to Christ. Paul explains in 1 Cor 15:45-49 how this participation in Christ will take full effect.

46. Ps 110:1 [LXX 109:1]: εἶπεν ὁ κύριος τῷ κυρίῳ μου κάθου ἐκ δεξιῶν μου ἕως ἂν θῶ τοὺς ἐχθρούς σου ὑποκάτω τῶν ποδῶν σου; Ps 8:6 [LXX 8:7]: καὶ κατέστησας αὐτὸν ἐπὶ τὰ ἔργα τῶν χειρῶν σου πάντα ὑπέταξας ὑποκάτω τῶν ποδῶν αὐτοῦ. This method of interpretation was known as *gezera shawah*; see Heil, *Rhetorical Role*, 205–19; R. Collins, *First Corinthians*, 548–50. It seems that the combination of Psalm 8 and Psalm 110 is a pre-Pauline interpretation that refers to Christ's resurrection and subjugation of powers (cf. Mark 12:36; Rom 8:34; Col 3:1; Eph 1:20; 1 Pet 3:21b-22; Heb 1:3; 2:8); Martinus C. de Boer, "Paul's Use of a Resurrection Tradition in 1 Cor 15,20-28," in Bieringer, *Corinthian Correspondence*, 639–51. Lambrecht convincingly contends that Paul interpreted Psalm 110 and 8:6 christologically and eschatologically ("Paul's Christological Use of Scripture in 1 Cor,20-28," 502–27). He also thinks that 15:23-28 is part of the Adam typology in vv. 20-21 and vv. 44b-49.

47. See Conzelmann, *First Corinthians*, Hermeneia, CD-ROM, 273.

48. Cf. Wis 1:16; 2:24b. This is particularly telling, since the portrayal of death as a personified power is found in the context of the exaltation of the righteous who share in God's immortality and incorruption (ἀφθαρσία and ἀθανασία) (Wis 1:15; 3:4; 6:18-19; cf. also Dan 12:1-3). Indeed, "all dominion, authority, and power" as well as death are to be *destroyed* (καταργήσῃ, v. 24c, and καταργεῖται, v. 26).

The First Adam from Dust and the Last Adam from Heaven: 1 Corinthians 15:45-49

In section C (15:35-58), Paul responds to someone (τις) who asks, "How are the dead raised? With what kind of body (σώματι) will they come?" (v. 35). This section is divided into three parts: first, the metaphor of sowing that describes the different kinds of bodies found in the cosmos (15:36-44); second, the contrast between the first and the last Adam as paradigms of the earthly and heavenly men (15:45-49); and third, the description of the eschatological transformation from perishable and mortal into the imperishable and immortal (15:50-57; cf. 15:26). The entire chapter concludes with a short *peroration* exhorting the believers to "stand firm" in the gospel, "abounding in the work of the Lord" (15:58).[49]

In the first part (15:36-44), Paul responds to a hypothetical interlocutor with the metaphor of sowing (three times), "You fool! What you *sow* (ὅ σπείρεις) does not come to life (ζῳοποιεῖται) unless it dies (ἀποθάνῃ). And what you *sow*, it is not the *body* (σῶμα) that will be what you *sow*, but a naked seed (γυμνὸν κόκκον). . . . But God gives it a *body* (σῶμα) as he has determined (καθὼς ἠθέλησεν)" (vv. 36-38; cf. Gen 1:11-13).[50] Then Paul explains that there are different kind of "flesh" (σάρξ), that of men, animals, birds, and fish (v. 39; cf. Gen 1:20-28). Finally, he describes the heavenly and earthly bodies (σώματα ἐπουράνια καὶ σώματα ἐπίγεια), each with a different splendor (δόξα) (vv.40-41; cf. Gen 1:14-19).[51] Paul concludes with an anaphora that contrasts what is sown (σπείρεται) to what is raised (ἐγείρεται) to illustrate that

49. Mitchell regards v. 58 as the ἐπίλογος of the whole letter (*Rhetoric of Reconciliation*, 290–91).

50. The sowing motif was a common topos used in Hellenistic Judaism perhaps under the influence of the Stoic doctrine of the λόγος σπερματικός as found in Philo (*Leg. All.* 2.37, 227; 3.40, 68, 185, 242; *Vit. Mos.* 279;); see S. Schulz, σπέρμα, κτλ, *TDNT* 7:543–44.

51. According to R. Collins, "That Paul uses the creation story to provide analogies for the resurrection of the body suggests that the resurrection might be considered as a 'new creation'" (*First Corinthians*, 564). However, Paul is not concerned with the sequence of the days of creation—as the loose sequence of the third, fifth, sixth, and fourth days suggests. Rather he uses the metaphor of sowing to explain the process of transformation (vv. 51-51) and that there are different kinds of bodies in the universe, according to God's will (καθὼς ἠθέλησεν). Philo rejects the notion that there are upper and lower levels in the universe; rather that is said "in relation to our own position" (*Decal.* 57). In *Spec. Leg.* 1.13-14, Philo presents the "the heavenly bodies" as the magistrates of those who exist "below the moon, in the air or on the earth" (1.13). Turid Karlsen Seim argues that the function of the "taxonomy" of vv. 38-41 is to demarcate the difference between the heavenly and earthly realms ("The Resurrected Body in Luke–Acts," in *Metamorphoses. Resurrection, Body and Transformative Practices in Early Christianity*, ed. Turid Karlsen Seim and Jorunn Økland, [Ekstasis 1; Berlin: de Gruyter, 2007], 19–39).

in the same way (Οὕτως καὶ . . .) it happens with the resurrection of the dead (vv. 42–44; cf. v. 36).[52]

Contrast between What Is Sown and What Is Raised (15:42–44a)

It is sown in corruption (ἐν φθορᾷ)	It is raised in immortality (ἐν ἀφθαρσίᾳ)
It is sown in dishonor (ἐν ἀτιμίᾳ)	It is raised in glory (ἐν δόξῃ)
It is sown in weakness (ἐν ἀσθενείᾳ)	It is raised in power (ἐν δυνάμει)
It is sown a natural body (σῶμα ψυχικόν)	It is raised a spiritual body (σῶμα πνευματικόν)

The first antithesis (φθορά/ἀφθαρσία) anticipates the eschatological transformation from perishable into imperishable at both the ethical and ontological levels (vv. 50–54).[53] The second antithesis (ἀτιμία/δόξα) recalls the different kinds of "splendor" of the heavenly and earthly bodies (vv. 40–41).[54] The third antithesis shows the contrasts between weakness and power (ἐν

52. Jeffrey R. Asher argues that "Paul's metaphor of sowing in vv. 42–44 is used antithetically to contrast not the burial or human existence, but human origins with the resurrection," "ΣΠΕΙΡΕΤΑΙ: Paul's Anthropogenic Metaphor in 1 Corinthians 15:42–44," *JBL* 120 (2001): 102. He claims that Paul demonstrates "two essential points: the cause and effect of the resurrection." Paul indeed explains that God is the cause or agent who transforms the earthly body into a celestial body. However, Paul does not explain this to "comply with the strictures of the Corinthians' cosmological system," nor does he demonstrate that "the bodies are distributed in the universe between two realms of habitation [and that ultimately] the resurrection of the dead conforms to the requirements of a dichotomous cosmology by means of the creative power of God" (p. 103). Rather, Paul emphasizes God's power to *transform* the natural body that is sown, into the spiritual body that is raised (v. 44); his emphasis is on the transformation of the body and not on the distribution of the different kinds of bodies in the cosmos. Furthermore Paul's perspective is not etiological ("anthropogenic") but eschatological.

53. Cf. G. Harder, φθείρω, κτλ, TDNT 9:100–102. The terms "perishable/imperishable" convey both ontological and ethical meanings. Thus, incorruption (ἀφθαρσία) leads into immortality (ἀθανασία); cf. Wis 1:15; 3:4; 6:18–19; 9:15.

54. Fee (*Corinthians,* 785) suggests that it may allude to the righteous as found in Dan 12:3; *1 Enoch* 62:15; 105:11; *2 Bar.* 51:10.

ἀσθενείᾳ/ἐν δυνάμει) in which the body is sown and will be raised. The fourth antithesis between the natural and spiritual body (σῶμα ψυχικόν/σῶμα πνευματικόν) (v. 44) anticipates the contrast between the first and natural Adam (τὸ ψυχικόν) and the last and spiritual Adam (τὸ πνευματικόν) (15:45-49).[55] Thus, Paul introduced the metaphor of the sowing as part of the creation motif (Genesis 1–2) to explain the bodily resurrection of the believers in terms of a new creation as a process of transformation ultimately determined by God. As he created different kinds of bodies, he also raised Christ from the dead and will give the believers a spiritual and imperishable body in the future resurrection.

In the second part (15:45-49), Paul further illustrates the bodily resurrection by means of the antithesis between the first Adam from dust and the last Adam from heaven. He supports his argument with a passage from Gen 2:7, introduced with the formula, "It is also written" (οὕτως καὶ γέγραπται).[56] The conjunction καὶ implies that the previous metaphor of the sowing (vv. 35-44) referred also to the biblical creation account. Now Paul focuses on the creation of humankind, which he modifies from the LXX Gen 2:7.

Parallel between 1 Corinthians 15:45-47 and Genesis 2:7

1 Cor 15:45-47	Gen 2:7
The first man Adam became (ἐγένετο ὁ πρῶτος ἄνθρωπος Ἀδάμ) a natural being (εἰς ψυχὴν ζῶσαν), 15:45a.	and man became (καὶ ἐγένετο ὁ ἄνθρωπος) a natural being (εἰς ψυχὴν ζῶσαν), 2:7c.
the last Adam (ὁ ἔσχατος Ἀδάμ), a life-giving spirit (εἰς πνεῦμα ζῳοποιοῦν), 15:45b.	and he breathed into his face the breath of life (πνοὴν ζωῆς), 2:7b.

55. The antithesis between ψυχικόν and the πνευματικόν recalls one of the main issues of the letter (cf. 2:14-15). This contrast is not simply the ontological transformation that will take place at the eschaton, but it entails also a moral transformation in the present in order to inherit the kingdom of God (15:50); see Witherington, *Conflict & Community*, 308.

56. This formula introduces other biblical passages in 1 Corinthians as well; see 1:19, 31; 2:9; 3:19; 4:6; 9:9; 10:7; 14:21. Stanley includes other texts under variants that also refer to Scripture, such as 15:54, ὁ λόγος γεγραμμένος, but surprisingly he omits 15:45 (*Arguing with Scripture*, 75-96). For further discussion on Paul's use of scriptural quotations, see Steve Moyise, "Quotations," in Porter and Stanley, *As It Is Written*. 15-28.

ἀλλ’ οὐ πρῶτον τὸ πνευματικόν ἀλλὰ τὸ ψυχικόν, ἔπειτα τὸ πνεθματικόν, 15:46.	
ὁ πρῶτος ἄνθρωπος ἐκ γῆς χοϊκός, ὁ δεύτερος ἄνθρωπος ἐξ οὐρανοῦ, 15:47.	καὶ ἔπλασεν ὁ θεὸς τὸν ἄνθρωπον χοῦν ἀπὸ τῆς γῆς, 2:7a.

Paul makes of the one man of Gen 2:7 two men, the ὁ πρῶτος Ἀδάμ and the ὁ πρῶτος ὁ ἔσχατος Ἀδάμ.[57] Paul moves on from his distinction between the "physical" and the "spiritual" body (v. 44) to the contrast between the "physical" Adam (ψυκὴν ζῶσαν; ψυχικόν) (15:45a), and the "life-giving spirit" Adam (πνεῦμα ζῳοποιοῦν; τὸ πνευματικόν) (15:45b). Paul's focus is on the sequence between the two, "the spiritual did not come first, but the natural (ψυχικόν), then the spiritual (τὸ πνευματικόν)" (v. 46). Then Paul explains the character of each man, "the first man was of the dust from the earth (ἐκ γῆς χοϊκός; cf. Gen 2:7a), while the second man (ὁ δεύτερος ἄνθρωπος) was from heaven (ἐξ οὐρανοῦ)" (v. 47).

Paul's brief allusion to the story of the creation of humankind presupposes that the Corinthians would have known interpretations that distinguished between the earthly man of Gen 2:7 and the heavenly-spiritual man who bears the image of God of Gen 1:26-27.[58] This kind of interpretation is found in several of Philo's exegetical works, but most clearly in *Opificio Mundi.* His sophisticated exegesis integrates both the literal and the metaphorical meaning of the text and reflects earlier exegetical traditions.[59] First, Philo distinguishes between the intelligible world created on day one, and the sense perceptible world created between the second and sixth days. Consequently, there is the

57. The LXX translates the Hebrew אָדָם as ὁ ἄνθρωπος in Gen 1:26-27 and 2:7; and it is not until Gen 2:16; 2:19-25 and Genesis 3 (the only exception is 2:18) where the LXX translates אָדָם as a proper name Ἀδάμ, that is, as an individual and ancestor of all humankind. The addition of "Adam" in Gen 2:7 also occurs in Theodotion and Symmachus; see Heil, who suggests that Paul is "dependent on a non-LXX version" (*Rhetorical Role,* 231–32).

58. See Sterling, "Wisdom among the Perfect," 359–60. Sterling suggests that "the Corinthians had already made the connection between Gen. 1:26-27 and 2:7 and that Paul co-opted their exegesis, but shaped it by his temporal eschatological perspective" (p. 361).

59. For the most extensive analysis of Philo's interpretation of the creation of man, see Thomas H. Tobin, *The Creation of Man: Philo and the History of Interpretation* (CBQMS 14; Washington, DC: Catholic Biblical Association of America, 1983); see above, chapter 2.

intelligible man created after the image of God (*Opif.* 25) and the sense-perceptible man created last on the fifth–sixth day as the crown of the entire sense-perceptible world (*Opif.* 129-30).[60]

However, when Philo turns to the interpretation of the creation of the earthly man (Gen 2:7; *Opif.* 134–47), he distinguishes between the man formed earlier after the image of God and this man, "for the man so formed is an object of *sense-perception* . . . consisting of body and soul (ἐκ σώματος καὶ ψυχῆς), man or woman, by nature mortal (φύσει θνητός); while he that was after the image (κατὰ τὴν εἰκόνα) was an idea (ἰδέα) or type (γένος) or seal (σφραγίς), intelligible (νοητός), incorporeal (ἀσώματος), neither male or female, by nature incorruptible (ἄφθαρτος φύσει)" (*Opif.* 134). Philo explains that "the individual man (ἐπὶ μέρους ἄνθροπου), the object of sense (αἰσθητοῦ), is a composite one (σύνθετον) made up of earthly substance (γεώδους οὐσίας) and of divine breath (πνεύματος θείου)." Thus, because the body (σῶμα) of the composite man was taken from clay (χοῦν), and his soul (ψυχήν) came from the divine breath (ἤ πνευμᾶ θεῖον) inbreathed (ἐνεφύσησεν) by "the Father and Ruler of all," he is at once "mortal with respect the body, but in respect of the mind (διάνοιαν) immortal" (*Opif.* 135).[61]

Philo calls this composite man "first man" (πρῶτος ἄνθρωπος) inasmuch as he was the "ancestor" and "forefather of our whole race" (*Opif.* 136, 140 [twice], 142, 145). Philo describes at length the features of the body and soul of the composite man (*Opif.* 136–47).[62] On the one hand, he explains that God made his body of the purest stuff in order to carry the soul "as a holy image, of all images the most Godlike" (*Opif.* 137). On the other hand, he claims that God made man's soul after "His own Word" (ἑαυτοῦ λόγῳ), so that "man was made a likeness and imitation of the Word, when the Divine Breath was breathed into his face" (*Opif.* 139). Thus, in his description of the composite man, Philo conflates the account of the creation of man after the image of God (Gen 1:26–27) and the account of God infusing breath of life into the face of man (Gen 2:7b). Subsequently, Philo argues that the descendants of the "first man," somehow as copies of the first copy, dwindle in the physical and moral qualities

60. Explaining why man was created *last*, Philo describes this man as mortal (θνητός), and yet deemed immortal (ῷ ἀπαθανατίζεται) (*Opif.* 77); "puny and perishable" (*Opif.* 73); "the noblest of things earthborn and perishable (γηγενῶν καὶ φθαρτῶν) (*Opif.* 82). After the interpretation of the creation of the sense-perceptible world, Philo explains largely the meaning of "seven" (*Opif.* 89–128).

61. Sterling notes that Philo's substitution πνεῦμα for the LXX πνοή of Gen 2:7b reflects "an exegetical tradition which equates the two" ("Wisdom among the Perfect," 364).

62. Philo also calls the "first made man" "heavenly (οὐράνιον), because by means of his sight . . . he draws near the sun and the moon" (*Opif.* 147).

of their ancestor (*Opif.* 140–45).[63] Yet the distinction between the man created earlier after God's image and the composite man is not chronological but "ontological."[64] While the man made earlier after the image was an idea (ἰδέα), intelligible (νοητός), incorporeal (ἀσώματος), and incorruptible (ἄφθαρτος) (*Opif.* 134), the body of the composite man was made up of earthly substance (γεώδους οὐσίας) taken from clay (χοῦν), and his soul (ψυχήν) came form the divine breath (ἤ πνεῦμα θεῖον; πνεύματος θείου) made in the likeness of the Word (*Opif.* 139).

It is plausible that the Corinthians knew this tradition as represented by Philo that distinguished between the man made after the image of God (Gen 1:26–27), incorporeal and incorruptible, and the earthly man infused with the divine breath of life (Gen 2:7).[65] Apparently those Corinthians who denied the resurrection of the dead believed they were already participating in a spiritual-heavenly existence and consequently were in no need of a bodily resurrection. Paul replies to the Corinthians' atemporal scheme with an eschatological perspective that opposed the earthly primordial (ὁ πρῶτος ἄνθρωπος) Adam to the heavenly and eschatological (ὁ ἔσχατος) Adam.[66] He emphasizes that it was "not first the spiritual (τὸ πνευματικόν) but the natural (τὸ ψυχικόν), and afterwards the spiritual" (v. 46).[67] Thus, on the one hand, "the first man" is simply a natural being (εἰς ψυχὴν ζῶσαν, ψυχικόν, 15:45a, 15:46),[68] made of earthly stuff (ἐκ γῆς χοϊκός) (15:47a; cf. Gen 2:7a, χοῦν ἀπὸ τῆς γῆς). His earthly condition calls to mind that he was destined to return to earth (ὅτι γῆ εἶ καὶ γῆν ἀπελεύσῃ, Gen 3:19). Paul's previous analogy of the natural

63. For Philo the "first man" was a virtuous man who "endeavored in all his words and actions to please the Father and King" (*Opif.* 144).

64. Sterling, "Wisdom among the Perfect," 362. He notes that in *Leg. All.* 2.5 "Philo refers to the molded *anthropos* as 'ὁ δεύτερος ἄνθρωπος'" (p. 363).

65. Sterling explains that it was probably Apollos who brought these "creation traditions" represented by Philo from Alexandria into the Synagogue in Corinth ("Wisdom among the Perfect," 382). Other scholars hold the same position.

66. Sirach contrasts the first and the last man to explain that no one could attain wisdom (24:28). *2 Baruch* also calls Adam "the first man," whose transgression brought "untimely death came into being" (56:5–6).

67. As we discussed in chapter 1, some suggest that Paul is correcting Corinthians who held Gnostic views (e.g., Rudolf Bultmann, Walter Schmithals, Egon Brandenburger). Others argue that some Corinthians were influenced by Hellenistic Jewish interpretations of the creation account (e.g., W. D. Davies, E. P. Sanders, C. K. Barrett, Robin Scroggs, James D. G. Dunn, A. J. M. Wedderburn, N. T. Wright).

68. The first Adam simply receives the breath of life (πνοὴ ζωῆς, Gen 2:7b). Ψυχή "identifies the human being as a vital, living creature" (R. Collins, *First Corinthians,* 571).

body that is sown as perishable and weak (15:42-44) suggests that the body of the first man was also perishable, that is, mortal (cf. 1 Cor 15:21-22). On the other hand, instead of having the first man endowed with the divine breath (ἥ πνεῦμα θεῖον; πνεύματος θείου; cf. *Opif.* 139), Paul presents "the last Adam" as "a life-giving spirit" (15:45b). The last Adam does not simply receives the "breath of life" (πνοὴ ζωῆς, Gen 2:7b); instead he becomes εἰς πνεῦμα ζῳοποιοῦν, that is, a Spirit-Giver of life to those who belong to him so that the spirit that raised Jesus from the dead will raise them also in the eschaton. The "spiritual" (τὸ πνευματικόν) (15:46) is also "the second man from heaven (ὁ δεύτερος ἄνθρωπος ἐξ οὐρανοῦ)" (15:47). Earlier Paul had distinguished between the heavenly and earthly bodies (15:40) and between the physical body that is sown perishable (ἐν φθορᾷ) and the spiritual body that is raised imperishable (ἐν ἀφθαρσίᾳ) (15:42-44).[69] Discussing the resurrection of the dead in 1 Thessalonians, Paul foretells that in his parousia the Lord will descend from heaven (καταβήσεται ἀπ' οὐρανοῦ; 1 Thess 4:16; cf. Dan 7:13). Thus, Paul identifies the second Adam with the spiritual and the heavenly man, imperishable and giver of life to those who belong to him.

After contrasting the first and the last Adam, Paul extends the contrast to their descendants,

> As the one of dust (οἷος ὁ χοϊκός), so those of dust (τοιοῦτοι καὶ οἱ χοϊκοί), and as the heavenly one (καὶ οἷος ὁ ἐπουράνιος), also those heavenly ones (τοιοῦτοι καὶ οἱ ἐπουράνιοι). Just as we have borne (ἐφορέσαμεν) the image (τὴν εἰκόνα τοῦ χοϊκοῦ) of the man of dust, we shall also bear (φορέσεμεν) the image of the man of heaven (τὴν εἰκόνα τοῦ ἐπουρανίου) (1 Cor 15:48-49).[70]

In this case, the earthly and heavenly Adams function as paradigms for their descendants, who bear the image (τὴν εἰκόνα) of their ancestors. On the one hand, the descendants of the first man bore the image of the earthly Adam (cf. Gen 5:3), and they have decayed even more after Adam's fall. On the other hand, the descendants of the last Adam *will* bear the image of the heavenly Adam who was made after the image of God (Gen 1:26-27). This apparent

69. Note Philo's distinction between the three orders in the cosmos: (a) the plants and animals, "devoid of reason" (ἄλογα) "partake neither of virtue nor of vice . . . for mind and reason (νοῦν καὶ λόγον) are as it were the dwelling place of vice and virtue"; (b) the heavenly bodies, "endowed with mind, or rather each of them a mind in itself, excellent through and through and unsusceptible of any evil" participate in virtue only; and (c) those "of mixed nature (τῆς μικτῆς ἐστι φύσεως)," as humankind (*Opif.* 72).

70. See the contrast between ἐπουράνια and ἐπίγεια, 1 Cor 15:40.

decay is found also in Philo, who argues that Adam's descendants are inferior copies of the original that decline in the physical and moral qualities after the "first man" (*Opif.* 140–45). He also distinguishes between two kinds of men, the heavenly (οὐράνιος) and the earthly (γήϊνος). The former, made after "the image of God (κατ' εἰκόνα θεοῦ), does not at all participate in corruptible (φθαρτῆς) and earthly substance, but the earthly was built out of scattered matter which he [Moses] called dust (χοῦς)" (*Leg. All.* 1.31-32; cf. 1.42, 53–55; 2.4; *Opif.* 134).[71] Philo explains that the creation of the "helper" for the earthly man refers to the senses, passions, and vices, "For sense and passions are helpers of the soul and come after the soul (*Leg. All.* 2.5; cf. 2.89).[72] Paul seems to know this tradition or presumes that his audience does; however, instead of dividing humankind into two realms, the earthly and the heavenly, he lays out a tension between the current status of the descendants of the primordial earthly Adam and the future status of the descendants of the heavenly and eschatological Adam. Therefore, although we still bear (ἐφορέσαμεν) the likeness of the earthly Adam and consequently are mortal and corruptible, we will also bear (φορέσομεν) the likeness of the heavenly and eschatological Adam, incorruptible and immortal.

The verb φορέω anticipates the metaphor of the clothing (ἐνδύω, vv. 53–54; cf. 2 Cor 5:1–4) but here φορέω conveys a more permanent quality.[73] Thus, we will bear permanently the "image" of the heavenly Adam and will be transformed into the Lord's likeness (εἰκόνα), who is the εἰκὼν τοῦ θεοῦ (cf. Rom 8:29; 2 Cor 3:18; 4:4; Col 3:10). However, the eschatological transformation requires an ethical transformation so that "to put on Christ" conveys "that one has to conform his/her life according to the moral qualities of Jesus Christ" (cf. Rom 13:12–14).[74] Therefore, although we still wear a weak and perishable body (cf. 15:53–54) after the image of the earthly Adam, in the eschaton we will wear (φορέσομεν) the likeness of the man of heaven (1 Cor

71. Translation from Sterling, "Wisdom among the Perfect," 364, slightly modified. Philo also identifies the first man as being mortal (θνητός) (*Opif.* 77), earthborn, and perishable (γηγενῶν) (*Opif.* 82).

72. See E. Schweizer, "χοϊκός, κτλ" *TDNT* 9:475–76.

73. φορέω, "*bear* (in contrast to φέρω) for a considerable time or regularly, hence *wear*," BAGD, 864. See also K. Weiss, *TDNT* 9: φόρος, κτλ, 83–84; Fee, *Corinthians,* 794 n. 34; Thiselton, *First Epistle,* 1289–90. Thiselton, following Barrett and Conzelmann, prefers the future indicative φορέσομεν, attested by B and other ancient manuscripts (*First Epistle,* 1289). R. Collins (*First Corinthians,* 572) with Fee prefers the aorist subjunctive attested by P46, ℵ, A, C, D, Ψ, and other ancient manuscripts and argues that "Paul concludes each of his proofs (vv. 34, 49) and his peroration (v. 58) with an exhortation;" therefore "the subjunctive reading is to be preferred.

74. L. T. Johnson, "Transformation of the Mind," 228.

15:49). Paul conveys that we still are subject to decay and death, but in order to share the glory of the future resurrection we must conform our lives to the heavenly man.[75] Consequently, those who belong to Christ must break with the old creation dominated by sin and resemble in their lives the mystery of the new Adam if they are to participate in the age to come.

In the third and last part (15:50-57), Paul concludes the entire argument on the bodily resurrection by means of the antithesis between "corruptible" (φθορᾷ) and "incorruptible" (ἀφθαρσίᾳ) (cf. 15:42b), and between and "mortal" (θνητόν) and "immortality" (ἀθανασία) (vv. 53-54; cf. 15:23-28). He describes this antithesis in terms of an eschatological event, when "we will all be transformed" (ἀλλαγησόμεθα) (15:51-52), and concludes with a *peroratio,* "Therefore, my beloved brothers, stand firm, immovable always" (15:58; cf. 15:1; 16:13-14).[76] The ethical tones of the antithesis between what is "corruptible" and "incorruptible" is found also in *2 Baruch,* which foretells "the end of that which is corruptible and the beginning of that which is incorruptible" (74:2; cf. 44:8-13).[77] Then, at the coming of the Anointed One "nobody will again die untimely, nor will any adversity take place suddenly" (73:3). The Sage explains that the wicked one who does not believe in the afterlife leads a dissolute life and consequently does not have a share in what is imperishable/immortal (ἀφθαρσίαν/ἀθανασία). Conversely, only the righteous who keep the commandments may share in the immortal/ incorruptible life (Wis 2:23-24; cf. Wis 1:15; 3:4; 6:18-19; 12:1; 18:4). It plausible that Paul was aware of Jewish interpretations of the story of the creation and fall, which often enough drew moral lessons. However, he emphasizes the eschatological dimension and exhorts believers to transform their lives according to the heavenly and incorruptible Adam in order to participate in the future immortality.

75. Paul urges the Corinthians "to conform to the life of the 'man of heaven' as those who now share his character and behavior" (Fee, *Corinthians,* 795).

76. Mitchell regards v. 58 as the ἐπίλογος of the entire letter (*Rhetoric of Reconciliation*, 290–91; likewise R. Collins, *First Corinthians,* 583). However, Paul continues to address his last question about the collection for the saints in 16:1-4, and further in vv. 5-12. Then Paul comes to his final exhortation in 16:13-14, 16 and gives his final greetings in 16:19-24. The "chiastic pattern" that R. Collins identifies in the first part (vv. 50-53) (*First Corinthians,* 573) is not so evident, for v. 54a still carries on the antithesis between perishable/mortal and imperishable/immortal, as well as the metaphor of "being clothed" (15:53-54a).

77. See earlier Philo, who suggests that the earthly man (γήϊνος) is corruptible (φθαρτῆς) *(Leg. All.* 1.31-32, 42, 53-55; 2.4; *Opif.* 134).

On the one hand, the expression "flesh and blood" (σὰρξ καὶ αἷμα) forms a synonymous parallel with "perishable" (φθορᾷ) (15:50).[78] "Flesh" looks back to the different kinds of flesh (σάρξ) found in the animated world, including men (v. 39), and "perishable" recalls the "perishable [body] that is sown" (v. 42b). Although "flesh and blood" here means primarily human vulnerability, elsewhere Paul also contrasts "flesh" and "spirit" as opposed desires or inclinations, κατὰ τοῦ πνεύματος/κατὰ τῆς σαρκός (Gal 5:16–17; Rom 7:14, 18; 8:3–11).[79] Thus, the synonymous parallel between "flesh and blood" and "perishable" conveys both what is physically perishable and what is morally corrupt (cf. Rom 8:7–8; Gal 3:3; 5:19–26; 6:1–6). On the other hand, "the kingdom of God" forms a synonymous parallel with "imperishable." The kingdom recalls the eschatological victory over death when Christ will hand over the kingdom of Christ to the Father in the end (15:24). More importantly, the inheritance in the kingdom of God conveys ethical overtones. Elsewhere Paul warns the believers that "the unrighteous will not inherit the kingdom of God" (1 Cor 6:9–10; cf. Gal 5:21; Rom 14:17), and he exhorts them to "lead a life worthy of God, who calls you into his own kingdom and glory" (1 Thess 2:12). Therefore, in order to participate in the eschatological and incorruptible kingdom and in immortality (ἀθανασία) (15:53–54; cf. 15:42b, 52b), believers are to transform their lives according to what is morally incorrupt; otherwise they cannot partake in the incorruptible kingdom of God.

Next Paul tells the Corinthians "a mystery" (μυστήριον), that is, the eschatological event, when "we will all be transformed" (ἀλλαγησόμεθα), the living and the dead (15:51–52).[80] This transformation resumes the contrast between the perishable and the imperishable (15:50–52; cf. 15:42), and implicitly between the earthly man and the heavenly man and their descendants (15:48–49). Earlier he explained that the hidden mystery of the wisdom of God was Jesus Christ crucified (1 Cor 2:1, 7; cf. Rom 11:25; 16:25),[81] of which he was servant and administrator (4:1–5). Paul explains with apocalyptic imagery that this eschatological transformation will take place suddenly (ἐν ἀτόμῳ, ἐν ῥιπῇ ὀφθαλμοῦ, 15:52), and the sound of "the last trumpet" will announce

78. According to R. Collins, "With this parallelism Paul has shifted from the language of Jewish apocalyptic to the language of Hellenistic philosophy and rhetoric" (*First Corinthians*, 579).

79. With Thiselton, *First Epistle*, 1291, contra Fee, who argues that "flesh and blood" "refers simply to the body in its present form . . . subject to weakness, decay, and death" (*Corinthians*, 799).

80. Note the textual variants in Fee, *Corinthians*, 796 n. 3; he appropriately opts for "We shall not all sleep, but we shall all be changed," with B and Maj. See also Thiselton, *First Epistle*, 1292–93.

81. As opposed to human wisdom (1 Cor 2:1–5). Furthermore, Paul praises love above the knowledge of human mysteries (1 Cor 13:3; 14:2).

God's judgment, and the dead will be "raised imperishable."[82] However, Paul introduces the metaphor of the clothing in order to illustrate both continuity and transformation and thus prevent a radical rupture between the present and the future, or between the higher and lower spheres.[83] This metaphor also suggests that the eschatological transformation requires the ethical transformation of both the individual and the community. Paul infers as a matter of necessity (δεῖ γάρ) that "this" (τοῦτο) perishable must clothe (ἐνδύσασθαι) itself with the imperishable, and "this" mortal must cloth itself (ἐνδύσασθαι) with immortality. "Once (ὅταν) this perishable has been clothed (ἐνδύσηται) with the imperishable, and this mortal has been clothed (ἐνδύσηται) with immortality, then (τότε) the saying that is written will come true" (vv. 53-54a; cf. vv. 37, 49). The fourfold "this" (τοῦτο) emphasizes the continuity between this corruptible and mortal body and this incorruptible and immortal body, which carries on the previous concept of transformation (vv. 52-53), and also the metaphor of the "naked seed" that is sown, which becomes "something else" (v. 37). Furthermore, the metaphor of "putting on clothing" (ἐνδύω), which was related earlier to the verb φορέω to express one's transformation into the likeness of his/her paradigm (v. 49), underlines again the need to be transformed into a new creation. Therefore, Paul directly relates the mystery of Christ's death and resurrection and the eschatological resurrection of the believers. On the one hand, this metaphor underlines the continuity between the perishable and imperishable body, so that, while we still bear the likeness of the first Adam, we are to bear also the likeness of the last Adam. On the other hand, it conveys the need of being transformed into or clothed in the new humankind after the paradigm of the last Adam, Christ.[84]

82. The apocalyptic features will accompany the coming of the Lord (1 Cor 15:51-52; 1 Thess 4:13-18); see R. Collins, *First Corinthians*, 574–75, 580–81; Fee, *Corinthians*, 800–802. Paul interprets metaphorically the sound of the last trumpet (ἐσχάτη σάλπιξ) used formerly to summon for battle (Jer 51:27; 1 Cor 14:8) but now to announce the coming of the Lord (cf. Zech 9:14) and the last judgment (cf. Joel 2:1; Matt 24:31; 1 Thess 4:16; Rev 8:2—9:14); see G. Friedrich, σάλπιγξ: *TDNT* 7:87; Fee, *Corinthians*, 801.

83. See Troels Engberg-Pedersen, "Complete and Incomplete Transformation in Paul: A Philosophical Reading of Paul on Body and Spirit," in Seim and Økland, *Metamorphosis*, 123–30. He argues that there is both continuity and a transformation of the individual; however, he speculates that "there is probably not much sense of individual subjectivity in the newly generated pneumatic body itself. For that body rather forms part of the *shared* pneumatic body that is Christ or, perhaps, God himself when God is everything in everything." In other words, "the pneumatic body . . . forms part of a pneumatic fellowship (*koinonia*)" (p. 129).

84. Jorunn Økland explains this transformation as "metamorphic" ("Genealogies of the Self," in Seim and Økland, *Metamorphoses*, 94).

Paul supports the metaphor of the clothing by conflating two scriptural passages that describe Christ's victory (τὸ νῖκος) over death: "Once (ὅταν) the perishable has been clothed with the imperishable . . . then (τότε) the saying that is written (ὁ λόγος ὁ γεγραμμένος) will come true" (vv. 54b–57; cf. 15:26). He cites Isa 25:8a and Hos 13:14b as a single passage (ὁ λόγος ὁ γεγραμμένος) by means of the catchwords "victory" and "death."[85] However, "victory" (τὸ νῖκος) is not found in the Septuagint in either of these Old Testament passages.[86] The future (γενήσεται) explains that, although Christ's resurrection has already occurred, the believers' victory over death will take place in the eschaton. Christ's victory over Death began with his resurrection and will be brought to completion only at the eschaton, at the resurrection of all who belong to him, the last Adam. Paul supplements Hosea's quotation, explaining that "the sting of death (τὸ δὲ κέντρον τοῦ θανάτου) is sin (ἡ ἁμαρτία) and the power of sin is the law (ὁ νόμος)" (15:56; cf. 15:21, 26). Given the allusions to Adam (15:21-22, 45-49), it is plausible that Paul and his audience also had in mind the story of the fall (Genesis 3). Although the narrative of Genesis 1–3 does not establish a direct link between Adam's transgression and his death, Hellenistic and apocalyptic Jewish interpretations of the story of the creation and fall of Adam often claim that Adam's disobedience brought death to him and his descendants (see Philo, *Opif.* 167-70; Wis 2:23-24; *L.A.B.* 13:8-9; *4 Ezra* 3:7; 7:48, 116-18; *2 Bar.* 17:2-4; 23:4-5; *L.A.E.* 14:1; also developed later by Paul in Rom 5:12-21).[87] Thus, Christ, in his death and resurrection defeated not only death but also its source, sin (cf. 1 Cor 15:3). More problematic is the relationship between sin and law. Raymond Collins argues that by "law" here Paul "refers generally to all human law."[88] Conversely, Gordon Fee claims that death "is the result of

85. This was a typical exegetical method called *gezera shawah* (Heil, *Rhetorical Role*, 247).

86. "Death has been swallowed up *in strength* (ἰσχύσας)" (LXX Isa 25:8a), and "Where, O Death, is your *punishment* (ἡ δίκη)? Where O Hades your sting (ποῦ τὸ κέντρον σου ᾅδη)? (LXX Hos 13:14b). It seems that behind Paul's κατεπόθη ὁ θάνατος εἰς νῖκος lies "a common tradition" as found in the Greek version of Theodotion and Aquila that read εἰς νῖκος instead of ἰσχύσας; see Heil, *Rhetorical Role,* 249. Heil notes, "Although the Theodosion version in uncial Q is identical to the Pauline version, it may be a later assimilation to 1 Cor 15:54b, especially since it occurs as a marginal gloss." Likewise, Paul changed Hosea's ἡ δίκη to τὸ νῖκος, and ᾅδη to θάνατε. See also Fee. *Corinthians,* 803–4; Thiselton, *First Epistle,* 1299–1301. Thiselton claims, "There is no evidence to suggest that these [passages] had been combined prior to Paul's use of them together" (p. 1299).

87. These interpretations do not waive human responsibility; rather they explain the origins of sin, human misfortunes, and death as an example of the consequences that disobedience to God's commands brings upon each individual and generation. Yet their message is also of encouragement and the hope of a new creation for those who abide by God's commands.

88. R. Collins, *First Corinthians,* 582.

the deadly poison, sin itself, which became all the more energized in our lives through acquaintance with the law."[89] Paul sees in the Mosaic Law not the cause of sin but an instrument that increases the awareness of sin, "Therefore no one will be declared righteous in his sight by observing the law; rather, through the law we become conscious of sin" (Rom 3:20; cf. 5:13, 20; 7:7-12).[90] Finally, Paul concludes praising God (τῷ δὲ θεῷ χάρις): "to the one who gives (τῷ διδόντι) us the victory (τὸ νῖκος) through our Lord Jesus Christ" (15:57; cf. 15:24-28). Although the victory is not complete for the believers yet, Christ's resurrection is the pledge for those who belong to him (cf. 15:20-28).

Paul concludes (ὥστε) this section and the entire chapter, exhorting believers to stand "firm, immovable (ἑδραῖοι, ἀμετακίνητοι), abounding (περισσεύοντες) in the work of the Lord always, knowing that your labor in the Lord is not in vain (οὐκ ἔστιν κενός)" (v. 58).[91] The "work of the Lord" (ἐν τῷ ἔργῳ τοῦ κυρίου) and "your labor" (ὁ κόπος ὑμῶν) refer primarily to the proclamation of the gospel. Thus, this exhortation evokes Paul's initial call to stand firm (ἑστήκατε and εἰ κατέχετε) in the gospel that he preached and they received (15:1-2; cf. 16:13). However, "your labor" may also refer to their daily activities, which should reflect their own faith (cf. 1 Thess 1:3).[92] Therefore, the believer's work, both their proclamation of the gospel and every action, is not in vain but have the assurance that Christ's resurrection will also be shared by those who belong to him. Ultimately, Christ's resurrection is the raison d' être of their faith and their very existence.

Summary

In 1 Corinthians 15, Paul addresses the crucial question of the resurrection of the dead. Apparently the lack of faith in the resurrection of the dead caused moral disorders among "some" who did not believe, and may have also caused divisions in the Christian community in Corinth (see 1 Cor 1:10; 11:18).

89. Fee, *Corinthians,* 806–7.

90. This controversial matter, found also in Galatians and Romans, lies beyond the scope of this study.

91. Watson claims, "This is the *peroratio* or conclusion for all of ch. 15. Like the *peroratio* of an entire work it recapitulates the main points of the argumentation of ch. 15 and arouses emotion. . . . In light of the resurrection and the continuity of the physical and spiritual bodies, their faith and Christian walk are not in vain" ("Paul's Rhetorical Strategy," 248).

92. Fee notes that "the work of the Lord" "may refer more broadly to whatever one does *as a Christian,* both toward outsiders and fellow believers; but along with the next word, 'labor,' Paul frequently uses it to refer to the actual ministry of the gospel" (*Corinthians,* 808). He cites 1 Cor 3:8-15; 9:1; 2 Cor 6:5; 10:15; 11:23; 1 Thess 3:5; 5:13; 2 Thess 3:8; 2 Tim 4:5. In 1 Cor 4:12 Paul describes his physical work, with his hands (κοπιῶμεν ἐργαζόμενοι ταῖς ἰδίαις χερσίν) to sustain himself while preaching the gospel.

Thus, Paul first recalls the Christian tradition of the resurrection of Christ from the dead, which they already have accepted (15:1–11). Then he introduces two Jewish traditions interpreting the story of the creation and fall of Adam that most likely the Corinthians knew. In the first passage (15:21-22), Paul introduces an apocalyptic tradition that attributes to Adam the beginning of sin and death (*L.A.B.* 13:8; 37:3; *L.A.E.* 7:1; 14:1; 21:5–6; *4 Ezra* 3:4–11; 7:116–18, 127–31; *2 Bar.* 17:2; 19:8; 56:5–10; cf. 54:14–15, 19). According to this tradition, Adam's sin brought death into the world, and those who follow his example would likewise face destruction and death. Yet the story of the creation and fall stands in contrast to the eschatological and new creation, which is promised to those who keep God's commands. In this context, some interpreters convey the need to keep God's commandments in order to attain an incorruptible life in the eschaton.

In the second passage (15:45–49), Paul introduces a tradition, represented by Philo, that distinguishes between the first and the second creation account of mankind.[93] Philo distinguishes between the man formed after the image of God, "an idea or type or seal; intelligible, incorporeal, neither male or female, by nature incorruptible (ἄφθαρτος φύσει)," and the man that is object of sense-perception "consisting of body and soul (ἐκ σώματος καὶ ψυχῆς), man or woman, by nature mortal (φύσει θνητός) (*Opif.* 134).[94] Since the composite man is "made up of earthly substance (γεώδους οὐσίας) and of divine breath (πνεύματος θείου)" (*Opif.* 135), he participates both in mortality and immortality. Philo claims that the Creator employed his own word (ἑαυτοῦ λόγῳ) as the pattern for the soul (ψυχή) or mind (διάνοια) of the first man, and breathed the divine breath (Gen 2:7) into his face (cf. *Opif.* 139). For Paul, however, the first man Adam "became a living being" (ἐγένετο εἰς ψυχὴν ζῶσαν), and "was of the dust of the earth" (ἐκ γῆς χοϊκός), whereas Christ is the second and last Adam, "a life-giving spirit" (εἰς πνεῦμα ζῳοποιοῦν), "from heaven" (ἐξ οὐρανοῦ) (1 Cor 15:44–47). Although Philo may have believed in some sort of eschatological reward,[95] he writes *De Opificio Mundi* so that, by keeping the Law, inscribed by God in the cosmos but revealed to Moses,

93. It has been argued before that Philo drew on and interpreted traditional material, especially on interpretations of Plato's *Timaeus*. Tobin argues, "Interpretations, then, of the creation of man as a double creation take over prior interpretations of Gen 1:27 and Gen 2:7 as complementary accounts of the creation of a single man and re-interpret them to refer to the creation of two different men, one heavenly and the other earthly [cf. *Opif.* 134-35, *L.A.* 1.31-32, and *Q.G.* 1.4]. Accounts of the double creation of man depend, then, on prior accounts of the single creation of man" (*Creation of Man*, 26–27).

94. However, earlier Philo described the first man as being mortal (θνητός) (*Opif.* 77), and earthborn and perishable (γηγενῶν καὶ φθαρτῶν) (*Opif.* 82).

and by leading a virtuous life, humankind may have a happy and blessed life (*Opif.* 2-3, 143, 170-72). Conversely, Paul's outlook is eminently eschatological, and he believes in an eschatological transformation "in the likeness of the man from heaven (φορέσομεν τὴν εἰκόνα τοῦ ἐπουρανίου) (1 Cor 15:49-52). This eschatological transformation, however, entails a transformation that Paul expresses in terms of being clothed with the imperishable (ἀφθαρσίαν) in order to attain immortality (ἀθανασίαν) (1 Cor 15:50-53; cf. Wis 2:23-24). Therefore, the first Adam represents what is corruptible (φθορά), which corrupts good character (ἤθη χρηστά) (15:33), and "cannot inherit the imperishable" (ἀφθαρσίαν) (15:50). On the other hand, the last Adam, Christ, represents what is "imperishable," and those who belong to him shall bear his likeness, that is, "shall we bear the likeness of the man from heaven (15:48-49). Yet they also must be "clothed with the imperishable" in order to be transformed in the eschatological resurrection of the dead (15:52-54).

In 1 Cor 15:21-22 and 45-49, Paul integrates these two Jewish traditions of the story of the creation and fall of Adam to illustrate the resurrection of Christ and believers and the impact that their faith should have in their lives in order for them to participate in the eschatological resurrection of the dead. Paul's appeal to these two different traditions shows how widespread these Jewish interpretations of the story of the creation and fall of humankind were. Although the interpretations explain the actual status of sin and the death of humankind, they convey also moral lessons and often exhort their audience to keep God's commandments. Paul introduces these traditions to illustrate the resurrection of Christ and believers. However, in this context he also conveys that believers should "stop sinning" (15:34) and be "clothed" with incorruption (15:52-53) in order to participate in the eschatological resurrection with Christ, the heavenly man.

The ethical implications that Paul draws from 1 Cor 15: 21-22 and 45-49 will be more explicit in Rom 5:12-21. In this passage, Paul will also lay the foundation for the new life in Christ that he explains in Romans 7 and 8.

95. See Thomas H. Tobin, "Philo and the Sibyl: Interpreting Philo's Eschatology," *Studia Philonica Annual* 9 (1997): 84–103. He argues that Philo proposed a nonsubversive eschatology "dependent on the observance of the Law and the practice of virtue by the Jewish nation," which the Gentiles could also share if they observe the Law and practice virtues (pp. 102–3).

Part 2: The Antithesis between Adam and Christ: Romans 5:12-21

Introduction

The interpretation of Rom 5:12-21 has been one of the most debated issues in theological and exegetical circles. As Paul did in 1 Corinthians 15, in this passage he carefully incorporates early traditions about Christ's expiatory death, as well as Jewish traditions that ascribed to Adam the beginning of sin and death. This passage occupies a crucial place within the larger literary context of the letter, which moves from the status of all humankind, Gentiles and Jews alike, under the wrath of God (1:18—3:20) to their new status in "this grace" because of Christ's faithfulness (see Rom 5:2). Since this grace is incompatible with sin, believers should die to sin and "walk" in the newness of life in the Spirit of the risen Lord (Romans 6). Romans 5:12-21 shows the transition from the state of sin and death of all humankind because of Adam's transgression to the state of grace and righteousness because of Christ's obedience. Yet its structure especially emphasizes God's grace, which exceeds all the more (πολλῷ μᾶλλον . . . ἐπερίσσευσεν) the effects of Adam's transgression on the many (5:15). Yet those who receive God's grace and righteousness will reign (βασιλεύσουσιν) in life through Jesus Christ in the eschaton (5:17-19). In the meantime, however, this grace initiates a transformation of believers: "So that . . . the grace also might reign (βασιλεύσῃ) through righteousness to eternal life through Jesus Christ" (5:21). Thus, this grace instills a transformation of believers, who should walk according to the newness of life (Romans 6), in the Spirit of the risen Lord (Romans 8).

Literary Context

Romans 5 occupies a central place within the letter, although its relationship with the previous and following sections is disputed.[96] Some scholars see this passage as the conclusion of the previous themes that describe the status of all humankind under the wrath of God, Gentiles and Jews alike, for all sinned as

96. For the different exegetical positions regarding the place of Romans 5 within the larger literary context, see Jean-Noël Aletti, *La lettera ai Romani e la giustizia di Dio* (Rome: Borla, 1997), 35-38; and Tobin, *Paul's Rhetoric*, 157 n. 4. See also Richard J. Erickson, "The Damned and the Justified in Romans 5.12-21: An Analysis of Semantic Structure," in *Discourse Analysis and the New Testament: Approaches and Results*, ed. Stanley E. Porter and Jeffry T. Reed (JSNTSup 170; Sheffield: Sheffield Academic Press, 1999), 282–307. Erickson describes Rom 5:12-21 as "the pivot point" of the entire letter, "In this comparison, the pith of the letter, are the grounds for the fears of libertinism which Paul addresses in the three chapters that follow 5.12-21" (pp. 306–7).

Adam sinned (1:18—3:20).[97] The "grace" that Christ's death and resurrection brought to all (5:1-11) may also evoke the righteousness by faith in Jesus Christ, stated in the *propositio* of the letter (1:16-17), and in the *subpropositio* of this section (5:1). It recalls the faith of Abraham, who believed "in him who raised Jesus our Lord from the dead, who was put to death for our trespasses and raised for our righteousness" (4:24-25). Other scholars identify Rom 5:12-21 as the introduction to the following themes of the superabundant gifts of grace and life brought by Christ's obedience, death, and resurrection, and the implications of standing in "this grace." [98] Thus, Paul exhorts believers to walk in the newness of life through their baptism, which inserts them into Christ's death and resurrection (Romans 6). Additionally, in order to dispel the concerns that some Christians in Rome may have had regarding Paul's standing regarding the Law, particularly the ethical elements of the Law (see Rom 5:13 and 20), Paul explains that the Law is not sin nor did it bring death, but that it is human weakness that leads us to sin and death (chapter 7).[99] Finally, in chapter 8 Paul

97. Ulrich Wilckens relates Romans 5 to the previous section: "tiene dispositivamente la función de una reflexión recopiladora de todo lo precedente y es, por consiguiente, el final y el vértice indiscutibles del raciocinio expuesto hasta ahora" (*La carta a los Romanos,* vol. 1, *Rom. 1–5* [Biblioteca de Estudios Bíblicos 61; Salamanca: Sígueme, 1997], 226; see also 348, 374–75). Simon J. Gathercole sees in Rom 5:11 "one of the points of conclusion in the literary structure of Romans," yet he also recognizes the difficulties in identifying the divisions, given the changes of "narrative mode, person, and number" (*Where Is the Boasting? Early Jewish Soteriology and Paul's Response in Romans 1–5* [Grand Rapids: Eerdmans, 2002], 255).

98. According to Tobin, Romans 5 introduces the larger section of chapters 6–7. He also notes that Rom 5:12-21 illustrates that "this grace in which we stand" (5:1) is incompatible with sin, which includes "all" Jews and Gentiles alike (5:12, 18), and serves "as the basis for his refutations of charges made against him that "this grace" leads to moral anarchy, which he explains in Romans 6–7 (*Paul's Rhetoric,* 186–87). Other scholars include chapter 8 as part of this introduction; see Fitzmyer, *Romans*, 98–99; Aletti (*La lettera ai Romani,* 39) regards Rom 5:20-21 as the *propositio* of chapters 6–8. See also Jean-Noël Aletti, "The Rhetoric of Romans 5–8," in *The Rhetorical Analysis of Scripture: Essays from the 1995 London Conference,* ed. Stanley E. Porter and Thomas H. Olbricht (JSNTSup 146; Sheffield: Sheffield Academic Press, 1997), 294–308. In this essay Aletti claims that the *synkrisis* between Adam and Christ (Rom 5:12-19) plays the role of *narratio,* which is developed by the *probatio* (chs. 6–8), which contrasts the "two types of humanity, the new one (those baptized in Christ) and the old one (those under the Law, unable to quit the orbit of sin)" (p. 304). See also Jean-Noël Aletti, "Romains 5,12-21," *Biblica* 78 (1997): 1–32. Brendan Byrne argues that "hope" "forms the main theme of the new section," specifically 5:1-11 and 8:31-39 (*Romans* [Sacra Pagina 6; Collegeville, Minn.: Liturgical Press, 1996], 163). See also Stanley E. Porter, "The Theoretical Justification for Application of Rhetorical Categories to Pauline Epistolary Literature," in Porter and Olbricht, *Rhetoric and the New Testament,* 100–122. Porter locates Romans 5 "within the dialogical flow of Romans 1–8 (p. 122).

99. Tobin explains that Paul meant to clarify some concepts he expressed in Galatians regarding the Law that eventually caused some concerns among some Christians in Rome (*Paul's Rhetoric,* 186–87).

explains that the Spirit of God "who raised Jesus from the dead," will also "give life to your mortal bodies" because it "dwells in you" (8:11).[100]

Therefore, the ethical significance of the antithesis between Adam and Christ is found especially within the wider argument of Romans 5–8, which presents the new status under the grace that Christ's death and resurrection brought to all. Furthermore, the antithesis between sin and death, on the one hand, and grace and life, on the other, lays the foundations of the new life in Christ for those who belong to Christ, as described in chapters 6–8. Thus, Adam and his descendants, despite the Law, sinned and consequently die, but those in Christ receive righteousness and life through the Spirit, and they must also walk according to the Spirit, and not according to the flesh.[101]

Internal Structure of Romans 5:12-21

This unit is introduced with the formula διὰ τοῦτο to contrast the status in which all humankind stood after Adam's transgression to the new status "in this grace," which Christ's death and resurrection brought to believers. The overall thrust of this unit is the comparison (ὥσπερ/ὡς and καὶ οὕτως) between Adam and Christ and the opposite effects that their actions brought upon all/the many.[102] This unit is also characterized by the third person singular represented in the main characters Adam and Christ (5:12-21), as opposed to the first person the plural in the previous unit (5:1-11), and then to the first person plural again (τί οὖν ἐροῦμεν;) in the following unit (6:1). The following structure could be outlined:[103]

100. Apparently Paul identifies the Spirit of God and the Spirit of Christ (8:9); see Scott Brodeur, *The Holy Spirit's Agency in the Resurrection of the Dead: An Exegetico-Theological Study of 1 Corinthians 15,44b-49 and Romans 8,9-13* (Tesi gregoriana, Serie teologia 14; Rome: Pontificia Università Gregoriana, 1996), especially 177–91. Accordingly "the hortatory point" is that "[t]o have the Spirit of Christ" means to give witness to the Spirit's presence by what one does" (p. 191).

101. See Christian Grappe, "Qui me délivrera de ce corps de mort? L'Esprit de vie! Romains 7,24 et 8,2 comme élements de typologie adamique," *Biblica* 83 (2002): 472–92. He claims that the figure of Adam runs through Romans 5–7, particularly in 7:7-25 and 8:2, as representative of the old self (6:6) and the of old creation, which are renewed by the spirit of life.

102. Christopher Forbes claims that, in Rom 5:12-21 and 1 Cor 15:35, Paul contrasted Adam and Christ by means of *synkrisis,* or "speech of comparison" ("Paul and Rhetorical Comparison," in *Paul in the Greco-Roman World: A Handbook,* ed. J. Paul Sampley [Harrisburg, Pa.: Trinity Press International, 2003], 134–71). See also R. Dean Anderson, *Ancient Rhetorical Theory and Paul* (Contributions to Biblical Exegesis and Theology; Kampen: Kok Pharos, 1996), 201-2; Aletti, "Rhetoric of Romans 5–8," 294–308; Byrne, *Romans*, 173, 178-182; Fitzmyer, *Romans*, 407–8. In Rom 5:6-21 T. Tobin identifies three types of Greco Roman arguments from comparison: "from the greater to the lesser in 5:9-10, from the lesser to the greater in 5:15-17, and between equals in [5]:18-21" (*Paul's Rhetoric,* 161; cf. 182–86).

A. The Coming of Death into the World through one Man's Sin (5:12-14)

- 1. Just as Sin and Death entered into the world through one man, likewise death came to all men because all sinned.
- 2. Before the Law sin was in the world, but sin is not taken into account without Law, and yet death reigned from Adam to Moses.

B. The Incomparability between the Trespass and the Gift (5:15-17)

- 1. The trespass is not like the gift, for God's grace overflows all the more.
- 2. The sin of one is not like the gift, for judgment came from condemnation of one, but from the many trespasses the gift brought righteousness.

3. If death reigned through the one man's transgression, how much more those who receive the abundance of grace and of the gift of righteousness will reign in life through the one man, Jesus Christ.

C. The Contrast between the *One* and the *Many* (5:18-19)

- 1. Just as through the transgression of one [man] all men incurred condemnation, likewise through the righteous act of one [man] all men came into righteousness of life.
- 2. For just as through the disobedience of the one man the many were made sinners, so also through the obedience of the one [man] the many will be made righteous.

D. The Incompatibility between the Trespass and God's Grace (5:20-21)

- 1. The Law came in so that the trespass might increase. But where sin increased, grace superabounded.
- 2. In order that, just as sin reigned in death, so also grace might reign through righteousness to bring eternal life through Jesus Christ our Lord.[104]

103. A tripartite structure is outlined also by Fitzmyer, *Romans*, 405; and Erickson, "Damned and the Justified," 288.

104. Cf. the ring that 5:21 (διὰ Ἰησοῦ Χριστοῦ τοῦ κυρίου ἡμῶν) forms with 5:1 (διὰ τοῦ κυρίου ἡμῶν Ἰησοῦ Χριστοῦ).

The New Status of Humankind after Christ's Righteousness

In order to illustrate the transformation Christ's expiatory death brought to all humankind (cf. Rom 3:25), Paul introduces the contrast between Adam and Christ and the opposite effects that their deeds brought to all/the many (Rom 5:12-21). Yet he claims that the effects of Christ's obedience are greater than those of Adam's disobedience. Additionally, he lays out a temporal contrast between the current effects of Adam's disobedience and Christ's righteousness upon the many, and the eschatological fulfillment of life (5:17) and righteousness (5:19) for those who receive God's grace. Thus, although "the many" already received God's grace through Christ's death and resurrection, they still await its fulfillment in the future. In the meantime, believers are to die to sin and to the old man (ὁ παλαιὸς ἄνθρωπος), and walk in the newness of life (καινότητι ζωῆς) by their participation in Christ's death and resurrection in their baptism (Romans 6). Therefore, the antithesis between Adam and Christ acquires its full significance within the larger context that describes the new status of the believers "in this grace" (5:2) and the exhortation to remain in this grace by dying to sin and walking in the newness of life.

As Paul did in 1 Corinthians 15, in this passage he integrates Christian traditions about Christ's death and resurrection, as well as Jewish interpretations of the story of the creation and the fall of Adam (Genesis 1–3), particularly those apocalyptic interpretations that ascribed to Adam the beginning of sin and death, as found in *4 Ezra* and *2 Baruch*, and also in *Liber Antiquitatum Biblicarum* and *Life of Adam and Eve*. Since Paul does not elaborate further on either of these traditions, it seems that these traditions already circulated at least among Christian communities in Corinth and in Rome.

The figure of Adam is explicitly mentioned also in 1 Tim 2:13-14 and Jude 14, but these texts date from a later time than Paul's letters, and they do not compare the figure of Adam with Christ and the consequences these figures passed on to future generations.[105] Thus, it seems that Paul drew on

105. 1 Timothy is considered by most scholars to be deutero-Pauline, dated ca. 80–90; see R. A. Wild, "The Pastoral Letters," *NJBC*, 897. The context is about instructions for men and women on how to behave during worship, and, according to Raymond E. Brown, these instructions were more specifically aimed at women, who were banned from teaching. Women were compared with Eve, who was formed second, after Adam, and then was deceived. See Brown, *Introduction to the New Testament* (New York: Doubleday, 1997), 651–56. Written probably ca. 90–100, Jude was intended to address the problems and errors caused by some intruders or the ungodly. After two sets of three examples where God punished the ungodly (vv. 5-10 and 11-13), the author introduces a Jewish tradition from *1 Enoch* 1:9 (cf. Gen 5:23-24). Besides these texts, the name of Adam also appears in Luke 3:18, but in the context of the genealogy of Jesus. In addition to the explicit mention of Adam, there is probably another allusion in Phil 2:2-11.

earlier Jewish traditions about the story of the fall that attributed to Adam's transgression the introduction of death to his descendants and on the Christian creed of Christ's expiatory death and resurrection.[106] Therefore, it is more likely that the contrast between Adam and Christ first found in 1 Cor 15:20-21 and now in Rom 5:12-21 is due to Paul himself.

The narrative of Genesis 3 describes the story of Adam's disobedience to God's commandment (Gen 2:16-17; 3:11, 17), but it does not mention that death was the result of his disobedience, let alone that sin and death passed to his descendants. As demonstrated above in chapter 2, there were Jewish traditions that ascribed to Adam's transgression the beginning of sin and death.[107] Thus, Pseudo-Philo claims that the *protoplastum*'s transgression brought death to all (*L.A.B.* 13:8; 37:3). Likewise, the *Life of Adam and Eve* explains that death was one of seventy plagues with which God punished Adam and Eve because they disobeyed his command (7:1) and forsook his covenant (8:2). Furthermore, Adam blames Eve for the destruction and wrath, that is, "death," that she brought to all (*L.A.E.* 14:1; cf. 21:5-6). *4 Ezra* also explains that Adam's transgression as well as those of subsequent generations brought death "for him and his descendants" (3:4-11). The author explains that their transgression was due to their "evil heart" or "root" (3:22-23, 27; 4:28-32; 7:92). Ezra claims that although Adam's sin was also that of his descendants (7:116-18), it was not the cause but the first of the transgressions of Israel and humankind (see *4 Ezra* 7:127-31). Finally, *2 Baruch* contrasts Adam's disobedience and the death that he brought to "those who were born of him" (*2 Bar.* 17:2; cf. 19:8; 56:5-10) with Moses' submission to God and the Law he brought to "the descendants of Jacob," who nonetheless followed after the example of Adam (*2 Bar.* 17:5; 19:1-3). Thus, despite the Law they did not keep God's commandments and died, "For although Adam sinned first and has brought death upon all who were not in his own time, yet each of them who has been born of him has prepared for himself the coming torment" (54:14-15). Therefore, "Adam is not the cause, except for himself, but each of us has become our own Adam" (54:19).

Although these authors interpret the story of the fall to explain the presence of sin and death in the world, their focus is again eminently eschatological. They envision a new creation and the vindication of the righteous. In this context, they often express an exhortation to keep God's commandments in

106. See Tobin, *Paul's Rhetoric,* 163, 177.

107. The Sage claims that death came into the world "through the envy of the devil; but those who have a share of it [envy] test it" (πειράζουσιν δὲ αὐτὸν οἱ τῆς ἐκείνου μερίδος ὄντες) (Wis 2:23-24).

order to have a share in the future restoration. Thus, *Liber Antiquitatum Biblicarum* anticipates that God will judge humankind and reward them according to their deeds (3:9-10; 19:12; 25:7). According to *Life of Adam and Eve*, after Adam pleads guilty and implores God's mercy, God assures him that he will raise him in the time of the resurrection and immortality forever "if you guard yourself from all evil" (28:4; cf. 10:2; 30:1; 41:3). In the same vein, *4 Ezra* envisions that the few righteous who defeat "their evil heart" will be saved in the eschaton because of God's mercy (6:35—9:25; 7:13-16, 92, 6:132—8:3; 8:37-40, 51-54). Finally, *2 Baruch* foresees that at "the coming of the Anointed One" the souls of the righteous "will enjoy themselves," and "the souls of the wicked will the more waste away" (30:1-5; cf. 40:1-4; 73:3), and there will be "the end of that which is corruptible and the beginning of that which is incorruptible" (74:2). Therefore, these authors interpret the story of the fall to explain the presence of sin and death in the world, but they also emphasize the judgment that will come at the eschaton. Thus, at the end the wicked will be punished and the righteous will be rewarded with life.

Paul was acquainted with these Adamic traditions, but his emphasis is not on Adam but on Christ. Furthermore, he underlines "the disparity" between the effects of the deeds of Adam and those of Christ: condemnation and death after Adam, and righteousness, life, and grace after Christ.[108] Thus, the effects of the grace brought by the obedience of the *one* man Jesus Christ "abounded" (ἐπερίσσευσεν, vv. 15, 20) much more (πολλῷ μᾶλλον, vv. 15, 17) upon the *many*, compared to the *one* transgression of the *one* man Adam.

The Coming of Death into the World through One Man's Sin: Romans 5:12-14

The formula διὰ τοῦτο (5:12) looks back to the previous passage, which describes the new status "in this grace" where we stand now after being justified through Christ's expiatory death (5:1-11; cf. 1:16-17).[109] Paul emphasizes this new status of grace by pointing out that, despite our condition as "weak" (ἀσθενῶν), "godless" (ἀσβεῶν) (5:6), "sinners" (ἁμαρτωλῶν) (5:8), and "enemies" (ἐχθροί) (5:10), God reconciled us through the death of his Son,

108. Karl Barth stresses the "essential disparity" between Adam and Christ: "Adam is subordinate, because he can only be the forerunner, the witness, the preliminary shadow and likeness, the *typos* (type) [v. 14] of the Christ who is to come," *Christ and Adam: Man and Humanity in Romans 5*, trans. T. A. Smail (New York: Collier, 1962), 72.

109. Paul also uses the same expression, διὰ τοῦτο, to connect the previous and the following thought in 1:26; 4:16; 13:6; and possibly 15:9, introducing a scriptural quotation.

and even more (πολλῷ μᾶλλον) we will saved (σωθησόμεθα) through his life in the eschaton (5:10). At this point Paul uses traditional material about the expiatory death of Christ but still needs to demonstrate that the status of humankind before Christ's death and resurrection was that of condemnation. Thus, in order to explain the status of humankind before Christ, Paul appeals to Jewish traditions that attributed to Adam the beginning of sin and death, which he contrasts to the gift of reconciliation that Christ's death and resurrection brought to all (cf. 1 Cor 15:21-22).

The terms of comparison in v. 12 initially are not evident, "just as (ὥσπερ) through one man (δι' ἑνὸς ἀνθρώπου) sin entered into the world, and through sin also death; likewise (καὶ οὕτως) death came to all men on the basis that (ἐφ' ᾧ) all sinned" (5:12). Some scholars notice the difficulty of the inverted order of καὶ οὕτως and contend that v. 12 is an anacoluthon (ὥσπερ δι' ἑνὸς . . .) that is not resumed until v. 18 (ὡς δι' ἑνος . . .).[110] However, καὶ οὕτως εἰς πάντας ἀνθρώπους ὁ θάνατος διῆλθεν is better understood as a consecutive clause that complements ὥσπερ δι' ἑνὸς ἀνθρώπου ἡ ἁμαστία/θάνατος εἰς τὸν κόσμον εἰσῆλθεν in the same v. 12.[111] The terms of comparison are (a) the sin (ἡ ἁμαστία) of one man (δι' ἑνὸς ἀνθρώπου) and (a′) the fact that all (πάντας) sinned (ἥμαρτον).[112] In the first case, sin represents an entity (ἡ ἁμαρτία), in the second case it is verbalized (ἥμαρτον). Thus, the focal point is the coming of death (ὁ θάνατος) (b) into the world (εἰς τὸν κόσμον) through one man's sin, and (b′) into all men (εἰς πάντας ἀνθρώπους) on the basis

110. See, among others, Rudolf Bultmann, "Adam and Christ According to Romans 5," in *Current Issues in New Testament Interpretation: Essays in Honor of Otto A. Piper*, ed. William Klassen and Graydon F. Snyder (London: SCM, 1962), 152; Wilckens, *La carta a los Romanos*, 1:375; Fitzmyer, *Romans*, 411. Nevertheless, vv. 18, 19, and 21 are three self-contained consecutive clauses, ὡς δι' ἑνὸς παραπτώματος . . . οὕτως καὶ δι' ἑνὸς διακιώματος . . . ὥσπερ γὰρ διὰ τῆς παρακοῆς τοῦ ἑνὸς ἀνθρώπου . . . οὕτως καὶ διὰ τῆς ὑπακοῆς τοῦ ἑνὸς . . . ὥσπερ ἐβασίλευσεν ἡ ἁμαρτία . . . οὕτως καὶ ἡ χάρις βασιλεύσῃ. . .
.

111. See Anne H. Groton, *From Alpha to Omega: A Beginning Course in Classical Greek* (Newburyport, Mass.: Focus Information Group, 1995), 205. Tobin also takes καὶ οὕτως as a consecutive clause of ὥσπερ in the same v. 12 (*Paul's Rhetoric*, 178).

112. See Richard H. Bell, "The Myth of Adam and the Myth of Christ in Romans 5.12-21," in *Paul, Luke and the Graeco-Roman World: Essays in Honour of A. J. M. Wedderburn*, ed. Alf Christophersen, Cart Claussen, Jörg Frey, and Bruce Longenecker (JSNTSup 217; Sheffield: Sheffield Academic Press, 2002), 21–36. Bell claims that in Rom 5:12-21 "Paul believes that all human beings participate in Adam's sin and in Christ's 'righteous act'. . . . Understanding the Adam-myth in terms of identical repetition solves the seemingly intractable problem of competing causality in regard to sin. . . . This pattern of identical repetition break down, however, in the Christ-myth" (p. 36). Nevertheless, Paul clearly affirms the uniqueness of Adam's trespass (5:14b, 15, 17-19).

that (ἐφ' ᾧ) all (πάντες) sinned (ἥμαρτον), where the one man's sin is co-related (ὥσπερ/καὶ οὕτως) to the sinning of all men resulting in the coming of death into the world/all. The correlation between the one man's sin and the fact that all sinned depends on how ἐφ' ᾧ is interpreted, either as a relative or as a consecutive clause.[113] According to the context, it seems that it is better understood as a relative clause, "on the basis that all sinned," or "because all sinned" "death came to all men."[114] Thus, Paul regards both Adam's sin and the sinning of all as the reason for the coming of "death" into the world/all. Yet, later on Paul underscores the significance of Adam's transgression, for "through the disobedience of the one man the many were made sinners" (v. 19a), setting off a series of further sinning that brings death into the world. In this way, although both Adam's sin and the sin of each one and of every generation bring death into the world, Adam's disobedience occupies a prominent place as the first transgression in the process of further sinning and death in the world.

In vv. 13–14, Paul introduces a digression in which he sketches out an age "before the Law" (ἄχρι νόμου), from the time of Adam to Moses (ἀπὸ Ἀδὰμ μέχρι Μωϋσέως), and another age from Moses to "the one to come" (μέλλοντος) (cf. Rom 5:20a; Gal 3:19) to explain the presence of sin and death in the world. Thus, in the age when there was no Law, "sin was in the world." Paul had already argued that "all sinned" (5:12b), Gentiles and Jews alike, whether the Jews against the precepts explicitly stated in the Law, or the Gentiles against nature (Rom 2:12–15; 3:9–10). Then, despite the Jewish axiom that "sin is not taken into account (ἐλλογεῖται) while there is no Law (νόμου)" (5:13b),[115] it is a fact that "death ruled (ἐβασίλευσεν ὁ θάνατος) from Adam until Moses, even over those who did not sin in the likeness (ἐπὶ τῷ ὁμοιώματι) of Adam's trespass" (5:14). Paul may have in view Adam's trespass (παράβασις, cf. 5:15, 17–19) as the specific transgression of God's command not to eat from the tree (Gen 2:16–17; 3:11, 17). Nevertheless, despite the distinction between Adam's sin and the sinning of those after Adam, the end result was the same, death. Thus, Paul shows that the Law was ineffective to prevent sin and death from

113. Fitzmyer discusses at length scholarly interpretations of ἐφ' ᾧ and concludes that it is better understood as a "consecutive conjunction," expressing "a result": "The primary causality for its sinful and mortal condition is ascribed to Adam, no matter what meaning is assigned to ἐφ' ᾧ, and a secondary causality to the sins of all human beings" (*Romans,* 413–17).

114. See Aletti, "Romains 5,12–21," 15–16. He regards ἐφ' ᾧ as a relative, "sur la base de quoi." See also Erickson, "Damned and the Justified," 303–4.

115. Cf. οὗ δὲ οὐκ ἔστιν νόμος οὐδὲ παράβασις (Rom 4:15b), and διὰ γὰρ νόμου ἐπίγνωσις ἁμαρτίας (Rom 3:20). These expressions presuppose "the Jewish conception of heavenly books in which human deeds were recorded" (Fitzmyer, *Romans,* 417). For the "heavenly books" Byrne cites *1 Enoch* 104:7; *Jub.* 30:19–23; *T. Benj.* 11:4; *2 Apoc. Bar.* 24:1 (*Romans,* 184).

ruling over humankind; furthermore, he claims later that "the Law was added so that the trespass (τὸ παράπτωμα) might increase" (5:20a). Finally, Paul declares that Adam is the "type of the one who was to come" (τόπος τοῦ μέλλοντος). In terms of "type" and "antitype," both Adam and Christ are heads of the old and new humankind respectively, with the antithetic features that Paul describes below. "The one who was to come" is identified with the coming of the Messiah, who brings to an end (τέλος) the Law (Rom 10:4; cf. Gal 3:24). Then, at his parousia he will judge the righteous and the wicked and will destroy death itself.[116] Therefore, the age "from Adam to Moses" has come to its end, and the eschatological times have already begun in Christ.[117]

The Incomparability between the Trespass and the Gift: Romans 5:15-17

In order to clarify that the antithesis between the "type" Adam and the "antitype" "Christ" is not between equal terms, Paul now contrasts the one man's transgression and wrongdoing and the one man Jesus Christ's grace and gift. He also contrasts the effects of their deeds upon the many: judgment, condemnation, and death, on the one hand, and righteousness and life, on the other. Furthermore, by means of the comparison "from the lesser to the greater" he underscores the greater effects (πολλῷ μᾶλλον) of the one man Christ and his righteous act upon the many (5:15d, 17b; cf. 5:9, 10).[118]

The conjunction "but" (ἀλλά) introduces a double asymmetrical comparison (οὐχ ὡς . . . οὕτως καί): "the transgression (παράπτωμα) is not like the grace (χάρισμα) (v. 15a); and the wrongdoing of one man (δι' ἑνὸς ἁμαρτήσαντος) is not like the gift (δώρημα) (v. 16a).[119] The contrast between παράπτωμα and χάρισμα is intended to reflect a wordplay with the suffix -μα.[120] Both statements are followed by an explanation why the transgression and grace are asymmetrical (οὐχ ὡς . . . οὕτως καί).[121] On the one hand, the transgression of one (τῷ τοῦ ἑνὸς παραπτώατι) (v. 15b), and the judgment

116. Cf. 1 Cor 15:23-26; 2 Tim 4:1; *2 Bar.* 21:3; 23:5. Jesus Christ is also portrayed as the one "who is to come to judge the living and the dead" (τοῦ μέλλοντος κρίνειν ζῶντας καὶ νεκρούς) (2 Tim 4:1).

117. Fitzmyer claims that, although the title "Adam of the *Eschaton*" does not appear in Romans, but only in 1 Cor 15:45, this title is implicit in "the type of the one who was to come" (Rom 5:14) (*Romans*, 418).

118. A "speech of comparison," or *synkrisis,* is identified in the overall structure of Rom 5:12-21; see Forbes, "Paul and Rhetorical Comparison," 134–71; R. D. Anderson, *Ancient Rhetorical Theory*, 201-2; Aletti, "Rhetoric of Romans 5-8," 294–308. Nevertheless, this specific comparison runs "from the lesser to the greater" or "a minori ad maius"; see Fitzmyer, *Romans,* 419; Tobin, *Paul's Rhetoric,* 161.

119. The second οὕτως καὶ, in v. 16a, is implied.

120. Cf. also τὸ δώρημα, κρίμα, κατάκριμα, χάρισμα, and δικαίωμα (vv. 16-18, 20).

of one (κρίμα ἐξ ἑνός) (v. 16b) resulted in the death of the many (οἱ πολλοὶ ἀπέθανον) (v. 15c; cf. 1 Cor 15:21b), and in condemnation (εἰς κατάκριμα) (v. 16c). On the other hand, God's grace (χάρις) and the gift (δωρεά) in the grace of the one man (ἐν χάριτι τῇ τοῦ ἑνὸς ἀνθρώπου) Jesus Christ abounded (ἐπερίσσευσεν) much more (πολλῷ μᾶλλον) for the many (εἰς τοὺς πολλούς) (v. 15d). Furthermore, out of many transgressions (ἐκ πολλῶν παραπτωμάτων) grace (χάρισμα) resulted in righteousness (εἰς δικαίωμα) (v. 16c).

In v. 17, the argument progresses "from the lesser to the greater" to demonstrate that, "if by the trespass of the one man death reigned through one man, how much more (πολλῷ μᾶλλον) will those who receive the abundance of grace and the gift of righteousness through the one man Jesus Christ reign in life" (v. 17). Paul had established earlier too that, if while we were still sinners, weak, and God's enemies we were made righteous (δικαιωθέντες) and reconciled (κατηλλάγημεν) in Christ's death, "how much more" (πολλῷ μᾶλλον) we will be saved (σωθησόμεθα) in Christ's life (Rom 5:8–10).[122] However, the contrast here is between death (ὁ θάνατος) and those who receive (λαμβάνοντες) God's grace. Thus, death represents an entity that in the past ruled (ἐβασίλευσεν) through Adam's trespass, but those who receive God's abundant grace will reign in the eschatological life (ἐν ζωῇ βασιλεύσουσιν), that is, eternal life (εἰς ζωὴν αἰώνιον) through Jesus Christ (5:21), and will be saved (σωθησόμεθα) (cf. Rom 5:9; 1 Cor 15:22). Therefore, Christ's expiatory death put an end to the reign of death and brought the many into the new status of grace (χάρις). Yet, in order that God's grace may reign (βασιλεύσῃ) in the eschatological life (5:21), believers are to remain in God's grace, that is, are to die to sin and walk in the newness of life (cf. Rom 6:1–4).

121. *Pace* Chrys C. Caragounis, "Romans 5.15-16 in the Context of 5.12-21: Contrast or Comparison?" *NTS* 31 (1985): 142–48. He interprets vv. 15a and 16a as rhetorical questions that expect an affirmative answer, *But does not the free gift operate just like the trespass did?* (v. 15a); *And is not the free gift transmitted in the same way as sin was transmitted by the one who sinned?* (v. 16a) (p. 145). However, the essential point that Paul emphasizes is precisely the difference between the trespass and the grace; furthermore, that God's grace and its effect on the many surpass all the more the one trespass of the one man Adam. In the same way, Aletti ("Romains 5,12-21," 8) criticizes Porter ("The Argument of Romans 5: Can a Rhetorical Question Make a Difference?" *JBL* 110 [1991]: 655–77) and notices that Porter follows and modifies Caragounis's hypothesis: "Au niveau sémantique l'interpretation de Porter se voit aussi infirmée. Car, en ces vv. 15-17, les différences l'emportent sur les resemblances."

122. Bultmann ("Adam and Christ According to Romans 5," 157) sorts out the difficulty of the meaning of ἐκ πολλῶν παραπτωμάτων (v. 16), explaining that, while "[i]n the line of Adam one transgression stands in the beginning, at the beginning of the line of Christ stand many transgressions."

The Contrast between the One and the Many: Romans 5:18-19

In the previous section, Paul explained why the transgression and wrongdoing were not like the gift, and he emphasized the greater impact of the abundance of the gift (πολλῷ μᾶλλον . . . τὴν περισσείαν τῆς χάριτος . . . ἐπερίσσευσεν) over against the trespass (5:15-17). In this section he infers (ἄρα οὖν) two sets of antitheses. First, between the one transgression (δι' ἑνὸς παραπτώματος) that leads into condemnation (ἐις κατάκριμα) and the one act of righteousness (δι' ἑνὸς δικαιώματος) that leads into righteousness of life (ἐις δικαίωσιν ζωῆς) for all men (εἰς πάντας ἀνθρώπους) (5:18; cf. 5:16). Second, between the many (οἱ πολλοί) who were made sinners (ἁμαρτολοὶ κατεστάθησαν) through the disobedience of the one man, and the many (οἱ πολλοί) who will be made righteous (δίκαιοι καταστα θήσονται) through the obedience of one (5:19).

The first comparison establishes that just as (ὡς) one act of transgression (δι' ἑνὸς παραπτώματος) led into condemnation for all men (εἰς πάντας ἀνθρώπους), likewise (οὕτως καί) the one act of righteousness (δι' ἑνὸς δικαιώματος) will lead into righteousness of life for all men (εἰς πάντας ἀνθρώπους) (v. 18). In this comparison, the verb is implied and its tense may be deduced from its immediate context, which sets a temporal contrast between the past kingship of death (ἐβασίλευσεν) and the future reign in life (ἐν ζωῇ βασιλεύσουσιν) of those who receive God's abundant grace (v. 17), and between the many who were made (κατεστάθησαν) sinners and the many who will be made (κατασταθήσονται) righteous (v. 19). The second comparison (ὥσπερ . . . οὕτως καὶ) is between the many (οἱ πολλοί) who were made sinners (ἁμαρτωλοί) through the disobedience of the one man (διὰ τῆς παρακοῆς τοῦ ἑνὸς ἀνθρώπου), and the many (οἱ πολλοί) who will be made righteous (δίκαιοι) through the obedience of the one man (ὑπακοῆς τοῦ ἑνός) (v. 19). The passive form and the tense of κατεστάθησαν and κατασταθήσονται demonstrates that, whereas through Adam's disobedience "the many" were made sinners, through Christ's obedience "the many" will be made righteous.

On the one hand, the "one transgression" and disobedience of the "one man" refers to Adam's specific act of disobedience to God's command (Gen 2:16-17; 3:11, 17), which made "the many" sinners and resulted in condemnation (κατάκριμα) for all men, that is, death (cf. 5:16, 18).[123] Yet, since the sentence of death upon all men is a tradition not explicitly found in the biblical narrative of Genesis, Paul may again have relied on Jewish

123. Transgression (παραπτώματος) and disobedience (παρακοῆς) are synonyms along with sin (ἁμαρτία) and trespass (παράβασις).

interpretations that ascribed to Adam the beginning of death upon all (see above). On the other hand, the one act of righteousness (δικαιώματος) and obedience of the "one man" evidently refers to Christ's expiatory death, which is God's surpassing gift of grace that made "the many" righteous and gave them righteousness of life. Furthermore, the verbs lay out a tension between the past dominion of death over the many that was overcome with the coming of the Messiah, in his death and resurrection, and the future participation of the believers in the new life brought in the gift of Jesus Christ.

The Incompatibility between the Trespass and God's Grace: Romans 5:20-21

In the last section, Paul contrasts again sin (ἁμαρτία) and God's grace (χάρις) (cf. 5:15–17), but now in relation to the Law. Earlier he had argued that sin was in the world before the historical marker of the Law and that the Law was ineffectual to prevent death from reigning in the world (Rom 5:13–14). In Gal 3:10, Paul realizes that the Law was not simply ineffective but that it actually brought under its curse those who do not keep it (cf. Deut 27:26). He explains that the Law "was added (προσετέθη) because of transgressions (παραβάσεων)," and portrays the Law as a custodian (παιδαγωγός) who was necessary until the coming of the seed (τὸ σπέρμα) Christ, in whom all are justified and are made sons of God "through faith" (Gal 3:19–24).

In the context of Romans, Paul admits that "the Law slipped in (παρεισῆλθεν) so that the transgression (παράπτωματα) may increase (πλεονάσῃ) (Rom 5:20a). Earlier he declares that "through the Law we [the Jews] became conscious of sin" (ἐπίγνωσις ἁμαρτία) (2:20). Furthermore, "the Law brings about wrath (ὀργὴν κατεργάζεται); for where there is no Law, there is no trespass" (4:15). Later he explains this apparent oxymoron arguing that knowledge of sin came through the Law (διὰ νόμου), which aroused covetousness (ἐπιθυμία) and brought death (Rom 7:7–13; cf. 3:20).[124] However, in Rom 5:20a the Law has the explicit purpose (ἵνα) of increasing the trespass, making it accountable (cf. Rom 5:13b), and bringing judgment and condemnation (cf. 5:16). Nevertheless, in this context the contrast is not between the Law and God's grace, but between sin and grace, so that "where sin increased (ἐπλεόνασεν) grace super-abounded (ὑπερεπερίσσευσεν)" (Rom 5:20b; cf. 5:15–17). This clause is closely related to the following comparison

124. The author of *Life of Adam and Eve* explains that covetousness led Adam and Eve to eat of the fruit, which started the beginning of sin. After the fall, they realize their nakedness and lose their glory and righteousness (*L.A.E.* 20:1—21:6). Josephus interprets the opening of Adam and Eve's eyes and their awareness of their nakedness (Gen 3:5–11) as an awareness (συνειδώς) of their crime (*Ant.* 1.45).

between sin and grace, "in order that (ἵνα) just as (ὥσπερ) sin reigned with death (ἐν τῷ θανάτῳ), so also (οὕτως καὶ) grace may reign through righteousness to eternal life through Jesus Christ our Lord" (5:21). Thus, the Law has a subordinate function with regard to God's grace, so that by increasing sin, either literally or by increasing the awareness of sin, the Law makes even more apparent the superabundance of God's grace. Sin "increased" not only in Israel, but actually in the world, for all sinned, Jews and Gentiles alike, a point well established already in the first three chapters of the letter, whereas grace "super-abounded" for "the many."[125] Although Paul omits the names of Adam and Christ, it is evident that they stand behind sin and grace respectively as representatives of the entire human race.

Finally, Paul portrays sin and death as personified powers who reigned over humankind until the Christ-event.[126] Thus, sin and death reigned (ἐβασίλευσεν) over humankind for a period of time through one man's transgression (διὰ τοῦ ἑνός) (cf. 5:14a, 17, 21), but their reign came to an end with the coming of God's grace through the one man (τοῦ ἑνὸς ἀνθρώπου) Jesus Christ (cf. 5:15). Then, those who receive "the abundance of the grace and the gift of righteousness will reign in life (ἐν ζωῇ βασιλεύσουσιν) through the one man Jesus Christ" (5:17),[127] "so that just as sin reigned (ἐβασίλευσεν) with death, grace may reign (βασιλεύσῃ) through righteousness (διὰ δικαιοσύνης) to eternal life (εἰς ζωὴν αἰώνιον) through Jesus Christ our Lord" (διὰ Ἰησοῦ Χριστοῦ τοῦ κυρίου ἡμῶν) (5:21; cf. 6:23). This final clause encircles the entire chapter 5 about "this grace" in which we stand after "we have been justified (δικαιωθέντες) through our Lord Jesus Christ" (διὰ τοῦ κυρίου ἡμῶν Ἰησοῦ Χριστοῦ) (5:1). As "Lord," Jesus Christ has put an end to sin and death and has brought eternal life to the many through his righteousness (5:21; cf. 1:4-7).

Although Adam is not mentioned anymore after this passage, the themes of sin, death, grace, and the Law, continue well into chapters 6–8.[128] First, in chapter 6 Paul relates the experience of baptism to the transformation that believers should undergo, from death into new life. In order to remain in this

125. *Pace* Byrne (*Romans,* 182), who claims that sin increased in Israel through the operation of the law; where God's grace superabounded "in the person and work of Israel's Messiah." However, grace superabounded not only for Israel but for "the many," that is, all humankind.

126. See Fitzmyer, *Romans,* 422, who also includes *Nomos.*

127. More precisely, his one act of righteousness (δι' ἑνὸς δικαιώματος) resulted in righteousness of life (εἰς δικαίωσιν) for all men (5:18).

128. Aletti ("Romains 5,12-21," 28–30) regards Rom 5:20-21 as the *propositio* that is explained in the *probatio* in Romans 6–8. In addition to the themes of sin, death, grace, and the Law that I mention, he also identifies the terms "abound" (5:15, 17, 20; 6:1), "reign" (5:14, 17, 21; 6:12), and "(eternal) life" (5:17, 18, 21; 6:4, 22, 23; 7:10; 8:2, 6, 10, 38).

grace Paul exhorts them to consider themselves "dead to sin but alive to God in Christ Jesus; consequently, do not let sin reign (μὴ βασιλευέτω) in your mortal body so that you obey its evil desires" (6:11-12). Thus, if we are dead to sin, "sin does not rule (οὐ κυριεύσει) over you; for you are not under the Law but under grace" (6:14). Second, in Romans 7 Paul explains and clarifies the place and function of the Law (cf. Rom 5:13, 20). Thus, although the Law is not sin, knowledge of sin and covetousness came through the Law (Rom 7:7-13). Third, Paul introduces a new law, "the law of the Spirit of life," which "set me free from the law of sin and death through Christ Jesus." Paul concludes that, "if by the Spirit you put to death the deeds of the body (πράξεις τοῦ σώματος), you will live, because those who are led by the Spirit of God are sons of God" (Rom 8:13-14). Therefore, the age of sin and death that ruled the Adamic generation and the age of the Law, which increased sin in the world, came to an end in the coming of Christ, whose death and resurrection brought us God's grace and assured us of the eschatological life in a new creation.

Summary

The proper interpretation of the Adam typology in Rom 5:12-21 and its ethical implications are better explained within the larger literary context of Romans 1–8. The passage represents a watershed in the argumentative flow between the state of sin of all humankind, Gentiles and Jews alike (chapters 1–3), and the state of righteousness by faith through Jesus Christ's death and resurrection, which introduced believers into this grace, hope, and peace (5:1-11). Believers must remain in this grace by their effective participation in Jesus Christ's death and resurrection through their baptism; that is, they are to die to sin and rise to the newness of life (Romans 6). Thus, with the coming of the Messiah, believers are no longer under the Law, which increased sin (Romans 7), but under the law of the Spirit of life (Romans 8).

In order to illustrate this transformation from sin and death to grace and life, Paul introduces the antithesis between Adam and Christ as heads of all humankind. He integrates two sets of traditions accepted by the Christian community: first, the creedal formula that proclaimed Christ's expiatory death and resurrection; and, second, a Jewish tradition that ascribed to Adam the beginning of sin and death in the world. As other Jewish authors did, Paul interpreted the story of the fall to explain the broken status of Israel and of the entire humankind, whereas the Christian *kerygma* proclaimed the redemption of all humankind through Christ's righteousness.

Paul carried on this contrast between Adam and Christ and their opposite deeds by means of a comparison in which he emphasizes the greater effects of

Christ's righteous act over against Adam's disobedience. In the fashion of other apocalyptic interpreters, Paul anticipated an eschatological and incorruptible creation for the righteous in opposition to the old and perishable creation represented by Adam. However, for Paul, this new creation has already been inaugurated in the coming of Jesus Christ, in his death and resurrection. Although believers have already been made righteous and are in God's grace through Jesus Christ, those who receive this grace will reign in life (ἐν ζωῇ βασιλεύσουσιν) through Jesus Christ (5:17). Thus, for believers the contrast lies between their past status as sinners (ἁμαρτωλοὶ κατεστάθησαν) and their future status as righteous (δίκαιοι κατασταθήσονται) (5:19), "so that just as sin reigned (ἐβασίλευσεν) in death, so also grace may reign (βασιλεύσῃ) through righteousness to bring eternal life through Jesus Christ our Lord" (5:21). In other words, although the new creation has already been inaugurated in Christ's righteous act, and has been granted to believers, their participation in eternal life (εἰς ζωὴν αἰώνιον) is still to come.

This eschatological tension gives Paul an opportunity to exhort believers to remain in this grace, to die to sin and walk in the newness of life (ἐν καινότητι ζωῆς περιπατήσωμεν) (6:2-4) in order to attain eternal life. Thus, from the passive form expressed mostly in the third person (Rom 5:12-21), Paul turns to direct discourse, in which he interprets the experience of baptism as being dead to sin but alive to God in Jesus Christ. In other words, the new creation and life are incompatible with sin, and consequently the process of transformation already inaugurated in Christ should be appropriated and expressed by believers in order for them to have a share in the eschatological, incorruptible, and eternal life. This new life is attained apart from the Law (Romans 7) and is empowered by the Spirit of life (Romans 8). Therefore, the antithesis between Adam and Christ does not simply explain the status of believers in this grace attained through Christ's righteousness but also conveys that they are to receive that grace and remain in that grace by dying to the old creation represented in Adam and by waking in the newness of life inaugurated in Christ. Whereas Adam represents the old creation dominated by sin and death, Christ inaugurates the eschatological and new creation where grace and eternal life are offered to believers. They in turn are to receive this grace and stand firm in it in order to attain eternal and incorruptible life.

4

Conclusion

The Adam and Christ antithesis in Rom 5:12-21 and 1 Cor 15:21-22, 45-49 occupies a crucial place in Paul's theology. This antithesis in Romans represents the watershed between the status in sin and death of humankind that came in Adam's transgression, and the new status of all in grace and eternal life brought through Christ's death and resurrection. In 1 Corinthians 15, Paul arrives at the climax of his letter and reminds the audience that faith in the resurrection of the dead has an ethical impact on the lives of believers. In these passages, Paul reflects contemporary Jewish interpretations of the story of the creation of humanity and of the fall that explain the beginning of sin and death in the world and, in some cases, anticipate a new and eschatological creation. Within this framework, these authors draw ethical implications that require keeping God's commandments in order to attain happiness and bliss in this life and/or in the eschaton.

Paul's interpretation of the story of Adam reflects some of these features, but he uniquely explains that the new creation has already been inaugurated in Christ's death and resurrection and that a moral transformation of believers is achieved by their participation in Christ's Spirit. Thus, he contrasts Adam as the representative of the old creation dominated by sin and death, and Christ as both the representative and agent of the new creation, who with his death and resurrection has inaugurated the eschatological times and has brought grace and eternal life to all. In Romans, Paul conveys that, in order to participate in the new creation, believers should undergo a moral transformation from sin into righteousness (Rom 5:12-21), and they should walk in the newness of life, dying to sin and living to God in Jesus Christ (Rom 6:4-14). In 1 Corinthians, Paul also exhorts the audience to stop sinning and "put on the imperishable" (1 Cor 15:34, 53). Furthermore, Paul contrasts the "already" of the new creation inaugurated in Christ's death and resurrection and the "not yet" for believers, who will not participate in Christ's resurrection until the eschatological times.

Therefore, the eschatological transformation should be preceded by a moral transformation according to the image of the heavenly Adam, Christ.

The figure of Adam appears in numerous Jewish documents between 200 b.c.e. and 100 c.e.[1] The documents selected in this study demonstrate how the interpretation of the story of the creation of humanity and of the fall during this time was prevalent, and how their authors most of the time inferred ethical implications from this story. Although Jewish authors seem to be aware of some of the inconsistencies of the story of Genesis 1–3, they read it not as two creation accounts but as a continuous narrative that describes the origins of Israel and of humankind, and they see in Adam a paradoxical paradigm of human freedom and responsibility, magnificence and weakness. On the one hand, they often see in the man, made after the image of God, the human attributes of the soul. On the other hand, they see in the earthly man human weakness, bound back to earth. They relate the earthly man Adam to the story of the garden and the fall, who suffered the consequences for disobeying God's command. Furthermore, Jewish authors turn to the story of Genesis 1–3 not simply to explain the origins of Israel and of humankind and their turmoil, but also to instill an ethical and social transformation. They saw in Adam not only the ancestor of Israel but also the archetype of humankind; and in his transgression and punishment they identify their own transgressions and sufferings for disobeying God's commands. Thus, in this context they typically convey the need to keep God's commands to prevent annihilation and to enjoy bliss and happiness in this life. The problem arises when they see that, despite their apparent faithfulness, Israel and the righteous still suffer. Consequently, some interpreters respond that the righteous will be rewarded and the wicked will be punished in the eschaton.

The ten interpretations treated in this study were classified in three groups, Hellenistic interpretations, "Rewritten Bible," and apocalyptic interpretations. They were classified according to their main trends of interpretation, although a clear and definitive distinction is unfeasible, for they all cope with the pressing questions of freedom and human responsibility and often convey ethical implications. For the first group, Sirach, Wisdom, and Philo, Adam is not simply the ancestor of Israel but also the paradigm of all humankind. These writings typically substitute the name "Adam" for "man." They regard the "image of God" (Gen 1:26-27) and the "breath of life" (Gen 2:7) as the human soul and the locus of the intellectual abilities that make man capable of distinguishing between what is good and bad, and what makes him or her responsible for his or her actions. On the other hand, they regard the earthly

1. The figure of Adam appears also in the Dead Sea Scrolls; see below.

man as bound back to earth, that is, mortal by nature. The story of the fall serves as an example of Israel's disobedience to God's commands and human wickedness that leads to misfortune and untimely death. Conversely, the authors of these works suggest that a virtuous life would bring happiness and bliss in this life. Nevertheless, each author underlines certain aspects of the story of the creation of humanity and the fall. For instance, the author of Sirach regards Adam as a representative of all humankind (15:14).[2] Made out of the ground (33:10), man is mortal by nature (17:30; 18:9; 37:25; 40:1-11; 41:3-4), although the wicked may also experience death as punishment for their own evil deeds (40:8-10). Sirach interprets "the image of God" (Gen 1:27) as the διαβούλιον or "deliberation" (cf. Sir 17:6-9; 15-20) that makes humankind free and capable of self-determination. Since humankind fails to attain God's wisdom, God gave wisdom to Israel in the Torah (17:15-20; 24:23-28). Although Sirach ascribes to the "woman" "the beginning of sin" and death (Sir 25:24), the context here refers to the wicked woman (25:13-26) in contrast to the virtuous wife (26:1-18). The author also divides humankind into two groups: "some [God] blessed, and exalted, and sanctified; and some He cursed" to distinguish the wise and keeper of the Law from the lawless and unwise (Sir 33:1-13).

Similarly, in Wisdom of Solomon the Sage explains that, although "God created man to be immortal (ἐπ' ἀφθαρσίᾳ) and made him an image of his own eternity (ἀϊδιότητος), death came into the world through envy of the devil, and those who have a share with [it] experience [death] (πειράζουσιν δὲ αὐτὸν οἱ τῆς ἐκείνου μερῖδος ὄντες)" (Wis 2:23-24). Thus, death represents an agent that subdues the wicked who fall under his dominion (cf. 1:16). In order to participate in God's own "eternity" (ἀθανασία) humans are to remain morally incorrupt (see Wis 1:15; 3:1-9; 5:15; 6:18-19; 12:1; 18:4). Even Solomon is "earthborn" (γηγενοῦς), descendant of the "first man made of the earth" (πρωτοπλάστου) (Wis 7:1-6; cf. 10:1), and consequently mortal (Wis 40:1). For this reason he prays for and receives God's Wisdom to rule in holiness and justice (ἐν ὁσιότητι καὶ δικαιοσύνῃ), and to judge in integrity of heart (ἐν εὐθύτητι ψυχῆς) (Wis 9:1-8). Wisdom represents also a personified power that saves the righteous and punishes the wicked (10:1—11:1). The author derides the potter, who was made out of the ground (ἐκ γῆς γενηθείς) and bound back to it, because he ignores his creator and estimates this life "a plaything" (παίγνιον) and "a holyday for gain" (πανηγυρισμὸν ἐπικερδῆ) (15:8-12). Consequently, the author exhorts the audience to seek God's wisdom

2. With the exception of Sir 49:16, where Adam stands as the first of Israel's ancestors endowed with glory (49:16).

and to order their lives in integrity and righteousness so as to share in God's immortality.

Philo's interpretation of the creation of humanity and of the fall in *De Opificio Mundi* was more complex. In the prologue and in the conclusion of *De Opificio Mundi,* Philo openly states the ethical purpose of his interpretation—that is, that by abiding by the Law, inscribed by God in the cosmos and revealed to Moses, and by leading a virtuous life, one may attain happiness and bliss in this life (*Opif.* 2-3, 172). Overall, Philo distinguishes between the creation of the intelligible world and that of the the sense-perceptible world. First, he regards the intelligible man created after the image of God as "the mind, the director of the soul (κατὰ τὸν τῆς ψυχῆς ἡγεμόνα)" (*Opif.* 69).[3] He also interprets the plural "let us make man . . ." (Gen 1:26) as the participation of co-workers in the fashioning of the "mixed nature of the perishable man," who are responsible for the internal conflict man experiences between "wisdom and folly, self-mastery and licentiousness, courage and cowardice, justice and injustice," and ultimately between "things good and evil, fair and foul," "virtue and vice" (*Opif.* 72, 73). Thus, the human soul (ψυχή) struggles against the passions and vices to pursue virtue but "irrational pleasures" overcame humankind, and so God punished man with difficulties in obtaining the necessities of life. Yet one recognizes that if self-control (σωφροσύνη) restrains the passions, God will provide good things for our race (*Opif.* 79-81). Second, Philo distinguishes between the "generic man" (γένος), made after the divine image, and "the individual man (ἐπὶ μέρους ἀνθρώπου), the object of sense (ἀισθητοῦ), made up of earthly substance (γεώδους οὐσίας) and of divine breath (πνεύματος θείου)" (*Opif.* 135). God breathed his own word (ἑαυτοῦ λόγῳ) into the face of the earthly man to be the pattern for the soul of the "first man" (*Opif.* 139), who excelled in qualities and virtues.[4] However, his descendants were "inferior copies" of their ancestor and morally and physically "feebler" (*Opif.* 136-45). Third, Philo describes that, after the woman was made after the first man's image (*Opif.* 151), "a desire (πόθος) for fellowship arose for each other with a view to the production of their like," but then this desire "begat bodily pleasure (σωμάτων ἡδονήν), which is the beginning of wrongs and violation of law," a pleasure "by which men bring on themselves the life of mortality and wretchedness

3. Philo also described the first man as being mortal (θνητός) (*Opif.* 77), and earthborn and perishable (γηγενῶν καὶ φθαρτῶν) (*Opif.* 82). David T. Runia leaves the question open and blames Philo "for this lack of clarity" (*Philo of Alexandria, On the Creation of the Cosmos according to Moses* [Philo of Alexandria Commentary Series 1; Leiden: Brill, 2001], 323).

4. The first man excels in virtues because "the divine spirit (θείου πνεύματος) had flowed into him in full current . . . and so all his words and actions were undertaken to please the Father and King, following Him step by step in the highways cut out by virtues (ἀρεταί)" (*Opif.* 144).

(κακοδαίμονα) in lieu of that of immortality and bliss (εὐδαίμονος)" (*Opif.* 152). Fourth, Philo interprets paradise as the place where "all plants are endowed with soul and reason, bearing virtues for fruit," and "insight and discernment," "and life free from disease, and incorruption (ἀφθαρσίαν)" (*Opif.* 153b). Thus, the "tree of life" represents the virtue of "reverence toward God" (θεοσέβειαν) "by means of which the soul attains immortality" (ἀθανατίζεται), and the tree that "discerns (γνωριστικοῦ) between good (καλῶν) and evil things (πονηρῶν)" stands for the "intermediate prudence (φρόνεσιν τὴν μέσην), which enables us to distinguish things by nature contrary the one to the other" (154b).[5] However, since the soul inclined toward wickedness (πανουργίαν) "and disregarded reverence of God (εὐσεβείας) and holiness, out of which comes immortal life," God "expelled [the human soul] from paradise" (*Opif.* 155). Philo concludes, explaining that the forefathers were "transformed from a state of simplicity (ἀκακίας) and innocence (ἁπλότητος) into one of wickedness" (πανουργίαν) (156b).

Philo infers further ethical implications in his allegorical interpretation of the fall. First, he interprets the snake as a "symbol of pleasure" (ἡδονῆς σύμβολον) who advocates for the sovereignty of pleasure (*Opif.* 160).[6] Against this snake stands the "snake fighter" (ὀφιομάχης) who represents "self-control" (ἐγκράτεια), and αν austere (φιλαυστήρω) and honorable (σεμνῷ) lifestyle, who fights "intemperance (ἀκρασίαν) and pleasure (ἡδονήν) (*Opif.* 163b). Second, Philo interprets woman as "sense perception" (αἴσθησις), who, deceived by the serpent or pleasure, ensnares man or the sovereign mind (ἡγεμόνα νοῦν), who "becomes subject instead of a ruler (ἡγεμόνος) . . . and a mortal instead of immortal" (*Opif.* 165–66). Third, Philo infers that the curse of the earth to fail to yield produce abundantly was meant to withhold its fruits from the wicked and to prevent humankind from laziness and overindulgence, and to "go astray and become insolent in their behavior" (*Opif.* 169). Philo concludes that, although the forefathers initially "enjoyed innocence and simplicity," they turned to "wickedness (κακίᾳ) instead of virtue (ἀρετῆς)" (170a). In sum, Philo explicitly infers ethical implications from the story of the creation of humanity and the fall. Although humans are mortal by nature, life is troublesome for the wicked, but for the righteous life is "a happy (μακαρίαν)

5. Philo attributes this interpretation to Moses. Similarly, Josephus distinguishes between the first and the second creation accounts and attributes the latter to Moses' interpretation of the former (*Ant.* 1.26, 34a).

6. This snake snares the lover of pleasure (φιλήδονος) who lacks self-control (ἀκρασίας) (cf. *Opif.* 164).

and blessed (εὐδαίμονα), molded by the doctrines of piety (εὐσεβείας) and holiness (ὁσιότητος)" (*Opif.* 156, 164, 172).

The Hellenistic interpretations of the story of the creation and the fall found in these three works, Sirach, Wisdom of Solomon, and *De Opificio Mundi*, demonstrate that there was a tendency in Alexandria to interpret the Scriptures allegorically in order to elicit ethical lessons.[7] This tendency was followed later by the Alexandrian Fathers of the Church, who integrated the interpretation of the Scriptures with philosophical and ethical values in order to adapt and transform their social and cultural context. This is a good example for contemporary interpretations of Scripture that seek an effective ethical and social transformation of individuals and communities.

The second group, broadly labeled "Rewritten Bible," regards Adam primarily as the ancestor of Israel and, in the story of the fall, as the first of Israel's transgressors of the Law. Only secondarily did they see in Adam and his fall the paradigm of humankind and human wickedness and weakness. From the beginning of his *Jewish Antiquities,* Josephus states the moral lessons he plans to draw from his interpretation of the story of the creation and fall (*Ant.* 1.40-51).[8] God's providence (πρόνοια) (see *Ant.* 1.46; 10.277-80; 16.395-404) is shown primarily to Israel and also to those who keep the Law and practice virtue, but God would also punish those who do not keep his commandments and pursue vices. Thus, Josephus explains that eating from the tree of wisdom (φρονησέως) in the Garden brought destruction (ὄλεθρον) to Adam and Eve (*Ant.* 1.40). The serpent deceives the woman and she persuades her husband to taste of the tree of wisdom so they may attain "a blissful existence (μακάριον βίον) no whit behind that of a God" (*Ant.* 1.42). The tree quickened their intelligence and made them believe they were happier (*Ant.* 1.44; cf. 1.14), but when God

7. This may be due to Hellenistic philosophical influences, particularly Stoicism and Middle Platonism.

8. Thus, it corresponds to "the main lesson to be learnt from this history, [that is] that men who conform to the will of God, and do not venture to transgress laws . . . prosper in all things beyond belief . . . , and for their reward are offered by God felicity (εὐδαιμονία); whereas, in proportion as they depart from the strict observance of these laws, things (else) practicable become impracticable, and whatever imaginary good thing they strive to do ends in irretrievable disasters (συμφοράς)" (*Ant.* 1.14; cf. 1.20, 23; 3.84). The proem of *Antiquities* resembles Philo's introduction to *De Opificio Mundi* 1.1—2.1; see Louis H. Feldman, *Josephus's Interpretation of the Bible* (Hellenistic Culture and Society 27; Berkeley: University of California Press, 1998), 52–53. Josephus combines the Deuteronomistic axiom of divine retribution (Deuteronomy 28) with the Stoic belief that human reason should agree with the order found in nature, so that a virtuous life is that which follows the order established in the universe (cf. Diogenes Laertius, *Lives* 7.86-88).

came into the garden Adam became conscious (συνειδὼς, *sic*) of his crime (*Ant.* 1.45) "through an evil conscience" (συνειδότι πονηρῷ) (*Ant.* 1.46-47), and they lost a long and unmolested (ἀπαθῆ) life of bliss (βίον εὐδαίμονα). Therefore, Josephus conveys that those who infringe God's commands bring upon themselves destruction and lose an untroubled life of bliss, whereas those who keep God's law may enjoy happiness and bliss in this life.

The author of the book of *Jubilees* portrays Adam in positive fashion and regards him as the first patriarch and priest of Israel who kept the ritual laws according to the proper calendar pertaining to the Sabbath (*Jub.* 2:17-33), the purification after childbirth (*Jub.* 3:8-14), and covering nakedness for the sacrifice (*Jub.* 3:26-31). The author also emphasizes the dominion and blessing God bestowed only upon Israel and Jacob and not upon all humankind (*Jub.* 2:14-23). He omits most of the second creation account (Gen 2:4b-17), the commandment not to eat from the tree (Gen 2:8-17), and most of the story of the fall (Genesis 3). Thus, the author of *Jubilees* focuses simply on the ritual laws and not on the ethical implications drawn from the story of the creation of man.

Similarly, Pseudo-Philo's *Liber Antiquitatum Biblicarum* (*L.A.B.)* omits the two creations accounts of man and alludes to Adam parenthetically as the ancestor of Israel (*L.A.B.*1:1; 32:15). Thus, when God showed Moses "the place of creation and the serpent," God explained that the *protoplastum* "transgressed my ways, and was persuaded by his wife," who was "deceived by the serpent." Consequently, they lost "the ways of paradise" and "death was ordained for the generations of men" (13:8-9; cf. 26:6). However, the author does not attribute to Adam the cause of sin and death, but he explains that men (*homines*) did not walk in his ways either, and consequently their misfortunes are due to their own transgressions. The only way to restore them in the ways of paradise is through God's mercy and by keeping God's commandments and the cultic ordinances (13:1-10). When Adam sinned, he also lost the "precious stones" (26.6) or wisdom, which God restored again later in the Law (11:1; 19:6; 32:7; 33:3; 37:3-4; 53:8; cf. *2 Bar.* 17:4). In the eschaton, God will restore this knowledge to his people Israel (*L.A.B.* 26:13-14; 32:17). Thus, Pseudo-Philo interprets the fall as the loss of "the ways of paradise" or wisdom revealed originally by God to the *protoplastum* and revealed again to Moses in Sinai. He also anticipates the eschatological restoration of these "ways" and knowledge for Israel on the condition that they "walk on His ways."

Book 1 of the *Sibylline Oracles* describes the creation of man and woman excelling in beauty and "removed from evil heart" (*Sib. Or.* 1:22-37). However, after the fall they are expelled from "the place of immortals" and die (*Sib. Or.*

1:38–58, 80–82). The following seven generations sin even more and decay, until finally they are annihilated (1:100, 107, 115–19, 125–282). However, the author envisions an eschatological restoration when justice and "fair deeds" are practiced (1:4, 295–96). Similarly, book 5 predicts the annihilation of the nations because of their vices, idolatry, sexual offenses, homosexuality, and idolatry (5:214–80). Nevertheless, it foretells the restoration of the Jews and their city at the coming of a messianic figure, "one exceptional man from the sky" (5:238–85, 256–63; cf. 5.108–9, 155–61, 414–25; Num 24:7, 17). Therefore, the story of the fall is an example of the consequences of failing to obey God's commands, but the author(s) also anticipate(s) an eschatological restoration for those who remain faithful to the one God and his law (cf. 5.281–86).

The author of the Greek *Life of Adam and Eve* (*L.A.E.*) exhorts the audience to "watch yourselves so that you do not forsake the good" (30:1), and to repent and plead for God's mercy (27:1—29:17). Thus, although initially Adam blames Eve for their sufferings and death (7:1; cf. 10:1–2; 14:1; 21:5–6), he clarifies that both disobeyed the "one commandment" (7:1; 24:1, 4b). The author interprets the evil poison that the serpent sprinkled in the fruit as desire (ἐπιθυμία), "for the covetousness is every sin" (19:3). He also interprets Adam and Eve's awareness of their nakedness as the loss of "glory" and "righteousness" (19:3—21:6). After God chastised them with "seventy plagues," including death (8:1–3; cf. 11:1), and expelled them from paradise, Adam pleads for God's mercy, and he and his wife, Eve, mourn and do penance. The author describes Adam and Eve's death and burial (31:1—43:4), while the angels praise the Lord for forgiving Adam and Eve, because Adam was God's image (ὅτι εἰκών σου ἐστίν) (cf. 33:5; 35:2). The author summarizes how Adam lost his dominion and died (39:1–3) and how he now returns to the earth, because "you are dust and to dust you shall return" (41:1–2). At the climax of the narrative, God assures Adam of the resurrection, for "I shall raise you on the last day in the resurrection (ἀνάστασιν) with every man of your seed" (41:3; cf. 10:2; 28.4). Therefore, the author interprets the story of the fall in an eschatological perspective, and warns the audience to "watch yourselves so that you do not forsake the good" (30.1), and exhorts them to repent so God may have mercy on them on the Day of Judgment and raise them up on the day of the resurrection.

That the wicked suffer because of their transgressions was not a major theological problem for most Jewish authors, but that the righteous suffered and the wicked apparently prospered represented a significant predicament for them. Thus, the apocalyptic interpreters classified in the third group, *4 Ezra* and *2 Baruch*, emphasize the eschatological restoration of the righteous and the punishment of the wicked (see *4 Ezra* 3:1–4).[9] In *4 Ezra,* the angel Uriel leads Ezra into the proper "understanding" regarding the fate of the righteous and of the ungodly.[10] Ezra asks about the fate of Israel and the few righteous who still suffer, and Uriel replies that in the eschaton all will be judged and "the evil heart" will be removed (cf. 6:35—9:25; 7:26-131). Although Adam was the first who transgressed God's command and is blamed for the fall and the death appointed upon his descendants (7:116-18), each generation after him also disobeyed and was punished with death (3:4-7), and consequently each one is responsible for his or her own actions (7:127-31). The angel explains that, like Adam, Israel also transgressed the "one commandment" and the covenant (cf. 7:22-24, 70-72; 8:37-40, 46-58; 9:11-13). Yet Uriel invites Ezra not to be concerned with the many godless but with those who defeated the evil heart, and exhorts him to conform to the few righteous who will be rewarded in the eschaton with paradise and immortality (6:35—9:25; 7:13, 16, 78-99, 7:132—8:3; 8:37-40, 47-62, 51-54). Therefore, Adam is not the cause but the pattern of the dynamics of sinning and death so that each generation is responsible for their own transgressions (3:7-11, 20-22, 26-27; 7:127-31). The sufferings and the evil in the world are due to "the evil heart" or "seed" present in Adam and in every generation (3:20-22, 26; 4:4, 26-32; 7:48, 92).[11]

The author of *2 Baruch* believes that the destruction of the Second Temple is due to both the wicked among the Israelites and the enemies of Israel (1:4; 4:4-7; 5:3). Likewise, eschatological salvation is promised first to the faithful among Israel and second to the nations who "mingled with the seed of the people" (15:7-8; 42:3-8). The author contrasts Adam's life span and the death he brought to his descendants with Moses' lifetime and the Law he brought to his descendants too (*2 Bar.* 17:2-5; 19:3-8; cf. Gen 5:5; Deut 34:7).[12] *2 Baruch* also juxtaposes the "few who imitated Moses" and "took from the light" or the Law, and the "many whom he illuminated [but] took from the darkness of Adam and did not rejoice in the light of the lamp" (18:2). Thus, Adam represents "all the inhabitants of the earth" and particularly "the many" among

9. It has been argued before that the content, theodicy, eschatology, and sevenfold structure (among other elements) indicate that there was a literary dependence between *4 Ezra* and *2 Baruch*.

10. Uriel gradually leads Ezra to wisdom and the proper understanding of righteousness and eschatological salvation (*4 Ezra* 4:10-11, 20-21; 5:31, 37-38; 8:4, 22, 26; 14:34-35, 40-48).

11. *4 Ezra* describes the "evil" heart" or seed as an evil inner inclination or desire found in every person (cf. Gen 6:5; 8:21).

12. The contrast between Adam and Moses resembles Paul's contrast between Adam and Christ as found in Rom 5:12-21, but instead of Moses Paul introduces Christ, his obedient act of righteousness, grace, and the life he brought to the believers. This contrast as well as the place and function of the remnant of Israel and the Gentiles found in Rom 11:1-24 invite further analysis between Romans and *2 Baruch*.

Israel who did not remember the Law, as opposed to "the few" who kept the Law (48:29—52.7; cf. 14:2; 18:2). This contrast does not necessarily correspond to the distinction between Israel and the Gentiles but between those who keep the Law and those who transgress it. When the righteouses die, their souls rest in "the treasuries," while the souls of the wicked await in the "realm of death," until the coming of the "Anointed One" (21:23; 23:5; 30:1-5). At the coming of the Messiah, corruption and untimely death will disappear, "joy will be revealed and all misfortunes will pass away" (56:10; 73:3; 74:2). *2 Baruch* also distinguishes between the Gentiles who disregard God's works in creation and face destruction and those righteous who could participate in the coming glory and reward (14:17-19; 17:1—18:1-2; 41–42; 54:14-22b; cf. Rom 1:18—3:20). Therefore, for *2 Baruch* Adam and Eve's disobedience represents everyone's transgressions (48:40). The author underlines the responsibility of the individual so that "although Adam sinned first and has brought death upon all" each one has prepared his or her own torment or glory (54:14-16, 19; 56:5-10).

When we turn to Paul's writings, we see that he interpreted the story of the creation of humanity and of the fall through the prism of the Christ-event. Although a specific literary dependence on any of the ten Jewish interpreters and Paul is untenable, the Adam motif in 1 Cor 15:21-22, 45-49 and Rom 5:12-21 reflects trends similar to those found in these interpretations. He contrasted Adam and his transgression with Christ and his obedience to explain that the eschatological times and the new creation have been inaugurated in Christ's death and resurrection. Paul believed that the reign of sin and death introduced with Adam came to an end with Christ's death and resurrection.

Thus, the apocalyptic trend that attributed to Adam the beginning of sin and death (see *L.A.B.* 13:8; 37:3; *L.A.E.* 7:1; 14:1; 21:5-6; *4 Ezra* 3:4-11; 7:116-18, 127-31; *2 Bar.* 17:2; 19:8; 56:5-10; cf. 54:14-15, 19) is reflected in 1 Cor 15:21-22 and in Rom 5:12-21. In the first passage, after reminding the Corinthians of their faith in Christ's resurrection from the dead (1 Cor 15:1-11), and showing them how vain their faith and lives would be if there were no resurrection of the dead (15:13-19), Paul presents Christ's resurrection as the first fruits (ἀπαρχή) of those who have fallen asleep (1 Cor 15:20-23). In this context he introduces a contrast between Adam and Christ and the death and resurrection that came through each one of them (1 Cor 15:21-22). Paul identifies a relationship between Adam and those who are in him (ἐν τῷ Ἀδάμ), and between Christ and those who are in him as well (ἐν τῷ Χριστῷ). This relationship entails that all humankind participate in Adam's death (ἀποθνῄσκουσιν) as well as in Christ's resurrection (ζῳοποιηθήσονται). On the one hand, the figure of Adam echoes the story of the fall and helps to explain the present broken status of all humankind. On the other hand, Christ's resurrection anticipates the eschatological victory over death of those who belong to him (οἱ τοῦ Χριστοῦ). The figure of Adam in this passage implicitly explains that, after his fall, other powers and death reigned over all, but that, in his resurrection, Christ brings to an end the dominion of death and he will also subdue all to God the Father. In this way, Christ's resurrection restores all creation according to the original order under the dominion of God (1 Cor 15:23-28). However, although Christ has already been raised from the dead, the resurrection of believers remains an eschatological event. Furthermore, faith in the resurrection of the dead should transform life and make it meaningful in the present, otherwise everything would be in vain and would lead to a dissolute way of life (15:29-33). Consequently, Paul shows that the faith in the resurrection of the dead has an impact on the morals of the community, and he exhorts them to "come back to your senses" and "stop sinning" (15:34).

In the following passage, 1 Cor 15:45-49, Paul contrasts the first Adam (ὁ πρῶτος ἄνθρωπος Ἀδάμ) with the last Adam (ὁ ἔσχατος Ἀδάμ), Christ. This passage reflects the influence of Hellenistic Jewish interpretations of the story of the creation of man that distinguished between the first and the second man as found in Philo. The first man, made after the "image of God," was "intelligible, incorporeal . . . by nature incorruptible (ἄφθαρτος); the second man was made "of body and soul (ἐκ σώματος καὶ ψυχῆς), man or woman, by nature mortal (θνητός)" (*Opif.* 134). The second man was also of mixed nature, "made up of earthly substance (γεώδους οὐσίας) and of divine breath (πνεύματος θείου)" (*Opif.* 135). Although a literary dependence between Philo and Paul is untenable, it is possible that this type of interpretation influenced the Christian community in Corinth. Apparently this view affected the faith of "some" in the Christian community who did not believe in the bodily resurrection of the dead and corrupted the moral values and principles of the Christian community (cf. 1 Cor 15:33-34). Thus, in this passage Paul reverses the order between the first and the second man that was probably held by "some" in the community. He clarifies that the first man, Adam, became "a living being" (ψυχὴν ζῶσαν), made out of "the dust of the earth" (ἐκ γῆς χοϊκός); conversely, the second and last Adam, Christ, is "a life-giving spirit" (πνεῦμα ζῳοποιοῦν) "from heaven" (ἐξ οὐρανοῦ) (1 Cor 15:44-47). Paul also relates the earthly man to those who are from the earth (οἷος ὁ χοϊκός, τοιοῦτοι καὶ οἱ χοϊκοί), and the heavenly man with those from heaven (οἷος ὁ ἐπουράνιος, τοιοῦτοι καὶ οἱ ἐπουράνιοι) (15:48). However, this comparison does not establish two kinds of men but entails an eschatological transformation from the earthly into the heavenly "so that as we bore the likeness of the earthly man (καθὼς ἐφορέσαμεν τὴν εἰκόνα τοῦ χοϊκοῦ), so shall we bear the likeness of the man from heaven (φορέσομεν καὶ τὴν εἰκόνα τοῦ ἐπουρανίου) (1 Cor 15:48–49). Furthermore, this eschatological transformation (ἀλλαγησόμεθα) (15:51–52) entails a moral transformation from what is perishable (φθαρτόν) into what is "imperishable" (ἀφθαρσίαν). Thus, Paul infers that "flesh and blood (σὰρξ καὶ αἷμα) cannot inherit the kingdom of God, nor does the perishable inherit the imperishable" (15:50). Earlier he warned that "the unrighteous will not inherit the kingdom of God" (1 Cor 6:9–10; cf. Gal 5:21; Rom 14:17; 1 Thess 2:12). Elsewhere Paul also contrasts "flesh" and "spirit" as opposed desires or inclinations (κατὰ τοῦ πνεύματος/κατὰ τῆς σαρκός) (Gal 5:16–17; Rom 7:14, 18; 8:3–11). Therefore, in order to participate in the eschatological and incorruptible kingdom and in immortality (ἀθανασία) believers are to transform their lives according to what is morally incorrupt (1 Cor 15:42b, 52–54; cf. Rom 8:7–8; Gal 3:3; 5:19–26; 6:1–6) and must put on what is incorruptible and immortal (1 Cor 15:53–54).

In the last passage, Rom 5:12–21, Paul contrasts Adam and Christ in order to illustrate the transformation from the state of sin and death of all humankind, Gentiles and Jews alike (cf. Romans 1–3), to the state of righteousness and grace by faith through Jesus Christ's death and resurrection, which brought hope and peace to all (5:1-11). This transformation entails for believers an effective participation in Jesus' death and resurrection through their baptism, so that they stand in this grace by dying to sin and to the old self and by walking in the newness of life (Romans 6). This transformation is achieved not by the Law, which instead increased sin (Romans 7), but by the Spirit of life that believers received (Romans 8). As in 1 Cor 15:21-22, in this passage Paul integrates a Jewish apocalyptic tradition that attributed to Adam the beginning of sin and death in the world and the confession of faith in Jesus Christ's expiatory death and resurrection (cf. 5:1-11). Thus, on the one hand, Adam represents the agent whose transgression (δι' ἑνὸς παραπτώματος) introduced sin and death to all; on the other hand, Christ is the one whose righteous deed (δι' ἑνὸς δικαιώματος) brought righteousness of life to all (5:18). However, in this antithesis between Adam and Christ, Paul underlines the greater effects (πολλῷ μᾶλλον) of Christ's righteousness over against Adam's disobedience (5:9–10, 17). As other apocalyptic Jewish interpreters did, Paul anticipates the restoration of the righteous and a new creation in the eschaton. However, although Paul believed that the eschatological times have been inaugurated already in Christ's death and resurrection and that believers have received God's grace, believers still await their future reign in life (ἐν ζωῇ βασιλεύσουσιν) (5:17), when they will be appointed righteous (δίκαιοι κατασταθήσονται) (5:19). Thus, their participation in eternal life remains an eschatological event, "so grace may reign (βασιλεύσῃ) through righteousness to bring eternal life (εἰς ζωὴν αἰώνιον) through Jesus Christ our Lord" (5:21). This tension between the "already" of Christ's resurrection and the "not yet" for believers in eschatological eternal life helps Paul to exhort the audience to remain in this grace, to die to sin and the old self, and to walk in the newness of life (Rom 6:1-6). Thus, the grace received through Christ's righteousness is incompatible with sin and the old order brought through Adam's disobedience. Furthermore, this new status in grace is attained not through the Law, which increases sin (Romans 7), but through the Spirit of life (Romans 8). Believers are to remain in this grace and walk in the newness of life in order to participate in the eschatological new creation with Christ.

The antithesis between Adam and Christ in these passages illustrates the contrast between the old and the new creation. It also demonstrates that all human beings somehow participate both in Adam's transgression and death and in Christ's righteousness and eternal life. Nevertheless, although Christ's death and resurrection have already inaugurated the eschatological times, the entire creation and believers still await the eschatological transformation. In the meantime, believers must also undergo an ethical assimilation to Christ, the last incorruptible and heavenly Adam in order to participate in the eschatological resurrection.

The analysis of the figure of Adam in the Dead Sea Scrolls requires further research to come to a better understanding of the dynamics of interpretation in this period. For instance, 4Q422 (*Paraphrase of Genesis and* Exodus) describes a double creation, darkness and light, and mentions the presence of the "evil inclination" in man (cf. also 1QS 3:17-18). The *Rule of the Community* says that "the nature of all the children of men is ruled" by both "the spirit of light" and the "spirit of falsehood," but that in the time of the visitation God will give to the "sons of heaven the glory of Adam" and will restore righteousness and wisdom (1QS 4:12-25). The *Thanksgiving Hymns* praise God's forgiveness and anticipate that God will give humans "the glory of Adam and abundance of days" (1QH 17:15). Likewise, the *Damascus Document* promises "the glory of Adam" to those who keep God's commandments and God's covenant (CD 3:20). These passages are further interpretations of the story of the creation of humankind and of the fall that illustrate the paradoxical nature of humanity, the internal struggles of the human heart, and often humans' eschatological restoration through God's mercy and forgiveness.

The story of the creation of humanity and of the fall influenced many other authors throughout the centuries who interpreted the figure of Adam as the paradigm of all humankind. Paul's interpretation of the figure of Adam is an example of the richness and creativity of biblical interpretation that aims to explain and transform humankind after the last Adam, Jesus Christ.

Bibliography

Primary Sources

Collins, John J. "The Sibylline Oracles." In *The Old Testament Pseudepigrapha.* Vol. 1, *Apocalyptic Literature and Testaments.* Edited by James H. Charlesworth. New York: Doubleday, 1983.

Diogenes Laertius. *Lives of Eminent Philosophers.* Translated by R. D. Hicks. 2 vols. Loeb Classical Library. Cambridge, Mass.: Harvard University Press, 1925.

Harrington, Daniel J. "Liber Antiquitatum Biblicarum." In *The Old Testament Pseudepigrapha.* Vol. 2, *Apocalyptic Literature and Testaments.* Edited by James H. Charlesworth. New York: Doubleday, 1985.

Johnson, M. D. "The Life of Adam and Eve. In *The Old Testament Pseudepigrapha.* Vol. 2, *Expansions of the "Old Testament" and Other Legends, Wisdom and Philosophical Literature, Prayers, Psalms, and Odes, Fragments of Lost Judeo-Hellenistic Works.* Edited by James H. Charlesworth. New York: Doubleday, 1985.

Josephus, vols. 6 and 7. Translated by Ralph Marcus and Louis H. Feldman. Loeb Classical Library. Cambridge, Mass.: Harvard University Press, 1965.

Klijn, A. F. J. "2 (Syriac Apocalypse of) Baruch." In *The Old Testament Pseudepigrapha.* Vol. 1, *Apocalyptic Literature and Testaments.* Edited by James H. Charlesworth; New York: Doubleday, 1983.

Metzger, Bruce M. "The Fourth Book of Ezra." In *The Old Testament Pseudepigrapha.* Vol. 1, *Apocalyptic Literature and Testaments.* Edited by James H. Charlesworth. New York: Doubleday, 1983.

Philo, vol. 1. Translated by F. H. Colson and G. H. Whitaker. Loeb Classical Library. Cambridge, Mass.: Harvard University Press, 1962.

Wintermute, O. S. "The Book of Jubilees." In *The Old Testament Pseudepigrapha.* Vol. 2, *Expansions of the "Old Testament" and Other Legends, Wisdom and Philosophical Literature, Prayers, Psalms, and Odes, Fragments of Lost Judeo-Hellenistic Works.* Edited by James H. Charlesworth. New York: Doubleday, 1985.

Wise, Michael, Martin Abegg Jr., and Edward Cook. *The Dead Sea Scrolls.* San Francisco: Harper, 1996.

Secondary Sources

Adams, Edward, and David G. Horrell, eds. *Christianity at Corinth: The Quest for the Pauline Church*. Louisville: Westminster John Knox, 2004.

Aletti, Jean-Noël. *La lettera ai Romani e la giustizia di Dio*. Rome: Edizioni Borla, 1997.

———. "The Rhetoric of Romans 5–8." In *The Rhetorical Analysis of the Scripture: Essays from the 1995 London Conference,* edited by Stanley E. Porter and Thomas H. Olbricht, 294–308. Journal for the Study of the New Testament: Supplement Series 146. Sheffield: Sheffield Academic Press, 1997.

———. "Romains 5,12-21: Logique, sens et function." *Biblica* 78 (1997): 1–32.

Alonso Schökel, Luis. "The Vision of Man in Sirach 16:24—17:14." In *Israelite Wisdom: Theological and Literary Essays in Honor of Samuel Terrien,* edited by John G. Gammie, Walter A. Brueggemann, W. L. Humphreys, and J. M. Ward, 235–45. Homage Series 3. Missoula, Mont.: Scholars Press, 1978.

Anderson, Gary A., and Michael E. Stone. *A Synopsis of the Books of Adam and Eve*. Rev. ed. Society of Biblical Literature Early Judaism and Its Literature 17. Atlanta: Scholars Press, 1999.

Anderson, Gary A., Michael E. Stone, and Johannes Tromp, eds. *Literature on Adam and Eve: Collected Essays*. Studia in Veteris Testamenti pseudepigrapha 15. Leiden: Brill, 2000.

Anderson, R. Dean. *Ancient Rhetorical Theory and Paul*. Contributions to Biblical Exegesis and Theology 18. Kampen: Kok Pharos, 1996.

Asher, Jeffrey R. "SPEIRETAI: Paul's Anthropogenic Metaphor in 1 Corinthians 15:42-44." *Journal of Biblical Literature* 120 (2001): 101–22.

Attridge, Harold W. *The Interpretation of Biblical History in the Antiquitates Judaicae of Flavius Josephus*. Harvard Dissertations in Religion. Missoula, Mont.: Scholars Press, 1976.

Aune, David E. "Distinct Lexical Meanings of ἀπαρχή in Hellenistic Judaism and Early Christianity." In *Early Christianity and Classical Culture Comparative Studies in Honor of Abraham J. Malherbe,* edited by John T. Fitzgerald, Thomas H. Olbricht, and L. Michael White, 103–29. Supplements to Novum Testamentum 110. Leiden: Brill, 2003.

Barclay, John M. G. *Jews in the Mediterranean Diaspora: From Alexander to Trajan (323 BCE–117 CE)*. Berkeley: University of California Press, 1996.

Barrett, C. K. *From First Adam to Last: A Study in Pauline Theology*. New York: Scribner, 1962.

———. "The Significance of the Adam-Christ Typology for the Resurrection of the Dead: 1 Co 15, 20-22. 45-49." In *Résurrection du Christ et des Chrétiens,* edited by Lorenzo De Lorenzi, 99–126. Série Monographique de "Benedictina": Section biblico-oecuménique 8. Rome: Abbaye de S. Paul, 1985.

Barth, Karl. *Christ and Adam. Man and Humanity in Romans 5.* Translated by T. A. Smail. New York: Collier, 1962.

Batto, Bernard F. "Creation Theology in Genesis." In *Creation in the Biblical Traditions,* edited by Richard J. Clifford and John J. Collins, 16–38. Catholic Biblical Quarterly Monograph Series 24. Washington, D.C.: Catholic Biblical Association of America, 1992.

Bell, Richard H. "The Myth of Adam and the Myth of Christ in Romans 5.12-21." In *Paul, Luke and the Graeco-Roman World: Essays in Honour of Alexander J. M. Wedderburn,* edited by Alf Christophersen, Carsten Claussen, Jörg Frey, and Bruce Longenecker, 21–36. Journal for the Study of the New Testament: Supplement Series 217. Sheffield: Sheffield Academic Press, 2002.

Bergen, Theodore A. "Christian Influence on the Transmission History of 4, 5, and 6 Ezra." In *The Jewish Apocalyptic Heritage in Early Christianity,* edited by James C. VanderKam and William Adler, 102–27. Minneapolis: Fortress Press, 1996.

Berthelot, Katell. *L*"*humanité de l'autre homme" dans la pensée juive ancienne.* Supplements to the Journal for the Study of Judaism 87. Leiden: Brill, 2004.

Betz, Hans Dieter. "The Concept of the 'Inner Human Being' (ὁ ἔσω ἄνθροπος) in the Anthropology of Paul." *New Testament Studies* 46 (2000): 315–41.

Blenkinsopp, Joseph. *The Pentateuch: An Introduction to the First Books of the Bible.* Anchor Bible Reference Library. New York: Doubleday, 1992.

Boer, Martinus C. de. "The Literary Development of the *Life of Adam and Eve.*" In *Literature on Adam and Eve: Collected Essays,* edited by Gary A. Anderson, Michael E. Stone, and Johannes Tromp, 239–49. Studia in Veteris Testamenti pseudepigrapha 15. Leiden: Brill, 2000.

———. "Paul's Use of a Resurrection Tradition in 1 Cor, 15,20-28." In *The Corinthian Correspondence,* ed.dited by R. Bieringer, 639–51. Bibliotheca ephemeridum theologicarum Lovaniensium 125. Leuven: Leuven University Press/ Peeters, 1996.

Borgen, Peder C. "Philo of Alexandria: Reviewing and Rewriting Biblical Material." *Studia Philonica Annual* 9 (1997): 37–53.

Boring, M. Eugene, Klaus Berger, and Carsten Colpe, eds. *Hellenistic Commentary to the New Testament*. Nashville: Abingdon, 1995.

Bouteneff, Peter C. *Beginnings: Ancient Christian Readings of the Biblical Creation Narratives*. Grand Rapids: Baker Academic, 2008.

Brandenburger, Egon. *Adam und Christus: Exegetisch-religionsgeschichtliche Untersuchung zu Röm. 5:12-21 (1 Kor 15)*. Wissenschaftliche Monographien zum Alten und Neuen Testament 7. Neukirchen: Kreis Moers, 1962.

Brodeur, Scott. *The Holy Spirit's Agency in the Resurrection of the Dead: An Exegetico-Theological Study of 1 Corinthians 15,44b-49 and Romans 8,9-13*. Tesi gregoriana, serie teologia 14. Rome: Pontificia Università Gregoriana, 1996.

Brown, Raymond E. *Introduction to the New Testament*. New York: Doubleday, 1997.

Bultmann, Rudolf. "Adam and Christ According to Romans 5." In *Current Issues in New Testament Interpretation: Essays in Honor of Otto A. Piper*, edited by William Klassen and Graydon F. Snyder, 143–65. London: SCM, 1962.

———. *The Old and the New Adam in the Letters of Paul*. Translated by Keith R. Crim. Richmond: John Knox, 1967.

———. *Theology of the New Testament*. Translated by Kendrick Grobel. 2 vols. New York: Scribner, 1951.

Byrne, Brendan. *Romans*. Sacra Pagina 6. Collegeville, Minn.: Liturgical Press, 1996.

Campbell, Williams S. *Paul and the Creation of Christian Identity*. Library of New Testament Studies 322. London: T&T Clark, 2008.

Caragounis, Chrys C. "Romans 5.15-16 in the Context of 5.12-21: Contrast or Comparison?" *New Testament Studies* 31 (1985): 142–48.

Charlesworth, James H., ed. *Old Testament Pseudepigrapha*. 2 vols. New York: Doubleday, 1983–85.

Chilton, Bruce D., and Jacob Neusner. *Classical Christianity and Rabbinic Judaism: Comparing Theologies*. Grand Rapids: Baker Academic, 2004.

Clifford, Richard J. *Creation Accounts in the Ancient Near East and the Bible*. Catholic Biblical Quarterly Monograph Series 26. Washington, D.C.: Catholic Biblical Association of America, 1994.

Clifford, Richard J., and John J. Collins. "Introduction: The Theology of Creation Traditions." In *Creation in the Biblical Traditions*, edited by Richard J. Clifford and John J. Collins, 1–15. Catholic Biblical Quarterly Monograph Series 24. Washington, D.C.: Catholic Biblical Association of America, 1992.

Collins, J. John, ed.*Apocalypse: The Morphology of a Genre.* Semeia 14. Missoula, Mont.: Scholars Press, 1979.

———. "Sibylline Oracles." In *The Old Testament Pseudepigrapha,* vol. 1, *Apocalyptic Literature and Testaments,* edited by James H. Charlesworth, 317–472. New York: Doubleday, 1983.

———. *The Sibylline Oracles of Egyptian Judaism.* Society of Biblical Literature Dissertation Series 13. Missoula, Mont.: Society of Biblical Literature, 1972.

Collins, Raymond F. *First Corinthians.* Sacra Pagina 7. Collegeville, Minn.: Liturgical Press, 1999.

Conzelmann, Hans. *1 Corinthians: A Commentary on the First Epistle to the Corinthians.* Translated by J. W. Leitch. Hermeneia on CD-ROM. Libronix Digital System Version 1.0. Print ed.: Philadelphia: Fortress Press, 1975.

Davenport, Gene L. *The Eschatology of the Book of Jubilees.* Studia Post-Biblica 20. Leiden: Brill, 1971.

Davies, W. D. *Jewish and Pauline Studies.* Philadelphia: Fortress Press, 1984.

———. *Paul and Rabbinic Judaism: Some Rabbinic Elements in Pauline Theology.* 2nd ed. New York: Harper & Row, 1955.

De Lorenzi, Lorenzo. "Presentazione." In *Résurrection du Christ et des Chrétiens,* edited by Lorenzo De Lorenzi, 5–16. Série Monographique de "Benedictina": Section biblico-oecuménique 8. Rome: Abbaye de S. Paul, 1985.

DesCamp, Mary Therese "Why Are These Women Here? An Examination of the Sociological Setting of Pseudo-Philo through Comparative Reading," *Journal for the Study of the Pseudepigrapha* 16 (1997): 53–80.

Di Vito, Robert A. "The Demarcation of Divine and Humans Realms in Genesis 2-11." In *Creation in the Biblical Traditions,* edited by Richard J. Clifford and John J. Collins. Catholic Biblical Quarterly Monograph Series 24. Washington, D.C.: Catholic Biblical Association of America, 1992.

Dunn, James D. G.*Christology in the Making: A New Testament Inquiry into the Origins of the Doctrine of the Incarnation.* Grand Rapids: Eerdmans, 1980.

———. *1 Corinthians.* New Testament Guides. Sheffield: Sheffield Academic Press, 1995.

———. "1 Corinthians 15.45: Last Adam, life-giving spirit." In *Christ and Spirit in the New Testament,* edited by Barnabas Lindars and Stephen S. Smalley, 127–41. Cambridge: Cambridge University Press, 1973.

———. "Reconstructions of Corinthian Christianity and the Interpretation of 1Corinthians." In Adams, Edward, and David G. Horrell, eds. *Christianity at Corinth: The Quest for the Pauline Church,* edited by Edward Adams and David G. Horrell, 295–310. Louisville: Westminster John Knox, 2004/

———. *The Theology of Paul the Apostle.* Grand Rapids: : Eerdmans, 1998.

Endres, John C. *Biblical Interpretation in the Book of Jubilees.* Catholic Biblical Quarterly Monograph Series 18. Washington, D.C.: Catholic Biblical Association of America, 1987.

Engberg-Pedersen, Troels. "Complete and Incomplete Transformation in Paul: A Philosophical Reading of Paul on Body and Spirit." In *Metamorphoses: Resurrection, Body and Transformative Practices in Early Christianity,* edited by Turid Karlsen Seim and Jorunn Økland, 123–46. Ekstasis 1. Berlin: de Gruyter, 2009.

Erickson, Richard J. "The Damned and the Justified in Romans 5.12-21: An Analysis of Semantic Structure." In *Discourse Analysis and the New Testament: Approaches and Results,* edited by Stanley E. Porter and Jeffrey T. Reed, 282–307. Journal for the Study of the New Testament: Supplement Series 170. Sheffield: Sheffield Academic Press, 1999.

Eriksson, Anders. "Elaboration of Argument in 1 Corinthians 15:20-34." *Svensk exegetisk årsbok* 64 (1999): 101–13.

Evans, Craig A. *Ancient Texts for New Testament Studies: A Guide to the Background Literature.* Peabody, Mass.: Hendrickson, 2005.

Fee, Gordon D. *The First Epistle to the Corinthians.* New International Commentary on the New Testament. Grand Rapids: Eerdmans, 1987.

Feldman, Louis H. *Josephus's Interpretation of the Bible.* Hellenistic Culture and Society 27. Berkeley: University of California Press, 1998.

———. "Prolegomenon." In M. R. James, *The Biblical Antiquities of Philo,* 42–60. New York: Ktav, 1971.

———. *Studies in Josephus' Rewritten Bible.* Supplements to the Journal for the Study of Judaism 58. Leiden: Brill, 1998.

Fishbane, Michael. "Inner-Biblical Exegesis." In *Hebrew Bible/Old Testament: The History of Its Interpretation.* Vol. 1, *From the Beginnings to the Middle Ages,* part 1, *Antiquity,* edited by Magne Sæbø. Göttingen: Vandenhoeck & Ruprecht, 1996.

Fisk, Bruce Norman. *Do You Not Remember? Scripture, Story and Exegesis in the Rewritten Bible of Pseudo-Philo.* Journal for the Study of the Pseudepigrapha: Supplement Series 37. Sheffield: Sheffield Academic Press, 2001.

Fitzgerald, John T. "The Catalogues in Ancient Greek Literature." In *The Rhetorical Analysis of Scripture: Essays from the 1995 London Conference,* edited by Stanley E. Porter and Thomas H. Olbricht, 274–93. Journal for the Study of the New Testament: Supplement Series 146. Sheffield: Sheffield Academic Press, 1997.

Fitzmyer, Joseph A. *The Genesis Apocryphon of Qumran Cave I*: A *Commentary*. 2nd ed. Biblica et orientalia 18A. Rome: Biblical Institute Press, 1971.

———. *Romans: A New Translation with Introduction and Commentary*. Anchor Bible 33. New York: Doubleday, 1993.

Forbes, Christopher. "Paul and Rhetorical Comparison." In *Paul in the Greco-Roman World: A Handbook,* edited by J. Paul Sampley, 143–71. Harrisburg, Pa.: Trinity Press International, 2003.

Franxman, Thomas W. *Genesis and the "Jewish Antiquities" of Flavius Josephus*. Biblica et orientalia 35. Rome: Biblical Institute Press, 1979.

Gathercole, Simon J. *Where Is the Boasting? Early Jewish Soteriology and Paul's Response in Romans 1–5*. Grand Rapids: Eerdmans, 2002.

Georgi, Dieter. *Weisheit Salomos*. Jüdische Schriften aus hellenistisch-römischer Zeit3.4. Gütersloh: Gerd Mohn, 1980.

Gillman, John. "Transformation into the Future Life: A Study of 1 Cor 15:50-53, Its Context and Related Passages." Ph.D. diss., Katholieke Universiteit Leuven, Belgium, 1980.

Grappe, Christian. "Qui me délivrera de ce corps de mort? L'Esprit de vie! Romains 7,24 et 8,2 comme élements de typologie adamique." *Biblica* 83 (2002): 472–92.

Groton, Anne H. *From Alpha to Omega: A Beginning Course in Classical Greek*. Newburyport Mass.: Focus Information Group, 1995.

Gundry, Robert H. *Sōma in Biblical Theology with Emphasis on Pauline Anthropology,* Society for the New Testament Studies Monograph Series 29. Cambridge: Cambridge University Press, 1976.

Hay, David M. "Philo's Anthropology, the Spiritual Regimen of the Therapeutae, and a Possible Connection with Corinth." In *Philo und das Neue Testament: Wechselseitige Wahrnehmungen. 1. Internationales Symposium zum Corpus Judaeo-Hellenisticum, 1.–4. Mai 2003, Eisenach, Jena,* edited by Roland Deines and Karl-Wilhelm Niebuhr, 127–42. Wissenschaftliche Untersuchungen zum Neuen Testament 172. Tübingen: Mohr Siebeck, 2004.

Hays, Richard B. *The Conversion of the Imagination: Paul as Interpreter of Israel's Scripture*. Grand Rapids: Eerdmans, 2005.

———. Echoes of Scripture in the Letters of Paul. New Haven: Yale University Press, 1989.

Hayward, C. T. R. "The Figure of Adam in Pseudo-Philo's Biblical Antiquities." *Journal for the Study of Judaism in the Persian, Hellenistic, and Roman Period* 23 (1992): 1–20.

Hedrick, Charles W. *The Apocalypse of Adam: A Literary and Source Analysis.* Ancient Texts and Translations. Eugene, Ore.: Wipf & Stock, 2005.

Heil, John Paul. *The Rhetorical Role of Scripture in 1 Corinthians.* Studies in Biblical Literature 15. Atlanta: Society of Biblical Literature, 2005.

Henry, David Paul. *The Early Development of the Hermeneutic of Karl Barth as Evidenced by His Appropriation of Romans 5:12-21.* NABPR Dissertation Series 5. Macon, Ga.: Mercer University Press, 1985.

Hill, C. E. "Paul's Understanding of Christ's Kingdom in 1 Corinthians 15:20-28." *Novum Testamentum* 30 (1988): 297–320.

Hoegen-Rohls, Christina. "Κτίσις and καινή:. Κτίσις in Paul's Letters." In *Paul, Luke and the Graeco-Roman World: Essays in Honour of Alexander J. M. Wedderburn,* edited by Alf Christophersen, Carsten Claussen, Jörg Frey, and Bruce Longenecker, 102–22. . Journal for the Study of the New Testament: Supplement Series 217. Sheffield: Sheffield Academic Press, 2002.

Holleman, Joost. "Jesus' Resurrection as the Beginning of the Eschatological Resurrection (1 Cor 15,20)." In *The Corinthian Correspondence,* edited by R. Bieringer, 653–60. Bibliotheca ephemeridum theologicarum lovaniensium 125. Leuven: Leuven University Press/Peeters, 1996.

Horsley, Richard A. "'How Can Some of You Say That There Is No Resurrection of the Dead?' Spiritual Elitism in Corinth." *Novum Testamentum* 20 (1978): 203–31.

———. "The Politics of Cultural Production in Second Temple Judea: Historical Context and Political-Religious Relations of the Scribes Who Produced 1 Enoch, Sirach, and Daniel." In *Conflicted Boundaries in Wisdom and Apocalypticism,* edited by Benjamin G. Wright III and Lawrence M. Wills. Society of Biblical Literature Symposium Series 35. Atlanta: Society of Biblical Literature, 2005.

Hubbard, Moyer V. *New Creation in Paul's Letters and Thought.* Society for New Testament Studies Monograph Series 119. Cambridge: Cambridge University Press, 2002.

Hull, Michael F. *Baptism on Account of the Dead (1 Cor 15:29): An Act of Faith in the Resurrection.* Society of Biblical Literature Dissertation Series 22. Atlanta: Society of Biblical Literature, 2005.

Hultgren, Stephen. "The Origin of Paul's Doctrine of the Two Adams in 1 Corinthians 15.45-49." *Journal for the Study of the New Testament* 25 (2003): 343–70.

Hurst, L. D. "Re-enter the Existent Christ in Philippians 2.5-11?" *New Testament Studies* 32 (1986): 449–57.

Hurtado, Larry W. "Does Philo Help Explain Christianity?" In *Philo und das Neue Testament: Wechselseitige Wahrnehmungen. 1. Internationales Symposium zum Corpus Judaeo-Hellenisticum, 1.–4. Mai 2003, Eisenach, Jena,* edited by Roland Deines and Karl-Wilhelm Niebuhr, 73–92. Wissenschaftliche Untersuchungen zum Neuen Testament 172. Tübingen: Mohr Siebeck, 2004.

Jacobson, Howard. *A Commentary on Pseudo-Philo's Liber Antiquitatum Biblicarum.* 2 vols. Arbeiten zur Geschichte des antiken Judentums und des Urchristentums 31. Leiden: Brill, 1996.

Jervell, Jacob. *Imago Dei: Gen 1, 26 f. im Spätjudentum, in der Gnosis und in den paulinischen Briefen.* Forschungen zur Religion und Literatur des Alten und Neuen Testaments 58. Göttingen: Vandenhoeck & Ruprecht, 1960.

Jewett, Robert. *Paul's Anthropological Terms: A Study of Their Use in Conflict Settings.* Arbeiten zur Geschichte des antiken Judentums und des Urchristentums 10. Leiden: Brill, 1971.

Johnson, Luke Timothy. "Transformation of the Mind and Moral Discernment in Paul." In *Early Christianity and Classical Culture: Comparative Studies in Honor of Abraham J. Malherbe,* edited by John T. Fitzgerald, Thomas H. Olbricht, and L. Michael White, 215–36. Supplements to Novum Testamentum 110. Leiden: Brill, 2003.

Jonge, Marinus de. "The Christian Origin of the *Greek Life of Adam and* Eve." In *Literature on Adam and Eve: Collected Essays,* edited by Gary Anderson, Michael Stone, and Johannes Tromp, 347–63. Studia in Veteris Testamenti pseudepigrapha 15. Leiden: Brill, 2000.

Jonge, Marinus de, and Johannes Tromp, eds. *The Life of Adam and Eve and Related Literature.* Guides to Apocrypha and Pseudepigrapha; Sheffield: Sheffield Academic Press, 1997.

Jonge, Marinus de, and L. Michael White, "The Washing of Adam in the Acherusian Lake (Greek *Life of Adam and Eve* 37.3) in the Context of Early Christian Notions of the Afterlife." In *Early Christianity and Classical Culture: Comparative Studies in Honor of Abraham J. Malherbe,* edited by John T. Fitzgerald, Thomas H. Olbricht, and L. Michael White. Supplements to Novum Testamentum 110. Leiden: Brill, 2003.

Kennedy, George A. *Progymnasmata: Greek Textbooks of Prose Composition and Rhetoric*. Writings from the Greco-Roman World 10. Atlanta: Society of Biblical Literature, 2003.

Kim, Seyoon. *The Origin of Paul's Gospel*. Wissenschaftliche Untersuchungen zum Neuen Testament 2/4. Tübingen: Mohr Siebeck, 1984.

Kloppenborg, John S. "Isis and Sophia in the Book of Wisdom." *Harvard Theological Review* 75 (1982): 57–84.

Kolarcik, Michael. "Creation and Salvation in the Book of Wisdom." In *Creation in the Biblical Traditions,* edited by Richard J. Clifford and John J. Collins, 97–107. Catholic Biblical Quarterly Monograph Series 24. Washington, D.C.: Catholic Biblical Association of America, 1992.

Lambrecht, Jan. *Pauline Studies: Collected Essays by Jan Lambrecht*. Bibliotheca ephemeridum theologicarum lovaniensium 115. Leuven: Leuven University Press, 1994.

———."Paul's Christological Use of Scripture in 1 Cor,20-28." *New Testament Studies* 28 (1982): 502–27.

———. "Structure and Line of Thought in 1 Cor. 15,23-28." *Novum Testamentum* 32 (1990): 143–51.

Levison, John R. (Jack). "The Exoneration and Denigration of Eve in the *Greek Life of Adam and Eve*." In *Literature on Adam and Eve: Collected Essays,* edited by Gary A. Anderson, Michael E. Stone, and Johannes Tromp, 251-75. Studia in Veteris Testamenti pseudepigrapha 15. Leiden: Brill, 2000.

———. "The Exoneration of Eve in the Apocalypse of Moses 15-30." *Journal for the Study of Judaism in the Persian, Hellenistic, and Roman Period* 20 (1989): 135-50.

———. "Is Eve to Blame? A Contextual Analysis of Sirach 25:24." *Catholic Biblical Quarterly* 47 (1985): 617–23.

———.*Portraits of Adam in Early Judaism: From Sirach to 2 Baruch*. Journal for the Study of the Pseudepigrapha: Supplement Series 1. Sheffield: JSOT Press, 1988.

———. *Texts in Transition: The Greek Life of Adam and Eve*. Society of Biblical Literature Early Judaism and Its Literature 16. Atlanta: Society of Biblical Literature, 2000.

Long, A. A. "Allegory in Philo and Etymology in Stoicism: A Plea for Drawing Distinctions." *Studia Philonica Annual* 9 (1997): 198–210.

———. *Hellenistic Philosophy: Stoics, Epicureans, Sceptics*. 2nd ed. Berkeley: University of California Press, 1986.

Longenecker, Bruce W. *2 Esdras*. Guides to Apocrypha and Pseudepigrapha. Sheffield: Sheffield Academic Press, 1995.

Martin, Aldo. *La tipologia adamica nella lettera agli Efesini*. Analecta Biblica 159. Rome: Pontificio Istituto Biblico, 2005.

Mason, Steve. *Josephus and the New Testament*. Peabody, Mass.: Hendrickson, 2003.

Méasson, Anita, and Jacques Cazeaux. "From Grammar to Discourse: A Study of the *Questiones in Genesim* in Relation to the Treatises." In *Both Literal and Allegorical: Studies in Philo of Alexandria's Questions and Answers on Genesis and Exodus,* edited by David M. Hay, 132–44. Brown Judaic Studies 232. Atlanta: Scholars Press, 1991.

Metzger, Bruce M. "The Fourth Book of Ezra." In *The Old Testament Pseudepigrapha*. Vol. 1, *Apocalyptic Literature and Testaments*, edited by James H. Charlesworth, 518–20. New York: Doubleday, 1983.

Milik, J. T. *Ten Years of Discovery in the Wilderness of Judaea*. Studies in Biblical Theology 26. Naperville, Ill.: Allenson, 1959.

Mitchell, Margaret M. *Paul and the Rhetoric of Reconciliation: An Exegetical Investigation of the Language and Composition of 1 Corinthians*. Louisville: Westminster John Knox, 1991.

———. "Paul's Letters to Corinth: The Interpretive Intertwining of Literary and Historical Reconstruction." In *Urban Religion in Roman Corinth: Interdisciplinary Approaches,* edited by Daniel N. Schowalter and Steven J. Friesen, 307–38. Harvard Theological Studies 53. Cambridge, Mass.: Harvard University Press, 2005.

Moyise, Steve. "Quotations." In *As It Is Written: Studying Paul's Use of the Scripture,* edited by Stanley E. Porter and Christopher D. Stanley, 15–28. Society of Biblical Literature Symposium Series 50. Atlanta: Society of Biblical Literature, 2008.

Murphy, Frederick J. "Divine Plan, Human Plan: A Structuring Theme in Pseudo-Philo." *Jewish Quarterly Review* 77 (1986): 5–15.

———. "The Eternal Covenant in Pseudo-Philo." *Journal for the Study of the Pseudepigrapha* 3 (1988): 43–57.

———. *Pseudo-Philo: Rewriting the* Bible. New York: Oxford University Press, 1993.

Nickelsburg, George W. E. "Philo among Greeks, Jews and Christians." In *Philo und das Neue Testament: Wechselseitige Wahrnehmungen. 1. Internationales Symposium zum Corpus Judaeo-Hellenisticum, 1.–4. Mai 2003, Eisenach, Jena,* edited by Roland Deines and Karl-Wilhelm Niebuhr, 53–72.

Wissenschaftliche Untersuchungen zum Neuen Testament 172. Tübingen: Mohr Siebeck, 2004.

———. "Wisdom and Apocalypticism in Early Judaism: Some Points for Discussion." In *Conflicted Boundaries in Wisdom and Apocalypticism,* edited by Benjamin G. Wright III and Lawrence M. Wills, 17–37. Society of Biblical Literature Symposium Series 35. Atlanta: Society of Biblical Literature, 2005.

Nickelsburg, George W. E., and John J. Collins, eds. *Ideal Figures in Ancient Judaism: Profiles and Paradigms.* Society of Biblical Literature Septuagint and Cognate Studies 12. Missoula, Mont.: Scholars Press, 1980.

Noort, Ed. "The Creation of Man and Woman in Biblical and Ancient Near Eastern Traditions." In *The Creation of Man and Woman: Interpretations of the Biblical Narratives in Jewish and Christian Traditions,* edited by Gerard P. Luttikhuizen, 1–18. Themes in Biblical Narrative 3. Leiden: Brill, 2000.

Økland, Jorunn. "Genealogies of the Self." In *Metamorphoses: Resurrection, Body and Transformative Practices in Early Christianity,* edited by Turid Karlsen Seim and Jorunn Økland, 83–122. Ekstasis 1. Berlin: de Gruyter, 2007.

Pate, C. Marvin. *Adam Christology as Exegetical & Theological Substructure of 2 Corinthians 4:7—5:21.* Lanham, Md.: University Press of America, 1991.

Pearson, Birger A. *Ancient Gnosticism: Traditions and Literature.* Minneapolis: Fortress, 2007.

———. "Cracking a Conundrum: Christian Origins in Egypt." *Studia theologica* 57 (2003): 61–75.

———. *The Pneumatikos-Psychikos Terminology in 1 Corinthians: A Study in the Theology of the Corinthian Opponents of Paul and Its Relation to Gnosticism.* Society of Biblical Literature Dissertation Series 12. Missoula, Mont.: Society of Biblical Literature, 1973.

Perkins, Pheme. "Apocalypse of Adam: The Genre and Function of a Gnostic Apocalypse." *Catholic Biblical Quarterly* 39 (1977): 382–95.

———. *Gnosticism and the New Testament.* Minneapolis: Fortress Press, 1993.

Porter, Stanley E. "The Pauline Concept of Original Sin, in Light of Rabbinic Background." *Tyndale Bulletin* 41 (1990): 3–30.

———. "The Theoretical Justification for Application of Rhetorical Categories to Pauline Epistolary Literature." In *Rhetoric and the New Testament,* edited by Stanley E. Porter and Thomas H. Olbricht, 100–122. Journal for the Study of the New Testament: Supplement Series 90. Sheffield: Sheffield Academic Press, 1993.

Porter, Stanley E., and Christopher D. Stanley, eds. *As It Is Written: Studying Paul's Use of Scripture.* Society of Biblical Literature: Symposium Series 50. Atlanta: Society of Biblical Literature, 2008.

Quek, Swee-Hwa. "Adam and Christ according to Paul." In *Pauline Studies: Essays Presented to Professor F. F. Bruce on His 70th Birthday,* edited by Donald A. Hagner and Murray J. Harris, 67–79. Grand Rapids: Eerdmans, 1980.

Ruiten, J. T. A. G. M. van. "The Creation of Man and Woman in Early Jewish Literature." In *The Creation of Man and Woman: Interpretations of the Biblical Narratives in Jewish and Christian Traditions,* edited by Gerard P. Luttikhuizen, 34–62. Themes in Biblical Narrative 3. Leiden: Brill, 2000.

———. *Primaeval History Interpreted: The Rewriting of Genesis 1–11 in the Book of Jubilees.* Supplements to the Journal for the Study of Judaism 66. Leiden: Brill, 2000.

Runia, David T. *Philo in Early Christian Literature: A Survey.* CRINT, Section 3, Jewish Traditions in Early Christian Literature 3. Assen: Van Gorcum; Minneapolis: Fortress Press, 1993.

———. *Philo of Alexandria, On the Creation of Cosmos according to Moses.* Philo of Alexandria Commentary Series 1. Leiden: Brill, 2001.

Sanders, E. P. *Paul and Palestinian Judaism: A Comparison of Patterns of Religion.* Philadelphia: Fortress Press, 1952.

Sayler, Gwendolyn B. *Have the Promises Failed? A Literary Analysis of 2 Baruch.* Society of Biblical Literature Dissertation Series 72. Chico, Calif.: Scholars Press, 1984.

Schaller, Berndt. "Adam und Christus bei Paulus: Oder, Über Brauch und Fehlbrauch von Philo in der neutestamentenlichen Forschung." In *Philo und das Neue Testament: Wechselseitige Wahrnehmungen. 1. Internationales Symposium zum Corpus Judaeo-Hellenisticum, 1.–4. Mai 2003, Eisenach, Jena,* edited by Roland Deines and Karl-Wilhelm Niebuhr, 143–53. Wissenschaftliche Untersuchungen zum Neuen Testament 172. Tübingen: Mohr Siebeck, 2004.

Schmithals, Walter. "The Corinthian Christology." In *Christianity at Corinth: The Quest for the Pauline Church,* edited by Edward Adams and David G. Horrell, 124–30. Louisville: Westminster John Knox, 2004.

Schüssler Fiorenza, Elisabeth. "Rhetorical Situation and Historical Reconstruction." In *Christianity at Corinth: The Quest for the Pauline Church,* edited by Edward Adams and David G. Horrell, 145–60. Louisville: Westminster John Knox, 2004.

———. *Rhetoric and Ethics: The Politics of Biblical Studies*. Minneapolis: Fortress Press, 1999.

Scroggs, Robin. *The Last Adam: A Study in Pauline Anthropology*. Philadelphia: Fortress Press, 1966.

Segal, Michael. *The Book of Jubilees: Rewritten Bible, Redaction, Ideology and Theology*. Supplements to the Journal for the Study of Judaism 117. Leiden: Brill, 2007.

Seim, Turid Karlsen. "The Resurrected Body in Luke–Acts." In *Metamorphoses: Resurrection, Body and Transformative Practices in Early Christianity*, edited by Turid Karlsen Seim and Jorunn Økland, 19–39. Berlin: de Gruyter, 2007.

Sharpe, John L., III. "The Second Adam in the Apocalypse of Moses." *Catholic Biblical Quarterly* 35 (1973): 35–46.

Siegert, Folker. "Philo of Alexandria." In *Hebrew Bible/Old Testament: The History of Its Interpretation*. Vol. 1, *From the Beginnings to the Middle Ages (until 1300)*, part 1, *Antiquity*, edited by Magne Sæbø, 162–89. Göttingen: Vandenhoeck & Ruprecht, 2000.

Ska, Jean Louis. *Introduzione alla lettura del Pentateuco: Chiavi per l'interpretazione dei primi cinque libri della Bibbia*. Collana Biblica. Rome: Dehoniane, 1998.

Skehan, Patrick W., and Alexander A. Di Lella. *The Wisdom of Ben Sira: A New Translation with Notes*. Anchor Bible 39. Garden City, N.Y.: Doubleday, 1987.

Son Sang-Won (Aaron). *Corporate Elements in Pauline Anthropology: A Study of Selected Terms, Idioms, and Concepts in the Light of Paul's Usage and Background*. Analecta Biblica 148. Rome: Pontificio Istituto Biblico, 2001.

Songe-Møller, Vigdis. "'With What Kind of Body Will They Come?' Metamorphosis and the Concept of Change. From Platonic Thinking to Paul's Notion of the Resurrection of the Dead." In *Metamorphoses: Resurrection, Body and Transformative Practices in Early Christianity*, edited by Turid Karlsen Seim and Jorunn Økland, 109–22. Ekstasis 1. Berlin: de Gruyter, 2007.

Speiser, E. A. *Genesis: Introduction, Translation, and Notes*. Anchor Bible 1. Garden City, N.Y.: Doubleday, 1964.

Stanley, Christopher D. *Arguing with Scripture: The Rhetoric of Quotations in the Letters of Paul*. New York: T&T Clark International, 2004.

Steenburg, D. "The Worship of Adam and Christ as the Image of God." *Journal for the Study of the New Testament* 39 (1990): 95–109.

Sterling, Gregory E."Philo's *Questiones*: Prolegomena or Afterthought?" In *Both Literal and Allegorical. Studies in Philo of Alexandria's Questions and Answers on Genesis and Exodus*,edited by David M. Hay, 99–123. Brown Judais Studies 232. Atlanta: Scholars Press, 1991.

———."The Place of Philo of Alexandria in the Study of Christian Origins." In *Philo und das Neue Testament: Wechselseitige Wahrnehmungen. 1. Internationales Symposium zum Corpus Judaeo-Hellenisticum, 1.–4. Mai 2003, Eisenach, Jena*, edited by Roland Deines and Karl-Wilhelm Niebuhr, 21–52. Wissenschaftliche Untersuchungen zum Neuen Testament 172. Tübingen: Mohr Siebeck, 2004.

———. "'Wisdom among the Perfect': Creation Traditions in Alexandrian Judaism and Corinthian Christianity." *Novum Testamentum* 37 (1995): 355–84.

Michael E. Stone, *Features of the Eschatology of IV Ezra*. Harvard Semitic Studies 35. Atlanta: Scholars Press, 1989.

———.Fourth Ezra: A Commentary on the Book of Fourth Ezra. Hermeneia. Minneapolis: Fortress Press, 1990.

———. *A History of the Literature of Adam and Eve*. Society of Biblical Literature Early Judaism and Its Literature 3. Atlanta: Scholars Press, 1992.

Svebakken, Hans Richard. "Philo of Alexandria's Exposition of the Tenth Commandment." Ph.D. diss., Loyola University Chicago, 2009.

Terian, Abraham. "Back to Creation: The Beginning of Philo's Third Grand Commentary." *Studia Philonica Annual* 9 (1997): 19–36.

———. "The Priority of the *Questiones* among Philo's Exegetical Commentaries." In *Both Literal and Allegorical: Studies in Philo of Alexandria's Questions and Answers on Genesis and Exodus*, edited by David M. Hay, 29–46. Atlanta: Scholars Press, 1991.

Thiselton, Anthony C. *The First Epistle to the Corinthians: A Commentary on the Greek Text*. New International Greek Testament Commentary. Grand Rapids: Eerdmans, 2000.

Thompson, Alden Lloyd. *Responsibility for Evil in the Theodicy of IV Ezra: A Study Illustrating theSignificance of Form and Structure for the Meaning of the Book*. Society of Biblical Literature Dissertation Series 29. Missoula, Mont.: Scholars Press, 1977.

Tobin, Thomas H."The Beginning of Philo's *Legum Allegoriae*." *Studia Philonica Annual* 12 (2000): 27–43.

———. The Creation of Man: Philo and the History of Interpretation. Catholic Biblical Quarterly Monograph Series 14. Washington, D.C.: Catholic Biblical Association of America, 1983.

———. "Interpretations of the Creation of the World in Philo of Alexandria." In *Creation in the Biblical Traditions,* edited by Richard J. Clifford and John J. Collins, 108–28. Catholic Biblical Quarterly Monograph Series 24. Washington, D.C.: Catholic University of America Press, 1992.

———. *Paul's Rhetoric in Its Contexts: The Arguments of Romans.* Peabody, Mass.: Hendrickson, 2004.

———. "Philo and the Sibyl: Interpreting Philo's Eschatology." *Studia Philonica Annual* 9 (1997): 84–103.

Thrall, Margaret E. "The Initial Attraction of Paul's Mission in Corinth and of the Chruch He Founded There." In *Paul, Luke and the Graeco-Roman World: Essays in Honour of Alexander J. M. Wedderburn,* edited by Alf Christophersen, Carsten Claussen, Jörg Frey, and Bruce Longenecker, 59–73. . Journal for the Study of the New Testament: Supplement Series 217. Sheffield: Sheffield Academic, 2002.

Tuckett, Christopher M. "The Corinthians Who Say 'There Is No Resurrection of the Dead' (1 Cor 15,12)." In *The Corinthian Correspondence,* edited by R. Bieringer, 247–75. Bibliotheca ephemeridum theologicarum lovaniensium 125. Leuven: Leuven University Press/Peeters, 1996.

VanderKam, James C. *The Book of Jubilees.* Guides to Apocrypha and Pseudepigrapha. Sheffield: Sheffield Academic Press, 2001.

———. "The Putative Author of the Book of Jubilees." *Journal of Semitic Studies* 26 (1981): 209–17.

———. *Textual and Historical Studies in the Book of Jubilees.* Harvard Semitic Monographs 14. Missoula, Mont.: Scholars Press, 1977.

VanderKam, James C., and William Adler, eds. *The Jewish Apocalyptic Heritage in Early Christianity*. Minneapolis: Fortress Press, 1996.

Vermes, Geza. *The Dead Sea Scrolls in English.* Rev. and extended ed. London: Penguin Books, 1995.

———. Scripture and Tradition in Judaism. Studia Post-Biblica 4. Leiden: Brill, 1961.

Versteeg, J. P. *Is Adam a "Teaching Model" in the New Testament? An Examination of One of the Central Points in the Views of H. M. Kuitert and Others.* Translated by Richard B. Gaffin. Nutley, N.J.: Presbyterian and Reformed, 1977.

Watson, Duane F. "Paul's Rhetorical Strategy in 1 Corinthians 15." In *Rhetoric and the New Testament: Essays from the 1992 Heidelberg Conference,* edited by Stanley E. Porter and Thomas H. Olbricht, 213–49. Journal for the Study of the New Testament: Supplement Series 90. Sheffield: Sheffield Academic Press, 1993.

Wedderburn, Alexander John Maclagan. "Adam and Christ: An Investigation into the Background of 1 Corinthians XV and Romans V. 12-21." Ph.D. diss., Cambridge University, 1970.

———. "Adam in Paul's Letters to the Romans." *Studia Biblica* 3 (1978): 413–30.

———. *Baptism and Resurrection: Studies in Pauline Theology against Its Graeco-Roman Background*. Wissenschaftliche Untersuchungen zum Neuen Testament 44. Tübingen: Mohr Siebeck, 1987.

———. "The Problem of the Denial of the Resurrection in 1 Corinthians XV." *Novum Testamentum* 3 (1981): 229–41.

———. "The Theological Structure of Romans V. 12." *New Testament Studies* 19 (1972–73): 339–54.

Westermann, Claus. *Genesis 1–11: A Continental Commentary*. Translated by John J. Scullion. Minneapolis: Fortress Press, 1994.

Wilckens, Ulrich. *La Carta a los Romanos*.Vol. 1, *Rom. 1–5*. Biblioteca de Estudios Bíblicos 61. Salamanca, Sígueme, 1997.

Willett, Tom W. *Eschatology in the Theodicies of 2 Baruch and 4 Ezra*. Journal for the Study of the Pseudepigrapha: Supplement Series 4. Sheffield: JSOT Press, 1989.

Winston, David. *The Wisdom of Solomon: A New Translation with Introduction and Commentary*. Anchor Bible 43. Garden City, N.Y.: Doubleday1979.

Witherington, Ben, III. *Conflict & Community in Corinth: A Socio-Rhetorical Commentary on 1 and 2 Corinthians*. Grand Rapids: Eerdmans, 1995.

Wolfson, H. A. *Philo: Foundations of Religious Philosophy in Judaism, Christianity, and Islam*. 2 vols. Structure and Growth of PhilosophicSystems from Plato to Spinoza 2. Cambridge, Mass.: Harvard University Press, 1948.

Wright, Benjamin G., III. "Putting the Puzzle Together: Some Suggestions Concerning the Social Location of the Wisdom of Ben Sira." In *Conflicted Boundaries in Wisdom and Apocalypticism,* edited by Benjamin G. Wright III and Lawrence M. Wills, 89–112. Society of Biblical Literature Symposium Series 35. Atlanta: Society of Biblical Literature, 2005.

Wright, Benjamin G., III, and Lawrence M. Wills, eds. *Conflicted Boundaries in Wisdom and Apocalypticism*. Society of Biblical Literature Symposium Series 35. Atlanta: Society of Biblical Literature, 2005.

Wright, Nicholas Thomas. "Adam in Pauline Christology." In *Society of Biblical Literature Seminar Papers,* vol. 22, edited by Kent Harold Richards, 359–89. Chico, Calif.: Scholars Press, 1983.

Index of Names

Index of Biblical and Ancient References

1 Corinthians

1 Thessalonians

2 Thessalonians

1 Timothy

Hebrews

1 Peter

Jude

Revelation

PSEUDEPIGRAPHA

Wisdom of Solomon

Sirach (Ecclesiasticus)

2 Baruch

4 Ezra

QUMRAN TEXTS

1QH

1QS

4Q

CPSIA information can be obtained at www.ICGtesting.com
Printed in the USA
BVOW03s0922290114

343295BV00007B/144/P